The THREE STOOGES

The Triumphs and Tragedies of The Most Popular Comedy Team of All Time

Authored by **Jeff Forrester**
and **Tom Forrester**

Edited by **Joe Wallison**

Introduction by **Mousie Garner**

db
Donaldson Books
Los Angeles

Library of Congress Cataloging-in-Publication Data

Forrester, Jeff.
  and
Forrester, Tom.

The Three Stooges: The Triumphs and Tragedies of The Most Popular
    Comedy Team of All Time.

  1. Comedy / Comedians —- Biography.   2. Three Stooges films.
      I. Title.

Library of Congress card number: ISBN 0-9715801-0-3

Published by Donaldson Books

Photo credits: Joe Wallison, Babe Howard, Eddie Brandt, Mousie Garner, David Maska,
Tony Bonich, Mickey Gold, Frank Mitchell, C3 Entertainment, Inc., and Forrester Bros.
Communications, Inc.

Donaldson Books,
7095 Hollywood Boulevard, #492,
Los Angeles, California, 90028

Designed by Kurt Wahlner

Manufactured in the United States of America

10 9 8 7 6 5 4 3 2

Table of Contents

BREWERY CO.

Introduction

I HAVE BEEN in show business practically all my life. I got my start as a kid during the First World War, entertaining soldiers at training camps and then later performing in theaters. My Dad managed a theater in Washington, D.C., and he helped me put together a musical routine with my cousin Jack Wolf that later evolved into a professional vaudeville act. Our act was all music — we sang, we danced, we played instruments — but we did no comedy whatsoever. That all changed when we were hired to work for the great Jack Pepper, a popular vaudeville singer and joketeller who later influenced guys like Bob Hope, Bing Crosby and many others.

Pepper encouraged us to be funny, and before long, audiences responded. Getting laughs in front of an audience was an exhilarating experience, and the more laughs we got, the more comedy we worked into the act. Pretty soon we were full-fledged comedians, and we quickly abandoned our dreams of becoming "serious" musicians. We were now serious only about being funny.

Shortly after we joined Jack Pepper, we were hired by General David Sarnoff of RCA to appear in an experimental television program, one of the first ever, broadcast live from NBC-TV's original studio in Schenectady, New York. This was in 1928, and in those days, the only people with TV sets were scientists and technicians, so only a handful of Earthlings even saw the thing. But they tell me I am the first comedian ever to appear on television, thanks to that early broadcast. And when I appeared on NBC-TV in Los Angeles recently, they told me I've been performing on television longer than any other human being in history. All of that is well and good, but as far as I'm concerned, the most important thing I ever did in the entertainment business was working as a Stooge for the late Ted Healy.

Ted Healy created The Three Stooges, and I became one of his boys in 1930 when he was auditioning comedians for a Broadway show called *The Gang's All Here*. With Jack Pepper I had learned timing and verbal delivery, but with Healy I was introduced to the fine art of physical comedy. And what a rude introduction it was.

I showed up at the theater where the auditions were being held, and when I offered my hand to Healy, he responded by giving me a smack on the head! I had never seen this type of comedy before, so I jumped on him, grabbed his nose and bit his ear in retaliation. "Get in the corner, you're hired," said Healy, and I never looked back.

I worked with Healy off and on throughout the 1930s, with a variety of different Stooge partners including my cousin Jack, our good friend Dick Hakins, and several others. On one occasion in the early 1930s, I even appeared as "Third Stooge" opposite the legendary Moe Howard and Larry Fine. After Healy's death in 1937, "The Three Stooges" came into its own as a comedy team, and I later worked with this act as well. My last appearance with the Stooges was in the early 1970s, when I did a personal-appearance tour with my old pal CurlyJoe DeRita and another Ted Healy veteran, Frank Mitchell. That tour turned out to be the last hurrah for The Three Stooges, as CurlyJoe's failing eyesight forced him into more or less permanent retirement.

As for myself, I don't think retirement is in the cards. As long as there's an audience out there that wants to laugh, I'll keep working. And nowadays, people need to laugh more than ever. As Ted Healy himself used to say, "never underestimate the power of laughter."

I won't, Ted.

MOUSIE GARNER
Hollywood, California, 2002

Dedication

This book is dedicated to

the memory of our grandmother,

Elizabeth Healy-Kelly,

who always encouraged us to write.

— Jeff and Tom Forrester

Acknowledgments

We gratefully acknowledge the contributions of the following individuals, all of whom were interviewed by the authors and/or editor on the subject of The Three Stooges:

Jeff Abraham
Joey Adams
Steve Allen
Morey Amsterdam
Lucille Ball
Billy Barty
Billy Benedict
Bob Benjamin
Earl Benjamin
Milton Berle
Phil Berle
Edward Bernds
Ernie (Mr. Joe) Besser
Joe Besser
Joey Bishop
Mel Blanc
Adrian Booth
Lyla Feinberg Budnick
Nate Budnick
Candy Candido
Frank Capra
Jeanne Carmen
James Carone
Connie Cezon
Robert Colbert
Tim Conway
Diana Darrin
Fred DeCordova
Joe "CurlyJoe" DeRita
Jean (Mrs. Joe) DeRita
Elaine Howard Diamond
Phyllis Diller
Mike Douglas
Buddy Ebsen
Morris Feinberg
Christy Lynne Fine
John Fine, Jr.
Larry Fine
Ruth Foster
Joe Franklin
Henry Freulich

Milton Frome
Paul "Mousie" Garner
George Gobel
Dave Gould
Johnny Grant
Geri Howard Greenbaum
Buddy Hackett
Abby (Mrs. Dick) Hakins
Dick Hakins
Alan Hale, Jr.
Betty (Mrs. Ted) Healy
John Jacob "Ted" Healy
Richard Herd
Thomas W. Holland
Janet Lord Holt
Bob Hope
Babe (Mrs. Shemp) Howard
Jill Howard
Marilyn Howard
Moe Howard
Sandie Howard
Arline Hunter
George Jessel
Hal Kanter
Margaret Brown Kerry
Ted Knight
Don Knotts
Stanley Kramer
Christy Fine Kraus
Don Lamond
Eric Lamond
Phyllis Fine Lamond
Peter Lawford
Jack Lemmon
Sheldon Leonard
Ethelreda Leopold
Jerry Lewis
Irving Lippman
Earl Lord
Lucille Lund
Jock Mahoney

Jerry Maren
Rose Marie
Dean Martin
Ross Martin
Norman Maurer
Mike Mazurki
Chuck McCann
Patricia Medina
Sid Melton
Sidney Miller
Frank Mitchell
Howard Morris
Donald O'Connor
Lee Orgel
Evan Owen
Gary Owens
Patty Palma
Norman Powell
Eddie Quillan
Quinn Redeker
Carl Reiner
Mickey Rooney
Benny Rubin
Soupy Sales
Samuel Sherman
Frank Sinatra
Emil Sitka
Red Skelton
Hal Smith
Elwood Ullman
Beverly Warren
Jack White
Judy (Mrs. Jules) White
Jules White
Paul Winchell
Herb Wiere
Alan Thicke
Adam West
Warner Wolf
Sammy Wolfe
Henny Youngman

Chapter 1

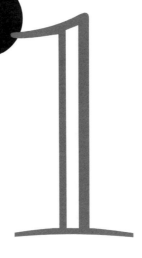

IT WAS ONE of the hottest days in the recorded history of Hollywood, that Los Angeles neighborhood recognized everywhere as the show-business capital of the world.

At high noon on August 30, 1983, thousands of people from all corners of the earth crowded themselves onto a small chunk of sidewalk at the corner of Vine Street and Selma Avenue. They were there to witness the unveiling of a commemorative "star," a chiseled plaque embedded in concrete on the world-famous "Walk of Fame." It was an honor granted exclusively to those performers who had established themselves as true Hollywood legends. The honorees in this case were The Three Stooges, the only major slapstick comedians in movie history who had never previously received such recognition. And despite the sweltering heat, the overflow crowd was the largest ever recorded for a so-called "star ceremony."

Most perplexing to the Hollywood Chamber of Commerce, the folks who threw the shindig, was the fact that none of the original members of The Three Stooges were alive to accept the honor. It was the Chamber's biggest turn-out ever, and yet none of those who truly made it possible were around to enjoy the applause. But that fact didn't stop the thousands of Stooge fans who jammed the intersection of Vine and Selma to observe this long-overdue tribute to their comedy idols.

During the ceremony it would be recalled that The Three Stooges made more movies than any other comedy team in Hollywood, that they enjoyed the longest-running studio contract in history. And that even though the Stooges starred in feature films, performed in radio revues, appeared in their own television series, headlined in vaudeville, toplined in nightclubs, trod the boards on Broadway, recorded musical albums, lectured at colleges, authored and promoted books, and turned up in every form of merchandising imaginable, their greatest legacy was their mammoth library of short-subject comedies, the first of which was filmed some fifty years earlier. This ceremony coincided with the golden anniversary celebration of that momentous event.

Gary Owens, who had campaigned for the Stooges' "star" on his radio and TV programs, masterfully hosted the proceedings. The audience shrieked with laughter as guest

Jennie and Solomon Horwitz (above), with their sons, from left, Samuel "Shemp," Harry "Moe" and Jerome "Curly."

speaker Milton Berle played straightman to surviving Stooge Joe Besser, in what turned out to be the latter's final public appearance. Meanwhile, veteran stage Stooges Mousie Garner, Frank Mitchell and Dick Hakins worked the crowd like politicians, shaking hands and signing autographs for starstruck onlookers. Character comedian Emil Sitka, the Stooges' favorite foil and the man who played more roles opposite them than any other performer, was greeted with deafening cheers when he recited dialogue from a popular Stooge film. Actor Adam West, who made his big-screen debut as leading man in a Stooge comedy, elicited a roar of approval when he described the boys as "just great guys."

There were endless speeches and testimonials from other friends and co-workers of the Stooges, including a number of prominent actors and comedians. Every living biographer of the Stooges was also present, as were dozens of writers, reporters, and photographers from all over the globe. But most poignantly, the Stooges' closest living relatives were on hand, bringing their own personal reminiscences to the occasion.

Shemp Howard, the man who started it all, the man considered by most who knew them to be the funniest of all the Stooges, was represented by his daughter-in-law Geri, and grandaughters Jill and Sandie. Moe Howard, Shemp's younger brother and the individual most responsible for keeping The Three Stooges alive, was canonized by his daughter Joan, son-in-law Norman, and grandsons Michael and Jeffrey. And Curly Howard, kid brother to Shemp and Moe, and indisputably the most beloved member of the Stooges, was remembered by his former wife, Elaine, and their only child together, Marilyn.

And then there were relatives of the Stooges who came from outside the Howard clan. These were the comedians who started out as "replacements" for the original members, but nevertheless became forever ingrained in the public consciousness as bona fide Stooges: Larry Fine, a Shemp stand-in who joined the act as a young man and became its longest-running member, was the subject of a brief speech by his daughter, Phyllis. Joe Besser, who became a temporary Stooge after Shemp's death, and subsequently found himself chronically typecast, was feted by his wife, Ernie. And finally CurlyJoe DeRita, Shemp's permanent replacement and the man who came to be known as The Last Stooge, was saluted in remarks by his spouse, Jean.

The event was widely covered on network television, and some local stations even pre-empted their afternoon programming in order to broadcast the lengthy

Shemp, Moe and Curly Howard: Three aspiring vaudevillians.

ceremony in its entirety. L.A. Mayor Tom Bradley issued an official proclamation, designating August 30th as Three Stooges Day throughout the City of Los Angeles. And the festivities continued long into the evening. The celebrity-studded premiere of the first-ever Three Stooges documentary was held at a movie theater just blocks from the site of the star unveiling. Numerous after-show parties, some of which continued until dawn, were thrown at various locations throughout greater Los Angeles. At one of these gatherings, Emil Sitka pronounced the eventful day as "the greatest in the history of The Three Stooges."

For the families of the Stooges, however, the whole thing constituted a rather bittersweet affair. Despite the heartfelt — albeit belated — recognition, the sad reality that none of the original members were there to enjoy the acclaim had finally hit home. As for the legacy of The Three Stooges, it was just the latest ironic twist in a half-century full of ironic twists.

This is the story of the most popular comedy team of all time. It is the story of movie stars and mobsters, of gloriously successful show-business achievements, and of criminally abusive career mismanagement. It is the story of The American Dream as pursued by the children of immigrants and their successors, with all of the hard work and heartbreak that necessarily accompany any such "grab for the brass ring."

But to understand the story of The Three Stooges, one must go back in time

A youthful Ted Healy, shortly after he decides to become a professional entertainer.

Ted Healy with his original "stooge," a stage-trained German Shepherd that appears in his very first vaudeville act.

long before the boys made their first Hollywood short subject in 1933. The story of the Stooges actually begins almost a quarter of a century before that, in the outer boroughs of New York City. Comedian Mousie Garner, who was born during the first decade of the twentieth century, and is still actively performing in the first decade of the *twenty-first* century, explains:

"I was born on July 31st in 1909.

"Around this same time, about mid-summer, a young fellow named Lee Nash first met the Horwitz brothers on the beach in Brooklyn. And that was really the beginning of The Three Stooges as we know the act today."

The rascally thirteen-year-old named Lee Nash later rechristened himself "Ted Healy," and became the father of modern standup comedy. The young Horwitz brothers, meanwhile, would Anglicize their name to "Howard," and develop the Stooge franchise that eventually became known throughout the globe.

Ted Healy, a native of Houston, Texas who spent his summers in New York, was the son of a wealthy Irish-Catholic businessman. The brothers Howard, on the other hand,

While Curly and his parents are visiting relatives in Europe, brothers Shemp and Moe rejoin Ted Healy on the beach at Coney Island for a circus-themed publicity stunt.

★★★ **The THREE STOOGES** ★★★

were the sons of a virtually unemployable Lithuanian Jew who emigrated to the United States from the old country and settled in Brooklyn in the late nineteenth century.

All of the boys' parents were dead-set against their sons entering show business. But Sol and Jennie Horwitz didn't know they were rearing a trio of Stooges, any more than Ted Healy's parents knew they were rearing the single most influential verbal comedian of the twentieth century.

Samuel "Shemp" Howard, Sol and Jennie's third son, was fourteen years old when he met Ted Healy in 1909. He was a clever but shy boy with an instinctive gift for making people laugh. His ability as a character comedian helped him overcome some of his shyness, and in the years to come Shemp would not only become one of the most popular funnymen in show business, but a legend in the annals of film comedy. He would also come to be regarded as the kindest and most affable of all the Howards, a true gentleman and sincere friend. Shemp and his wife Babe would have a son, Morton, and two granddaughters.

His brother, Harry "Moe" Howard, was two years younger than Shemp. Like Shemp, Moe was also somewhat shy, and, also like Shemp, he used entertaining as a means of connecting with others emotionally. He, too, would become a film legend, best known for the manic rages and bullying attitude of his screen character. In real life, Moe would be described by his wife Helen as a kind and gentle man and devoted husband, and the cou-

Curly, whose mother refuses to allow him to tour with Ted Healy, is now forced to do all of his entertaining at the beach.

ple would have two children, Joan and Paul, as well as several grandchildren.

Moe's younger brother, Jerome "Curly" Howard, was six years his junior and nicknamed "Babe" by the family. True to Howard tradition, Curly was also quite shy, especially around women, and he too used clowning as a means of breaking the ice. In the movies, Curly became the most beloved of the Howard boys, and his childlike screen personality was imitated by dozens of comedians. Married as a teenager, Curly would see that union annulled and two others dissolved before he would finally meet the woman of his dreams. His fourth and final wife, Valerie, would bear him a daughter, Janie, and provide him with the happiness and contentment intimates say he always longed for. By all accounts Curly was a lovable and generous man who made friends everywhere he went.

The content of the act that would become world-famous as The Three Stooges would evolve from the childhood antics of these three brothers.

★★★ **The THREE STOOGES** ★★★

Unlike Ted Healy, the scion of a well-to-do family, the Howards came from relatively modest circumstances. Their father barely made a living as a clothes-cutter, while their mother earned whatever she could selling real estate in and around the neighborhood. But *like* Healy, the Howards were natural comedians and entertainers, and for them, that was all that mattered.

Soon Healy and the Howards were wringing laughter from Brooklyn beachgoers on a regular basis. Ted played the ukelele, sang, and told jokes, while the Howards provided the physical comedy. From the outset, Ted was the undisputed ringleader of this fun-loving gang, with the Howard boys gamely following his example. And so their relationship would remain for decades to come, through good times and bad.

In 1909, however, bystanders were astounded by the quality of entertainment provided by Healy and his friends, especially considering they were all just kids at the time. But the desire to make people laugh, to hear that sweet, sweet music of applause, had already taken hold of all the boys.

And although they couldn't have known it at the time, their improvised tomfoolery and beachfront acrobatics had already marked the beginning of an act that was to revolutionize entertainment.

Young Ted Healy likes being seen in tailored suits and fedoras, as he believes the natty attire gives him an older, more sophisticated look.

★★★ **The THREE STOOGES** ★★★

Curly poses with brother Shemp's wife Babe (left), and brother Moe's sister-in-law Clarice.

Lifeguard Moe, with bride-to-be Helen Schonberger (at left) and her sister Clarice.

Shemp, drafted into the Army during World War I and stationed on the East Coast, is visited by his father, Sol Horwitz.

Chapter 2

TODAY, TED HEALY is all but unknown to the general public. Most historical references to Healy divulge little more than the fact that he introduced The Three Stooges to the silver screen. This is a shame, because during his day Ted was one of the top comedians in all of show business. By the late 1920s, Healy was probably the highest-paid performer in vaudeville, as well as a major Broadway personality and Hollywood veteran. He had established himself as a truly great improvisational entertainer, and his style, look and mannerisms were quickly imitated by dozens of vaudeville gagsters. In fact, Ted's performing style influenced virtually every major stand-up performer in American history. Jack Benny, Bob Hope, and Milton Berle are among the many superstar comedians who initially patterned themselves after Healy. In later years, Berle even cited Ted as his "idol."

Healy's physical appearance was also a significant part of his comedy. While he wasn't a true buffoon character, he nevertheless strived for a comic appearance. Always attired in a cheap suit and hat, he was often seen chewing on a cigar or cigarette as well. Ted's facial expression could be one of sour cynicism, a reflection of his acerbic comic personality, especially when dealing with characters outside the Stooge cadre. But perhaps the most memorable aspect of Healy's stage character was his walk. With arms swinging confidently at his sides, Ted walked

Ted and Betty Healy originally bill themselves as "The Philosopher and the Flapper," a comedy pairing that later influences the husband–and–wife vaudeville team of George Burns and Gracie Allen; at bottom, Shemp, Moe and Curly Howard as young vaudevillians.

briskly, gut first, giving him an air of assertiveness. (Benny, Hope and Berle all assimilated this aspect of Healy's stage persona into their own acts.)

Ted's stage character was that of the "citified yokel." As a native of central Texas who spent his summers on Riverside Drive in Manhattan, Healy filled that role in life as well as on stage.

By the winter of 1922, the Howard boys had not seen their "citified yokel" pal for a solid decade. In the interim, Ted had become a successful stage performer, and word had reached the Howards that their old beach buddy was now headlining the Prospect Theater in Brooklyn. Healy, who had started out in burlesque nearly a decade earlier, was now a vaudeville star, specializing in comedy, song and dance in a "double" act with his wife, Betty Braun Healy.

Shemp and Moe Howard, meanwhile, had developed a vaudeville act of their own

around the time of World War I, with kid brother Curly serving as their original stooge. Shemp was the comedian, spouting an endless array of corny jokes, while Moe served as his straightman. And it was Curly's job to sit in the front row and lead the audience in laughter, cheers and applause, especially when the theater was experiencing a slow night.

According to Shemp's wife Babe, her husband, Moe and Curly dropped by the Prospect Theater to visit with their old friend, and Ted invited them onto the stage for some ad-lib clowning. Their improvisation was so well-received that Healy asked the boys to join his act as stooges.

Nineteen-year-old Curly had hoped to tour with Ted and his brothers, but mother Jennie Horwitz considered him the "baby" of the family and refused to let him travel far from home. Curly, whose nickname among family members would forever be "Babe," was heartbroken, but sufficiently dominated by his mother so as not to put up a fight.

Instead, Curly's place was taken by Ted Healy's real-life valet, Kenny Lackey, a talented comic who comprised the original trio of Stooges along with Shemp and Moe. Lackey's goofy grin and haystack haircut were even said to have influenced comedian Stan Laurel's screen personality.

Ted and Shemp, who together create the concept of Stooge comedy, in the first known publicity photo for Ted Healy and his Stooges.

←

Also part of Healy's gang was Ted's brother-in-law, Sam "Moody" Braun, who would serve as understudy Stooge whenever one of the three regulars was unable to perform. In early 1923, Ted and his troupe of entertainers — including Shemp, Kenny, and Moe, wife Betty, and brother-in-law Moody — went out on the road for the first time.

"Stooge comedy was invented by Ted and Shemp," said Shemp's wife Babe. "In the early days, it was mostly the two of them, along with Betty Healy, who got the laughs. And it was mostly jokes, verbal humor, that they got laughs with, although Healy started slapping Shemp around from the very start. Shemp never liked getting hit, but the audience loved it when he would make a smart remark and Healy would let him have it. So the slapping was always part of it. Moe and the other Stooge had nothing to do with the slapping, or even the jokes, for that matter. They were more or less acrobats, not comedians."

In addition to their onstage services, their responsibilities also included taking care of the Healys' pair of German Shepherds, who had become an integral part of the act. Early snapshots reveal the well-dressed Stooges, Moe and Kenny, solemnly tending to Ted's four-legged companions.

After touring with Healy throughout most of 1924, however, Moe decid-

Dave Chasen (right), seen here in a tug-of-war with popular Broadway star Joe Cook, begins his comedy career as a Ted Healy Stooge and later founds Chasen's, for decades Hollywood's most popular restaurant–nightclub.

Ted Healy and his Stooges in *The Passing Show*, Chicago, 1926: Back row, eighth from left, Shemp Howard, Ted Healy, Betty Braun Healy; back row, fifth from right, Dick Hakins, Moody Braun, Lou Warren.

ed he had had enough of running errands for Ted and looking after his pets. He left the act — and show business in general — to marry Helen Schonberger, a cousin of vaudeville legend Harry Houdini, in 1925. He also decided to follow his mother's lead, and pursue a career in real estate in his home town of Brooklyn.

Meanwhile, Shemp also got married in 1925, to dancer Gertrude "Babe" Frank, but he left vaudeville only long enough to enjoy his honeymoon. The brothers Howard couldn't have picked a worse time to leave the act, however, as Ted Healy subsequently found himself booked into his first Broadway show, *Earl Carroll's Vanities*, in 1925. Kenny Lackey remained with Ted, while Shemp and Moe were replaced by two newly-initiated Stooges. They were pantomimist Dave Chasen (who is reputed to have influenced Harpo Marx), and acrobatic comedian Lou Warren (who served as the inspiration for Stooge-to-be Frank Mitchell).

Ted Healy was a smash in the *Vanities*, which was something of a racier version of Florenz Ziegfeld's *Follies*, and it made him a star. After a few months of convulsing New Yorkers with his zany brand of comedy, Ted was ready to take his act out on the road again. However, two of his Stooges were happy right where they were, with steady employment in a hit Broadway show, and they had no intention of leaving. Kenny Lackey and Dave Chasen stayed on in the *Vanities*, leaving Ted with only one full-time Stooge, Lou Warren.

Shortly after Ted and Lou left the Vanities, Shemp returned to the fold. And while appearing in vaudeville, Healy met Dick Hakins, a young musician, songwriter and student at Northwestern University. Ted and Dick got along famously, and the clever Hakins became the latest "Third Stooge" in 1926. Hakins also became the first "gagwriter" Stooge, regularly supplying Healy with topical comedy material and song parodies.

From *The Passing Show*: Ted Healy hangs from the trapeze, with Lou Warren at his right, Betty Healy directly below, Shemp Howard at his left, and Dick Hakins (with conductor's baton) behind chorus girls.

MAMMOTH CONGRESS OF FREAKS

"I was playing piano in a minstrel act, and Ted just pulled me out of the orchestra," remembered Dick. "He said 'I can make a Stooge out of anybody,' and that's exactly what he did. I had written gags before, but I had never done comedy as a performer. Ted said he thought I was funny and that I would make a good Stooge. So he helped me through it. And Shemp Howard, who was one of the funniest guys I ever knew, was also helpful. We rehearsed for a few hours one afternoon, and that same night I went onstage with Ted for the first time. Believe me, it was an education.

"Ted was the first guy ever to play comedy off of somebody else. He was the main comedian, but he would let the Stooge get the laughs. He could break up an audience just by *looking* at one of his Stooges."

By 1927, Ted Healy and his Stooges had become a huge success on the vaudeville circuit. As a result, they were summoned by the Shubert Brothers to return to Broadway for a major musical-comedy revue, *A Night in Spain*. But Dick Hakins was ill, in fact so ill he left the show after only a few performances and returned to his home town of Fargo, North Dakota to recuperate. Once again, this left Ted with a vacancy to fill in his Stooge ensemble. Hakins' place was taken by Bobby Pinkus, a song-and-dance man known for his acrobatic slapstick that Healy had pulled from the chorus of *The Passing Show*.

Ted and Shemp perform "The Old Army Game" in Shuberts' *The Passing Show*.

Ted and his new group of Stooges — Shemp, Lou Warren and Bobby Pinkus — were a tremendous hit in *A Night in Spain*, so the brothers Shubert decided to send the show out on the road. While Healy and the boys were playing Chicago in 1928, the man who was then America's greatest stage star, singer-comedian Al Jolson, was added to the cast of *A Night in Spain*. Local audiences, starved for big-name Broadway talent, clamored for tickets to what the *Chicago Tribune* was now calling

"the hottest show in town."

Meanwhile, Ted's wife Betty had left the act after the New York run of *A Night in Spain*, returning to the couple's palatial estate in Darien, Connecticut. Lou Warren had also decided to leave the group, but in search of greener pastures as a solo performer. This left Ted with the responsibility of finding a new Stooge to take his place in relatively short order. While enjoying a tribute to Jolson and the cast of *A Night in Spain* at Chicago's Rainbo Gardens nightclub, Ted, Shemp and Bobby were treated to an hilarious performance by the evening's master of ceremonies, a twenty-six-year-old comedian and impressionist named Larry Fine.

Larry had grown up in Philadelphia, Pennsylvania, and had already spent most of his life in one form of show business or another. As a child he had won amateur contests with his impersonation of screen star Charlie Chaplin, and as a teenager he even embarked on a lightweight boxing career, billing himself as "Kid Roth." By 1928 Larry was a successful vaudeville performer, co-starring with his wife Mabel Haney Fine and her sister Loretta in a song-and-dance act. But occasionally Larry performed as a single, serving up impersonations and dialect comedy, as he did the night he caught the eye of Ted Healy and his remaining Stooges at the Rainbo Gardens.

Shemp's wife Babe said it was her husband who convinced Ted Healy that he should hire Larry on the spot. Shemp believed Larry's improvisational skills and good-natured attitude would make him a Stooge of the first order. And Shemp had selfish interests in bringing Larry into the act — the elder Stooge was going to ask Healy for a leave of absence.

Before leaving the act, Shemp walked Larry through all of the Stooges' routines, and within a matter of hours the new Stooge trio was ready for audiences. Larry joined

From left, Larry Fine joins Shemp Howard and Bobby Pinkus as one of the Stooges in 1928, and the three young comedians embark on a whirlwind tour of the Midwest with Ted Healy.

Healy's entourage in 1928, just in time to embark on an extended tour of the Midwest with the Shuberts' *A Night in Spain*. Shortly thereafter, Shemp rejoined the group, and he, Larry and Bobby Pinkus fractured theatergoers with their semi-improvised clowning.

A Night in Spain was so successful that the Shuberts decided to hire Healy and his boys for a follow-up Broadway revue, *A Night in Venice*, slated for the following year. But now Bobby Pinkus had decided to go off on his own, leaving Ted with another vacancy in his Stooge trio just as he was about to open on Broadway.

Worse still was the fact that Larry Fine, although amenable to working with Healy, was nowhere to be found. After the conclusion of *A Night in Spain* in late 1928, Larry and his wife Mabel had headed for Atlantic City, where Larry began working in nightclubs as a solo comedian, and billing himself as "the star of the Shuberts' *A Night in Spain*." Larry had told Ted he would be available for more stooging when Healy went back to work, but hadn't bothered to let anyone know he was leaving New York City.

Unable to locate Larry, Healy hired another performer, an eccentric funnyman and musician named Freddie Sanborn, to take his place. And while auditioning comedians in search of a replacement for Bobby Pinkus,

An advertisement for the Shuberts' touring-company production of *A Night in Spain*, published in a Chicago newspaper in 1928.

Mabel and Larry Fine at the shore in Atlantic City, New Jersey, at precisely the same time Ted Healy is desperately trying to find the elusive Stooge.

Far left; Freddie Sanborn, a comedian and xylophonist who works on the bill with Ted Healy and his Stooges, eventually becomes a full-fledged member of the team, playing the middleman between Shemp and Moe in 1929.

24

Ted suddenly thought of a retired actor who was not only familiar with the act, but also lived in New York. What's more, Healy had a feeling he would be more than eager to get his feet back on the boards again.

By this time, Moe Howard had had a bellyful of the business world, having failed miserably in most of his endeavors. He longed to return to the stage, and when Ted Healy asked him if he'd like to appear as one of his Stooges in a new Broadway show, Moe jumped at the chance. Moe joined his brother Shemp and the newly-indoctrinated Freddie Sanborn in 1929, shortly before the debut of *A Night in Venice*.

While Shemp, Freddie and Moe were working the bugs out of their new act, Larry happened to show up in New York, having taken the train up from Atlantic City to pursue some business opportunities. While strolling down Broadway, and letting old friends know his wife had just given birth to his daughter, Phyllis, Larry ran into Mabel's brother-in-law, Harry Romm. A major theatrical talent agent, Romm informed Larry that Ted Healy was looking for him, that he wanted him to appear as one of his Stooges in a new show for the Shubert Brothers. Larry quickly tracked down Healy, and was just as quickly re-hired. Freddie Sanborn, meanwhile, was relegated to a subordinate role, that of "stooge for the Stooges," as Larry returned to his "middleman" position between Moe and Shemp.

Left: Larry, Moe and Shemp are Ted Healy's "Southern Gentlemen" in the Broadway smash *A Night in Venice* (1929), marking the first time these three legendary Stooges appear on the same stage.

It was this trio of Stooges that really clicked with audiences, and Ted and the boys emerged as the undisputed hit of the new Shubert revue. It also marked the first time the Stooges received billing as part of Healy's act, debuting as the Three Southern Gentlemen. Within weeks of the show's debut, Ted and his Stooges were the toast of the Great White Way, so much so that they even started making surprise appearances in other comedians' venues.

Frank Mitchell, a slapstick comedian who was then appearing in the 1929 edition of *George White's Scandals* with straightman Jack Durant, recalled the night Ted Healy and his Stooges showed up backstage and hastily put together a slapping routine:

"Healy had Moe and Larry with him, but for whatever reason, Shemp didn't come along. So I took his place, you might say. The boys came out on stage and we did a slap-fight, Moe, Larry and myself, that had the audience screaming. Big laughs, big laughs. Most of what the Stooges did in those days was off-the-cuff."

When *A Night in Venice* was closed by the Depression in 1930, Ted Healy and his partners returned to vaudeville, performing numerous crowd-pleasing routines from the

From right, onetime Ted Healy Stooge, Frank Mitchell, poses with musical–comedy headliners Alice Faye, Ray Walker, and his own straightman, Jack Durant, when all four are starring in feature films at Hollywood's Fox Studios.

Above, right: By the early 1930s, Ted (pictured here with Broadway star Anne Seymour) realizes his marriage to Betty is on the rocks, and the couple begins talking about divorce.

Shubert revue. That same year Ted and his Stooges — now called "Racketeers" — acquired a booking at New York's famed Palace Theater, then the most prestigious vaudeville house in the country. Meanwhile, a talent scout from Hollywood's Fox Studios, the forerunner of 20th Century-Fox, was in New York on the lookout for "talking" comedians to star in his studio's new "all-talking" pictures.

By 1930, silent films had all but disappeared, and Fox was in search of Broadway-trained stage performers to take advantage of the movies' latest technology. The Marx Brothers' "talkie" debut in the previous season's *The Cocoanuts* had proven a smash hit for Paramount, and Fox was eager to duplicate the rival studio's success. On an evening at the Palace when Ted and company were "laying them in the aisles" with laughter, Fox's scout caught their act and signed Healy and the Stooges — as well as Freddie Sanborn — for a feature film appearance.

Soup to Nuts (1930), written by cartoonist and humorist Rube Goldberg, marked the screen debut of the Stooges as a team. The film was actually conceived as a vehicle for Ted Healy, who enjoys not only top billing but the lion's share of screen time.

The plotline of *Soup to Nuts*, the team's big-screen endeavor for the 1930-31 season, simply served as an excuse to showcase the vaudeville routines of Ted and the Stooges. Shemp, Larry and Moe (here billed under his real name, Harry Howard) play big-city firemen, while Healy plays their kibitzing pal Ted, a rakish character who likes nothing more than accompanying the Stooges on emergency calls.

The film was clearly intended as a star vehicle for Ted Healy, and he receives top billing in the opening credits. The remainder of the cast, billed in smaller type, is listed as follows: "Charles Winninger, Frances McCoy, George Bickel, Lucile Browne, Shemp Howard, Stanley Smith, Harry Howard, Hallam Cooley, Fred Sanborn, Larry Fine." Not credited were former Mack Sennett comics Mack Swain, Heine Conklin and Roscoe Ates, nor the film's "inspiration," Rube Goldberg, who appears in a cameo.

Below, left: Ted and the boys — as well as that "stooge for the Stooges," Freddie Sanborn — in costume for Fox's feature film *Soup to Nuts* (1930).

While the Stooges' screen time is minimal (they don't even receive billing as a team), *Soup to Nuts* is significant in that the boys were offered a separate film contract as a result of their appearance. Thus, the Stooges made arrangements to leave their mentor and sign with Fox as a trio. Ted reportedly interfered, however, and Fox called the deal off.

Angry with Healy, the Stooges decided to go out on their own anyway. Jack Walsh, a handsome straightman of Irish descent, was hired to replace Ted in their act, and the Stooges began developing material of their own. The trio continued working without their mentor for a couple of years, building a reputation of their own as a starring act rather than as a group of sidemen.

Around this time, Healy's behavior started to become erratic and, sometimes, dangerous. He had developed a fondness for alcohol, but was not a happy drinker. Shemp

The Stooges, their screen girlfriends, and sidekick Freddie Sanborn pose on the set of *Soup to Nuts*, located on the Fox lot in what is now L.A.'s Century City district.

The Stooges and
their vaudeville
straightman, Jack
Walsh (far left),
clown between
shows with cham-
pion boxer Georges
Carpentier.

was, in the words of his wife Babe, "absolutely terrified of Ted when he was drinking." Larry felt that Ted was a full-blown alcoholic, incapable of turning down drink "even when he knew he needed to be sober." And Moe described Ted as "a Dr. Jekyll when sober, and a Mr. Hyde when drinking."

"Ted Healy was a good guy, but he suffered from depression," said Frank Mitchell. "That's why he drank. In those days, there was no medication you could take if you were depressed. A lot of people, especially show-business people, turned to liquor because it was the only thing that made their life tolerable. Remember, if you were a performer, you had to get out there on that stage and entertain people whether you were depressed or not. And for some people, the booze helped. For a while, anyway."

While Ted struggled with his addiction to alcohol, he also struggled to survive as a solo performer. For the first time in years, Healy was working without Stooges. During this period, both Ted and the Howard gang were using much of the same comedy material, even though they were working separately. Healy accused the Stooges of stealing material that he had created, or had hired writers to create specifically for his act. Shemp, however, managed to create a major new addition to the Stooges' repertoire, although in a rather unortho-dox manner.

According to Shemp's wife Babe, the addition came about one afternoon as the Stooges and their wives were relaxing between stage shows. "We were all sitting around playing cards, and passing time," said Babe. "Shemp had a terrible temper, and he thought Larry was cheating. So he jumped up and yelled 'I'm gonna stab your eyes out!' He actually poked Larry right in the eyes with his fingers! Moe, who was the brains of the outfit, always had a sharp eye for something new for the act. So he decided to include that bit in their routines."

By now Moe had established himself as the de facto business man-ager and spokesman of the trio. He became the driving force of the Stooges, securing performing dates for the group and making sure the boys got paid on time. Larry was in charge of music, with responsibil-ities ranging from the creation of the occasional song parody, to the selection of the team's entrance and exit numbers. And Shemp devot-ed much of his time to creating new comedy material for the act.

As Shemp and his partners began establishing themselves as an act independent of Healy, Ted, in turn, hired three other sidemen to replace the Howard gang in his act. These "replacement" Stooges had already had extensive vaudeville performing experience prior to team-ing with Healy. Each of them was a musician and comedian, and each had been a professional performer for years before becoming members of the second major Stooge dynasty. This newest Stooge trio was assembled in 1930, by a beloved old crony of Ted's from the previous decade.

Dick Hakins, who had worked with Healy in the Twenties along with Shemp Howard and Lou Warren, formed the new act and played its eccentric "lynchpin" character. After recovering from a lengthy ill-ness, Dick had re-entered show business as a musician, and had scored several Broadway shows prior to working again for Ted Healy. Dick was brought back into the act primarily because of his gagwriting skills, his dry sense of humor, and his ability to look "sappy" on demand.

Dick's pal Jack Wolf was the antagonist figure of the new group; he played the "underboss" that dished out all the slapping and eye-poking

While appearing in vaudeville in the early 1930s, Shemp takes time out for a snapshot with Petey, the lovable mascot of The Little Rascals.

From left, Ted Healy's Stooges — Dick Hakins, Jack Wolf and Mousie Garner — pose with oblivious straightman Jack Walsh in the early 1930s.

The original program from the stage revue *The Gang's All Here*, in which Ted enjoyed the starring role and introduced Mousie Garner, Jack Wolf and Dick Hakins as his "Stooges."

to his partners. Jack was an astute businessman, and he later arranged performing contracts and vaudeville engagements for the team. He was also a talented musician, and his musical abilities were often showcased in appearances with the Stooges.

Jack brought with him Mousie Garner, the new "Third Stooge," who initially played the act's lynchpin before evolving into its full-time "patsy." In real life Mousie was Jack Wolf's cousin, and they had broken into show business together as part of a musical comedy act prior to teaming with Dick Hakins as Ted Healy's Stooges. Like his partners, Mousie was also a musician, and his comic piano-playing routine eventually became the staple of the act.

All three of Healy's new Stooges — now called his "New Racketeers" — had met long before joining up with Ted. They had previously appeared together in a variety of vaudeville lineups. At that time, Dick was playing piano onstage while cousins Jack and Mousie were working as stooges (along with then-unknown Ginger Rogers) for song-and-dance man Jack Pepper. Pepper, a vaudeville star and Rogers' first husband, billed his act as "Jack Pepper with Ginger, Mustard and Ketchup," the latter two condiments portrayed by Jack and Mousie.

THE
IMPERIAL THEATRE

THE GANG'S ALL HERE

★★★ The THREE STOOGES ★★★

The Pepper group made its one and only movie appearance together in the late Twenties, starring in a talkie short subject titled *After the Show* that included a filmed version of their vaudeville act.

But it was Ted who first hired Jack, Mousie and Dick as a trio, with the specific goal of developing them into a Stooge team, and it wasn't until they appeared with Healy that they were called "Stooges." In fact, they were the *first* comics in history to be billed as Ted Healy's "Stooges," as evidenced in the 1931 program for the Broadway musical *The Gang's All Here.*

In 1932, Betty Healy is divorced from her hard-partying husband after a decade of marriage, and she embarks on a successful solo career as a comedienne.

All three "new" men were serious musicians, even though they played it primarily for laughs when appearing as Stooges. One routine, for example, had all three Stooges playing one piano at the same time. In addition to playing instruments, Ted's new trio also sang and danced. They introduced the popular Depression-era hit *Million Dollar Baby*, which they performed in their second musical revue, Billy Rose's 1931 Broadway hit *Crazy Quilt*. While appearing in that show, they also made film appearances, sans Healy, in Warner-Vitaphone's *Broadway Brevities* musical shorts.

In comparing the Howard family's Three Stooges with his own Stooge unit, Mousie Garner says, "Our act was like The Three Stooges with music. We did the same kind of physical comedy as the Stooges, but we could also play instruments and sing."

Dick Hakins also pointed out that their act wasn't as violent as that of the Howards' Three Stooges, even though they indulged in a lot of physical mayhem themselves. Newspaper reviews from the 1930s indicate that the content of both Stooge acts was somewhat similar. In addition, Healy's "new" threesome also sported gag haircuts and wore similar stage costumes. And, of course, they were also fairly short in stature, as were the original members.

As Jack Wolf put it, "Ted had a rule" that none of the Stooges who worked opposite the six-foot Healy could stand more than five-and-a-half feet tall.

After appearing with his new threesome on Broadway, in the national touring company of *Crazy Quilt*, and on the vaudeville circuit, Healy was forced to take a substantial salary cut due to the Depression. By 1932, Ted found himself temporarily out of work — and out of cash as well. As a result, he had to drop his second set of Stooges. They, in turn, went out on their own European stage tour (not as "Stooges," but as the more British-sounding "Gentlemaniacs"). The trio rehearsed some new material and departed for performing engagements in Great Britain. Healy's second ensemble spent more than a year overseas, headlining the London Palladium and playing before the crowned heads of Europe during an extended tour of the Continent.

Healy's new Stooges had developed a new act that was similar in many ways to the Howard family's "Three Stooges," but distinctly different in style. There was less emphasis on violence, even though they employed such traditional bits as the "poke in the eyes." One bit they used quite frequently was nicknamed the "mob scene." This consisted of the boys milling around in circles around each other, creating the effect of crowding and confusion!

For their 1932-33 tour, Mousie and company hired straightman Jack Walsh — the same vaudevillian who had worked with Shemp and his partners just weeks earlier.

Mousie explains, "Jack had been working with Shemp and the boys at the same time Hakins, Wolf and myself were working with Healy. But when Healy hired back his old Stooges, Walsh was out of a job, just like the three of us. It was Walsh who suggested we

★★★ **The THREE STOOGES** ★★★

work together. So the three of us went out on the road in vaudeville with Jack Walsh as our straightman."

While both sets of Stooges were establishing themselves in the early 1930s, their mentor Ted Healy also went back to work. Ted had just divorced his wife Betty, and was in desperate need of cash. Healy was thus relieved to be hired as star of the 1932 edition of the Shubert Brothers' Broadway revue *The Passing Show.* As a result, he was once again in a financial position to rehire his old sidemen.

Ted contacted his former Stooges now working in Europe, the Garner group, but they had just begun their overseas tour. In addition, Mousie and his partners also had a number of contractual obligations to fulfill upon returning to the States. Despite Ted's pleadings and promises, Garner and friends honored all of their performing dates.

CurlyJoe DeRita, pictured here in a dance routine with his mother and sister, recalled that the Stooges used material from *The Passing Show* until the end of their days as a team.

In time it became clear to Ted that he had only two options left: Either hire three brand-new comedians and try to make Stooges out of them, or bring the audience-proven Howard dynasty back into the fold. Healy opted for the latter.

With a major Broadway show about to open, the brothers Shubert were pressing Healy to mend fences with his old cronies. By now, however, a rift had formed between the former beach buddies. Moe felt that Ted was an opportunist who drank too much and, as a result, was moody and unpredictable. He also felt that Healy didn't pay his Stooges nearly enough money for the beatings they took and the bellylaughs they provided.

Ted, on the other hand, saw himself as an established star who knew how to get laughs with or without Stooges. He was also aware of the fact that the Stooges were struggling to make a name for themselves without him, and they weren't having much success. Their vaudeville tour, in which they billed themselves as "Three Lost Souls," brought them little in the way of income or acclaim.

Eventually both parties realized they needed each other, and, after much deliberation, Shemp, Larry and Moe returned to Ted's act. They began rehearsing day and night for *The Passing Show,* often sharing the stage with a zany young comedian named Joe Besser. Joe became a part-time Stooge, and frequently found himself dragged into Healy's act whenever Ted felt the urge to expand his troupe.

Strange as it may seem, all of Healy's various Stooges were friends at one time or another. They even socialized together on occasion. They had become acquainted with each other during their vaudeville days through their mutual association with Healy. If Shemp Howard was temporarily unavailable to play the "Third Stooge," for example, Ted might ask Mousie Garner or another so-called "rival" Stooge to leave his own act and take Shemp's place. Mousie Garner, in fact, worked opposite Moe and Larry on one occasion in the early 1930s, when Healy and the boys were trying out new material in Boston.

As members of Ted Healy's entourage, they were virtually interchangeable. This was primarily because they had not yet developed characters for themselves with distinct personality traits. The characters of the Stooges evolved into recognizable icons only after the boys left Ted's employment.

Ted Healy lords it over Stooges Jack Wolf, Mousie Garner and Dick Hakins, gagwriter Eddie Moran (at Ted's right), and an unidentified stagehand (under Ted's foot).

"But Healy really preferred working with Moe and Shemp," recalled Shemp's wife Babe. "They had grown up with him, and he knew Larry very well, too. He knew the way they ad libbed."

Even though they were more or less friends, Ted loved to give his Stooges a hard time. This was especially true when he was drinking, which became more and more frequent as the years progressed. "Healy was a conniver," said Shemp's wife Babe, "and he had a mean

sense of humor. He'd do terrible things to the boys, especially Shemp, just to see the terrified look on his face."

Reportedly Healy had a habit of inviting his Stooges over to his house as overnight guests. But when he started drinking, the Stooges quickly packed their suitcases and headed out of the building. Experience had taught them that that was the best thing to do. Because Healy, while drunk, would become angry and belligerent. He would take all of their clothes and personal belongings, and simply toss them out the windows, for no apparent reason other than to irritate the Stooges.

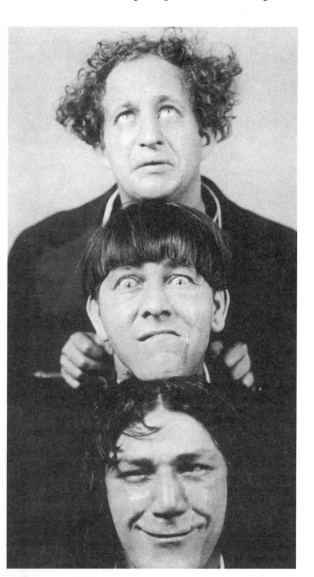

Healy also enjoyed pulling elaborate practical jokes on the Stooges, and, often, innocent bystanders. While living in a Santa Monica hotel in the 1930s, Ted once instructed his Stooges to gather up about a hundred telephone directories. The Stooges brought them up to Healy's penthouse suite, where the boys were instructed to soak each one of the heavy phone books in a bathtub full of water. Ted then amused himself by dropping the missile-like directories out the window, aiming for people on the sidewalk below.

And Dick Hakins remembered a story, told to him by Healy, about a trick Ted had pulled on Shemp, Larry and Moe. "Healy brought all three of them to a Catholic church," said Hakins. "Healy was Catholic, and the Stooges were Jewish. They asked Healy to show them what to do. He just told them to do whatever he did. So they all went up to the front pew, and sat down. Every time the priest turned around, Healy would stand up, or sit down, or kneel, just to watch the poor guys jumping up and down in confusion! Afterwards, Shemp told him he'd never go to a church again — too much jumping up and down!"

But these practical jokes were harmless compared to Ted's antics involving the criminal underworld. In a Manhattan nightclub, Healy had managed to offend Charles "Lucky" Luciano, then New York's most powerful and dangerous gangster, by making some smart cracks about Luciano's Italian heritage. Later, while appearing with the Stooges in Chicago, Ted had attempted to get the attention of that city's number-one mobster, Al Capone, through a series of risky stunts.

The wildest of these was his attempt at looting a safe Capone maintained in the back room of his brother's Chicago speakeasy. Big Al laughed it off, but Healy and his Stooges were forced to provide Capone with a private performance of their vaudeville act — free of charge. For Ted, it was all worth it. He had wanted an audience with the biggest gangster in America, and he got one.

The Stooges, however, were so terrified of Capone and his army of thugs, they could barely spit out their lines.

TO HEADLINE THE COMIC SECTION OF YOUR PROGRAM

An uproarious new laugh-star sensation . . . .

Discovered and developed to continue the comedy leadership of Vitaphone . . . .

Sky-rocketed to fame by the millions who go to the movies for the *fun* of it!

If you've never seen him, ask for a screening of one of his "Big V Comedies" . . . .

Be your own preview audience . . . . test him on yourself . . . .

You'll see why his name on your front is going to mean money in your cash-drawer!

SHEMP HOWARD in VITAPHONE SHORTS

Shemp leaves Ted Healy's act, and quickly becomes a star in his own right at Vitaphone Pictures, Warner Bros.' short-subject studio in New York.

So when Ted asked Shemp, Larry and Moe to join him in walking out on *The Passing Show* during a salary dispute, Shemp refused. Shemp had had enough of Healy's antics, both onstage and off.

"I was really the one that made Shemp go out on his own," said his wife Babe. "I was sick and tired of Healy, and of all his tricks, so I told Shemp to take a movie offer he had gotten."

Shemp did as his wife asked, and began his career as a solo comedian at Warner Bros.' "Vitaphone" Studios, working out of soundstages in Brooklyn, New York. He appeared in a vast number of short-subject comedies beginning in 1933, quickly becoming one of Warner-Vitaphone's biggest names. And although he couldn't have known it at the time, Shemp's career as a major star of shorts would continue until the literal end of his life.

Ted Healy, however, was less than pleased when his star "Stooge" left the act. Shemp had suggested that they use his younger brother, Jerry "Curly" Howard, as a replacement, but Ted wasn't interested. And he wasn't the only one unimpressed with the idea. Seasoned Stooges Moe and Larry thought the notion was ridiculous as well.

"Moe wrote Shemp a letter," said Shemp's wife Babe, "telling him that Jerry had absolutely no talent. Moe did not want him in the act. Jerry didn't have a lot of experience in show business, but he

Curly Howard, complete with Chaplinesque moustache, replaces his brother Shemp as one of Ted Healy's Stooges in 1932.

Opposite: Ted, the Stooges, and Ted's girlfriend Bonnie Bonnell on the set of their first starring film at Metro–Goldwyn–Mayer, *Nertsery Rhymes* (1933).

wanted to get in, even if Moe didn't want him."

So Shemp devised a scheme to get Curly into the act. He told him to shave his head and run on stage in a bathing suit, barefoot, carrying a tiny pail of water! Jerry did so, and, because of his newly-acquired hairstyle, officially acquired the stage name "Curly" as well.

As a result of his rather grotesque appearance, Curly got a tremendous laugh from the audience every time he stepped onto the stage. That was enough to convince all concerned that Curly would indeed serve as a suitable replacement for Shemp.

Curly eventually developed his own unique comic style, creating a character whose actions and personality suggested a blend of insanity and childlike ignorance. With his shaven head, rotund appearance and use of a cackling, high-pitched voice, Curly resembled, as Moe put it, "a fat fairy."

But Curly clicked with the Stooges, and he quickly became the star of the trio, outshining his partners as well as his highly-regarded predecessor.

"After Shemp quit," recalled his wife Babe, "Curly became the funniest Stooge."

Ted and the Stooges went back into vaudeville in 1932, and Curly quickly adapted to the style of the act. While making an appearance at a Hollywood, California night club the following year, Healy and his partners were enlisted by a representative from Metro-Goldwyn-Mayer Studios to perform at a charity benefit.

Following their performance, Healy met with Metro boss Louis B. Mayer, and signed a one-year contract to appear in films at that prestigious studio. Ted personally was responsible for pay-

↑ Character player Edward Brophy is scolded by the boys in Metro's backstage musical *Hello Pop* (1933), an early Technicolor short now believed to be a lost film.

↑ Ted and the Stooges resurrect their vaudeville act for Bonnie Bonnell in Metro's short subject *Plane Nuts* (1933).

↑ Metro's *Beer and Pretzels* (1933), which finds the boys as singing waiters who wreak havoc in a beer garden, is the funniest of the Healy-Stooge shorts.

ing the Stooges, whose names do not even appear in the contract! While at Metro, Healy and the boys made a handful of musicals and comedies, some of them lensed in primitive Technicolor. In each of these efforts Ted invariably received more attention and screen time than any of his three Stooges. Also along for the ride was Bonnie Bonnell, a chorus girl from *Crazy Quilt* who was Healy's real-life girlfriend and protégé. She played what might be described as the "Betty Healy" role in most of the group's Metro appearances.

The team's Metro feature film for the 1932-33 season was *Meet the Baron* (1933), an all-star "college"-themed comedy featuring radio comedian Jack Pearl (in the title role), singing funnyman Jimmy Durante, and character comedienne Zasu Pitts, among others. But it was Ted and the Stooges who walked away with most of the laughs, cast as campus

Solo comedian Shemp (far right) appears with Fatty Arbuckle (far left) in Arbuckle's last film, Warner–Vitaphone's *In the Dough* (1933); the rotund comedian dies of a heart attack the day after shooting is completed.

custodians who wreak havoc in a girls' dormitory.

Even though the Stooges were now working steadily in the movies, it was becoming clear that their development as a team was being hampered by their second-banana status. It was not until the Stooges decided to go out on their own on a permanent basis that they were able to fully develop their madcap style of comedy.

During their year at Metro, Ted and his Stooges were used both separately and as a team, appearing in feature films, short subjects and a handful of live appearances on behalf of the studio. Healy was especially prolific as a single, eventually co-starring with all of Metro's top personalities in feature-length "spectaculars." In most of these productions, Ted was entrusted with the role of lead comedian, and his inspired clowning saved many a scene that would otherwise have fallen flat. Metro even began grooming Healy as a solo star, casting him in both comedic and dramatic roles.

Edna May Oliver already regrets having summoned Healy and his Stooges to repair the plumbing in the girls' locker room in this scene from *Meet the Baron*.

A processional march on the Metro lot with Ted, the Stooges, and an array of supporting players.

Ted and the Stooges are about to provide the musical accompaniment for co-star Joan Crawford's chorus audition in this scene from *Dancing Lady* (1933).

The Stooges, meanwhile, worked occasionally without their mentor as well. But mostly they felt as if they were grabbing at whatever crumbs happened to fall from Ted's plate.

The success of Healy and his Stooges at Metro prompted an old friend of Ted's from military school, producer Bryan Foy, to offer the foursome their own starring feature-film vehicle. Foy had started out in vaudeville as part of his father's song-and-dance act, "Eddie Foy and the Seven Little Foys," but had made the transition from stage actor to Hollywood film producer. He owned the screen rights to the popular radio series *Myrt and Marge*, and felt that the visually-oriented comedy of Ted and his gang would carry the film.

Myrt and Marge, filmed independently by Foy for release by Universal Pictures, turned out to be the team's feature-film offering for the 1934-35 season. Advertising for the movie gave Healy top billing, with the Stooges again providing most of the laughs as stagehands traveling with a touring vaudeville company.

While Healy and his partners mulled the possibility of leaving Louis B. Mayer's studio in favor of working for independent producer Bryan Foy, they made one last major appearance in a Metro feature film. *Fugitive Lovers* (1934) was another all-star epic, this time casting Ted and the boys as passengers on a coast-to-coast bus trip along with Robert Montgomery, Madge Evans, Nat Pendleton and others. The film also provided the last straw in the professional relationship between Ted Healy and Moe Howard.

On the Metro lot, Healy and the boys clown with Hollywood's most popular actor, Clark Gable, their co-star from David O. Selznick's super-musical *Dancing Lady* (1933).

Ted had grown tired of Moe's constant complaining about their performing arrangement at Metro, in which the Stooges were employed by Healy, not the studio. Moe was constantly threatening that he, Larry and Curly might join the newly-formed Screen Actors Guild, a move that would force Metro to put them under studio contract — and out of Ted's control.

In what was apparently an attempt to oust Moe from the Stooges, Healy had brought in yet another comedian, a gagman and character actor named John "Red" Pearson, ostensibly to play the role of "a stooge for the Stooges." This was Ted's own description of the part, and Red appears on-camera with the Stooges as a fellow bus passenger.

But Moe believed Red was being groomed to take over the role of the Stooges' leader, the part that had fallen to Moe once Shemp left the act. Moe felt he was being squeezed out of the team, and he convinced Curly and Larry that the best idea for all concerned was for the Stooges to make a clean break with Healy. From this moment forward, Moe

Howard would forever control the destiny of The Three Stooges, and this would eventually lead to the formation of the Stooges' own film-producing and licensing company, Comedy III Productions.

Moe and his partners left Ted for good this time, certain they now had what it took to successfully pursue an independent career. Healy, in turn, granted them permission to use the name "The Three Stooges." The boys had first appeared billed as Ted's "Three Stooges" in Metro's *The Big Idea*, their final film with Healy, and they liked the sound of the name. At least it was more upbeat than "Three Lost Souls."

Immediately after disengaging themselves with Ted, the Stooges' agent signed them to a deal with Universal Pictures, in which they would star in ten short-subject comedies per year. At first this sounded like a great arrangement, until Moe realized that

Balding Ted wears a toupee in this publicity photo for *Fugitive Lovers* (1934), the film that provides the last straw in the relationship between Healy and his boyhood buddy Moe Howard.

At Columbia Pictures, the boys try to frighten head honcho Harry Cohn for a change.

they would be working at Universal under the supervision of Healy's best friend, Bryan Foy. Moe suspected that Ted had allowed them to use the name "Three Stooges" because he knew they would be working for Foy. Through Healy's influence with Foy, Ted would essentially still be in control of the Stooges' destinies. And this was not something Moe felt he could tolerate.

So the Stooges got out of their Universal contract, and instead signed with Columbia Pictures, then regarded as something of an embarrassment among Hollywood studios. Columbia was best known for its cheap-looking movies and its lack of major stars. The studio was located in an area of Hollywood called "Poverty Row," so named because of the numerous low-budget film companies that operated there.

The Stooges' new boss, tough-talking Columbia president Harry Cohn, was known to have connections to the New York Mafia. This in and of itself was not unusual in Hollywood's early days, as Louis B. Mayer of Metro, Jack Warner of Warner Bros., and

What's a Stooge?
TED HEALY TELLS YOU!

By ROBERT FENDER

TED HEALY, the man who made the United States stooge-conscious, had just finished a scene with Robert Montgomery in a picture when I cornered him. I had been hanging around some time, waiting to get the answer to "What is a stooge?" So when I sprang it on him he replied:

"A stooge is a *****! /////
---- #### !!!!!——"

"*Wait* a minute, Ted," I soft-pedaled. "We can't print that. Give me a definition I can use in the magazine!"

Ted scratched his head. "It's going to be tough to give you a definition of a stooge in decent language," he pleaded, "but here's a go. A stooge is a guy who never has a light for a ciga-rette he is trying to borrow.

"A stooge is something that's there when you look around. It's a sort of something—something awful." He shuddered. "Some-thing really awful, like *Dr. Jekyll* and *Mr. Hyde* without the *Dr. Jekyll*. A stooge is two helpings

This is Ted Healy. You can tell him by his hat. The three lads who are practically in his hair are his "stooges." Between them, they have brought a brand-new kind of clowning to films!

of awful. A stooge is some-thing that, when you dream about it, you have to get up and turn on the lights.

"All of us," Ted continued, "have a little stooge in us. If our Mr. Mayer and President Roosevelt are walking down the street, one of them's a stooge, but if Mr. Mayer reads this, I'm only joking."

"What do you call your stooges?"

"I call 'em N. R. A. be-cause, like prosperity, they're always around the corner when I want 'em. But my stooges ought to get along fine in Hollywood. They have lots of company. This is Stooge Cen-ter here, the land where all good little stooges go. If," he added, "they're real, real good or bad. All my stooges have to do here is keep real quiet and pretty soon they'll all be supervisors."

"Where," I asked, "did you find your stooges?"
(*Continued on page 63*)

51

The March 1934 issue of *Movie Classic Magazine* features an interview with Ted Healy in which he states, "Whenever I'm in doubt or feel mixed up, I always hit the nearest stooge."

many other so-called moguls routinely took orders from the Mob. But Harry Cohn prid-ed himself on his ruthlessness, and he would soon come to be regarded as the most hated man in Hollywood. It was a label Cohn not only accepted, but actually relished. He ruled his studio with an iron fist, delighting in intimidating lower-rung employees and instilling fear into the hearts of his top creative people.

In the thirty years The Three Stooges made motion pictures for Columbia, they would appear in ten original feature-length movies, more than two hundred short films, and more than three thousand personal appearances, all on behalf of the studio. And although the Stooges themselves would never be made aware of it, the income produced by Columbia's "Three Stooges" comedies would help transform the studio from a Poverty Row outfit into the most profitable film factory on earth, a major amongst majors.

In 1934, a young craftsman named Jules White, formerly a producer and director at

On location at Columbia's Burbank "ranch" facility in the 1930s, the Stooges confer with Jules White, their longtime producer–director and founder of the studio's Shorts Department.

Charlie Chaplin, who first met the Stooges while visiting with old friend Ted Healy on the set of *Soup to Nuts*, occasionally drops by Columbia's Shorts Department as well.

Metro, had just been put in charge of developing Columbia's short-subject comedy department. He had known the Stooges when they were part of Ted Healy's act, and thought they would do fairly well in shorts.

The Columbia Shorts Department, or "Jules' Fun Factory," as it was also known, was a hectic place in the 1930s. A separate entity from the company's feature-film division, the department occupied a building on Beechwood Drive in Hollywood, across the street from Columbia's main studio. The close-knit Shorts Department had its own sound stages, its own producers and directors, and its own stars.

By the time the Stooges signed with Columbia, its short-subject unit was already regarded as a haven for has-been comedians, as well as old favorites who had nowhere else to go. By the end of the 1930s, Columbia was the only film studio in the world regularly producing Mack Sennett-style slapstick. Sooner or later, most of the comedy legends of the silent screen would find themselves on Columbia soundstages.

Harry Langdon was the first of the previous decade's comedy giants to make shorts at Columbia. He was hired to star in his own films, as well as create gags for the department's other comedians. Langdon was followed shortly thereafter by Buster Keaton, who also signed on as a performer and gagman. Even Charlie Chaplin occasionally dropped by the Shorts Department, just to kibitz with old colleagues and suggest gag ideas on the set of whatever film might be in production. Other top comedians of the silent era, including Charley Chase, Andy Clyde, Chester Conklin, Leon Errol, Tom Kennedy, Franklin Pangborn, Monty Collins, Slim Summerville, Max Davidson, and Snub Pollard, also found themselves appearing in Columbia shorts and on soundstages alongside The Three Stooges.

In addition to former stars from the silent era, future stars began their movie careers at Columbia as well. For example, Lucille Ball, Lloyd Bridges, Walter Brennan and several other prominent film actors had supporting roles in early Three Stooges shorts. Also, "name" broadcast personalities, like Bob Hope's stooge Vera Vague, George Burns' stooge Harry von Zell, and Eddie Foy's stooge (and Bryan's brother) Eddie Jr., were among Columbia's "up-and-comers" who found themselves stars in the Shorts Department. Headliners were constantly coming and going at Columbia, finding short-term work in shorts between feature-film assignments at Columbia and other studios.

These shorts, each less than twenty minutes in length, were produced by the studio as "curtain-raisers" to be shown before the feature film presentation. Studio management considered the shorts to be "throwaways," and they paid little attention to their production — as long as they were completed on schedule.

Because each short had to be shot in less than a week, time was of the essence. At Columbia most of them were filmed in three days. The Stooges, however, were usually accorded an extra day of shooting time, because of the often-elaborate sight gags their comedies required. Character comedian Emil Sitka, who began working at Columbia during Curly's tenure with the Stooges, reported that sometimes half a day would be spent preparing and filming a single gag.

"I was surprised they shot the entire film in only a few days," he said. "It was a tight schedule, believe me! We really had

Future television superstar Lucille Ball (above center) is featured in her first major comedy role in the Stooges' 1934 short *Three Little Pigskins.*

to squeeze it in. We'd work a full day, and get a good many scenes in the can, but on the last day there was always a rush to get it in before five o'clock."

Indeed, Columbia's comedy factory was among the busiest lots in Hollywood. By the late 1930s, Columbia had the largest short-subject comedy unit in operation. The Stooge shorts, in turn, were among Columbia's most consistently popular attractions.

But in 1934, not many people would have guessed that the Shorts Department's newest acquisition, a slapstick comedy team called The Three Stooges, was about to become Columbia's most valuable on-screen property.

"I had dozens of great comedians," said Jules White, a silent-film veteran who had rubbed shoulders with Griffith, Sennett, and Chaplin, and who in his thirties founded Columbia's comedy department. "Some of 'em were world-renowned . . . So the Stooges were not the only ones I made pictures with. But television has boosted them to the sky, and they've overshadowed anything else we've ever done as far as public taste is concerned."

At the time the Stooges were hired by Columbia, the studio was developing its short-subject comedy unit and was in search of new talent. Comedy veteran White headed the department during the first several years of its existence. Hugh McCollum, former secre-

tary to Columbia president Harry Cohn, later split production duties with White, but White would eventually regain complete control of the Shorts Department.

White had many years of experience under his belt as both a producer and director. He started out as a child actor, and as an adolescent appeared in the landmark feature film of the mid-Teens, *The Birth of a Nation*, under the direction of cinema pioneer D.W. Griffith. After working an apprenticeship as a gag creator, or "gagman," at the Mack Sennett Studio, White decided upon a career behind the camera as producer-director of film comedies.

By the early Thirties, Jules White was one of Hollywood's best-known short-subject producers. He had worked his way up from gag man and film editor at Fox-Educational Pictures, to producer and director at Metro-Goldwyn-Mayer. Shortly after White became ensconced at Metro, Harry Cohn "hired away"

While The Three Stooges are establishing themselves in Hollywood, Shemp is still in New York starring in hilarious shorts for Warner-Vitaphone like *Dizzy and Daffy* (1934), in which the former Stooge pitches to baseball legends Dizzy and Daffy Dean.

Jules and his childhood pal Zion Myers, assigning them the task of organizing Columbia's short subjects division.

White had crossed paths with The Three Stooges when they were working at Metro under Ted Healy's employment. Jules had been a sequence director on the feature-length *Turn Back the Clock* the previous year, the trio's first film in which Healy does not appear with them on camera. White and partner Zion Myers felt the Stooges might be successful in their own vehicles, and they advised Columbia to hire the boys and try them out with a one-or two-picture deal.

After hiring the Stooges for Columbia, they saw to it that they were supplied with good writers and directors, as well as talented supporting players.

Columbia paid each of the Stooges a yearly salary of between $20,000 and $25,000. Even though they started at that figure in 1934, during the depths of the Depression, they never received a substantial raise in pay in all the years they toiled for Harry Cohn and his studio.

"Columbia made millions off the Stooges, and they're still making money" reflected

Right: Edward Bernds, who begins his career in Hollywood as head of Columbia's sound-recording division, serves as soundman on all of the Stooges' earliest films for producer Jules White.

Far right: director Del Lord, pictured at the peak of his career, exerts more influence on the Stooges' screen characterizations than any other craftsman.

Edward Bernds, who began working with the Stooges as soundman in 1934, and eventually wrote and directed some of their best films.

But Shemp"s wife Babe pointed out that the Stooges made most of their money from personal appearances, not through their studio salary. "At Columbia, they worked for peanuts," she said.

During the Depression, however, $25,000 was an enormous amount of money for a year's labor, and the Stooges were happy to sign with Columbia. They were assured by Harry Cohn that the men creating their comedies would be the top craftsmen in the field, many of whom were personal friends of Jules White.

Under the direction of Del Lord, the Stooges appear in what many believe are their funniest films; here the boys are seen trying to put one over on straightman Eddie Laughton.

White had already hired a number of film comedy "giants" to work in the Shorts Department, including former partner Del Lord. White and Lord had started out in the business together, working for the Mack Sennett Studio during the silent era. While White went to work behind the scenes, Lord became an on-screen performer as one of the "Keystone Kops," Sennett's in-house squadron of knockabout comics.

According to White, Lord also worked as a stunt driver for Sennett, appearing in films with Charlie Chaplin and other legends. Eventually the versatile Lord began directing films as well. By the mid-Twenties, Del was Sennett's top director, renowned for his ability to shoot complicated "chase" sequences with a minimum of difficulty.

By the 1930s, however, the short comedy business was on a definite decline. Del Lord subsequently found himself out of the movies and selling used cars. Upon hearing of this, White hired him immediately.

"He had no business ever getting out of the business," said White, "but he had a funny habit of eating."

Released weeks after the Stooges begin making their own films at Columbia, Metro's all-star feature musical *Hollywood Party* (1934) originally includes a scene in which Ted and the boys are pitted against boxing champ Max Baer (seen here with actress Mary Carlisle).

The inimitable Charley Chase, posing here with frequent co-star (and occasional offscreen lover) Thelma Todd in the early 1930s.

Metro's *The Big Idea* (1934) is released with the boys billed as Ted Healy's "Three Stooges" — *before* they use that name at Columbia.

At Columbia, Lord turned out to be one of the comedy department's greatest assets; his filmmaking experience and knowledge of physical comedy were invaluable. As a director, Lord even threw his own pies. Mack Sennett himself credited Lord as being the foremost "pie thrower" in the business.

"Del Lord made some terrific films for me," commented White. "He was a great gag man, a great story man, and he was good on the stunts because he had done them. He was really very valuable to me."

Most of the Stooges' best work was, in fact, accomplished under Lord's direction, whose sense of timing and flair for comedy was unparalleled. Lord would remain at Columbia as producer-director throughout the Thirties and Forties. During this period he found himself directing people like Buster Keaton, Harry Langdon and Andy Clyde (all of whom had also worked in shorts with Lord's mentor, Mack Sennett), as well as The Three Stooges. Lord even wrote several Stooge scripts, all of which were loaded with familiar gags from his silent comedy days.

Another comedy great who eventually found himself on the Columbia roster and working with the Stooges was Charley Chase. Chase was one of the most versatile people in the business, just as much at home serving as comedian, producer, director, screenwriter or even songsmith. During the silent era, Chase had been the star of his own hugely successful series with comedienne Thelma Todd, and he continued to be a top draw when talkies became popular, working in shorts at the Hal Roach Studio.

Roach and Sennett had been the two major comedy factories of the late Twenties and early Thirties. By the late 1930s, however, the Sennett Studios had closed down and Roach, although still in business, had decided to abandon its Shorts Department. As a result, Chase was dropped by Hal Roach, and he soon found himself unemployed. Jules White grasped this opportunity and Chase, too, was signed by Columbia. Chase directed a number of films with the Stooges, and, like Del Lord, he lifted many of his favorite gags and routines from

★★★ **The THREE STOOGES** ★★★

earlier comedies and simply reshaped them for the boys.

Yet another comedy veteran whom White hired — described by Jules himself as "a genius" — was his brother Jack, a lifelong colleague and advisor. Jack White, who would come to create some of the Stooges' most popular films, was something of a prodigy in early Hollywood. By the time he was in his late teens, the savvy and creative Jack was one of the industry's most successful comedy directors.

White worked initially for Mack Sennett, but became head of his own short-subject movie company, Jack White Productions, upon reaching the ripe old age of twenty. White also personally produced the company's double-reel comedies, all of which were released through Fox under the Educational Pictures banner. He soon found himself a mini-mogul of sorts, overseeing the Fox-Educational studio on Santa Monica Boulevard in Hollywood, and enjoying friendships with people like Charlie Chaplin and other early legends of the comedy-film industry.

Following his tenure with Fox-Educational, Jack White was forced to file for bankruptcy and he closed Jack White Productions. Fortunately, he was immediately hired as a writer and director by brother Jules. Jack had shown Jules "the ropes" of the short-subject business, and now Jules called upon his elder brother to help him in organizing Harry Cohn's new comedy division at Columbia, with specific emphasis on The Three Stooges.

Jack directed several of the Stooges' earliest comedies under the pseudonym "Preston Black," occasionally doubling as screenwriter, and later contributed to their film scripts as Jack White. As a writer, White often missed his mark when working with the Stooges, although several of his directorial efforts were better than average. White continued to work with the Stooges as a screenwriter and director throughout their years of service at Columbia, remaining there until their final year of production.

Jack White, in fact, wrote the last shorts the Stooges ever made at Columbia, which were produced and directed by brother Jules, and edited by Jules' son Harold. During the Stooges' final years in the Shorts Department, the White family was responsible for every major creative aspect of their films. (There was even a third White brother, Sam, who also began his career in silent shorts and later became a short-subject comedy director at Columbia.)

An army of film comedy experts was quickly assembled by White. "I have a theory," Jules White often said, "that old talent never dies. It may hide for a while, but it never dies.

And all of these men verified that."

Curiously enough, with all that experience and talent available, the first film the Stooges appeared in at Columbia was *Woman Haters* (1934), an odd musical comedy in which the dialogue is spoken completely in rhyme. Even stranger is the fact that the Stooges appear separately, not as a team, with character names used only in this film.

Curly and Moe are pushed into the background, while Larry receives a generous amount of screen time as the crooning romantic lead and central character. Larry plays a member of the Woman Haters Club who, despite his professed philosophy, falls in love with a gal named Mary (comedienne Marjorie White) and secretly gets married. Although the film is supplied with a fine cast of supporting actors, many of them talented comedians in their own right, the results are rather weak.

Woman Haters, a full-fledged musical, was in many ways reminiscent of the shorts the boys had made with Ted Healy at Metro. And again as with Healy, Larry found himself the center-piece of the Stooges. *Woman Haters* was definitely his film, and he reportedly was more than delighted with his starring debut. His partners, however, bristled at their subordinate roles. More than ever, Moe Howard and his kid brother Curly were being relegated to supporting-comic status, and Moe in particular wasn't happy about it. As far as he was concerned, he had not gone to the trouble of getting the Stooges a deal away from Healy so that he and Curly could play second fiddle to *Larry*.

As far as the Stooges saw it, the one unarguably positive aspect of *Woman Haters* was that it introduced them to the man who would quickly become their leading on-screen foil. Bud Jamison, cast as the president of the Woman Haters Club, was the first of several movie straightmen who would play the role of "authority figure" opposite the generally lawless Stooges. A veteran of silent films — and onetime co-star of Charlie Chaplin, Buster Keaton and Harold Lloyd — Jamison enhanced the Columbia shorts with his acting versatility and innate sense of comedy. His characterizations in the Stooge comedies are among his most memorable performances, and his chemistry with the boys is evident even in their very first film together.

Meanwhile, the Stooges' old boss, Ted Healy, was enjoying a little chemistry of his own. According to Mousie Garner, Healy had begun an affair with Thelma Todd, the popular Hal Roach comedienne and co-star of Charley Chase, in 1934. Ted had been introduced to Todd by their mutual friend Stan Laurel, who had directed Healy in his first Hollywood film, a Stooge-less Hal Roach comedy titled *Wise Guys Prefer Brunettes*, back in the mid-Twenties.

As Mousie explains it, Ted was seeing Thelma Todd in 1934. This was while she was

Bud Jamison (right), who quickly becomes the number-one onscreen straightman for The Three Stooges, is seen tangling with Thelma Todd (center) and comedy partner Zasu Pitts at the Hal Roach Studios in the early 1930s.

still married to Pasquale "Pat" DiCicco, gangster Charles "Lucky" Luciano's "eyes and ears" in Hollywood. DiCicco was a well-known pimp and hustler with a reputation for being violent, and he was friendly with most of the big shots in the film business.

The following year, some time after she had last seen Ted Healy on the sly, Todd was found dead in her garage, slumped over the steering wheel of her automobile. She supposedly died of carbon monoxide poisoning, which did not explain why her nose was broken. It was widely reported that ex-husband Pat DiCicco was somehow involved, but the L.A. coroner ruled her death "accidental." Many observers believed, however, that it was never fully determined if her death was caused by accident, suicide, or murder.

As a result of Todd's untimely demise, Ted swore off actresses and subsequently fell in love with a beautiful UCLA student named Betty Hickman. Betty would provide the love and stability that had been lacking in Ted's life, and as far as he was concerned, he had at long last found true happiness.

Meanwhile, Ted's former Stooges were struggling to establish themselves at Columbia. To add insult to the injury of *Woman Haters*, the Stooges' first feature film assignment at Columbia — as per their original double-picture deal — consisted of but a tiny cameo in *The Captain Hates the Sea* (1934).

This was a seafaring switch on Metro's smash hit *Grand Hotel*, the highly-praised comedy-drama of the previous season. In what amounted to a big-budget, all-star epic for Columbia, the boys play a trio of shipboard musicians who unfortunately have lit-

The Three Stooges make their Columbia feature-film debut in the comedy-drama *The Captain Hates the Sea* (1934), but despite the action depicted in this publicity photo, the boys indulge in no physical humor whatsoever in the released movie.

tle to do with advancing the plot. Worse still was the fact that Larry was the only Stooge supplied with dialogue! Neither of his partners had any scripted lines whatsoever, and they had to resort to ad libbing to get their voices heard on the soundtrack at all. Not surprisingly, little of what wound up in the film was reminiscent of "Stooge" comedy, with or without the presence of Ted Healy.

Moe began to wonder if signing with Columbia might not have been such a great idea after all.

If The Three Stooges were to survive in Hollywood without Ted Healy, they would have to establish themselves as a real comedy team, not just a trio of guys who happened to appear in the same movies. The best solution to this problem was to fashion a screenplay tailored to their individual personalities.

Their second Columbia short, *Punch Drunks* (1934), was a vast improvement over their initial effort. Directed by comedy specialist Lou Breslow, who had co-written *Soup to Nuts*, it was also the first film in which the Stooges actually received top billing. In fact, Columbia would eventually refer to *Punch Drunks* as its first official "Three Stooges" comedy.

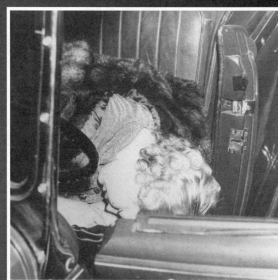

Thelma Todd, whose screen career started during the Chaplin era, co-starred with such comedy luminaries as Buster Keaton, Harry Langdon, Stan Laurel, Oliver Hardy, and The Marx Brothers before meeting Ted Healy in 1934.

Los Angeles Police Department photo-graphs of Thelma Todd's death scene.

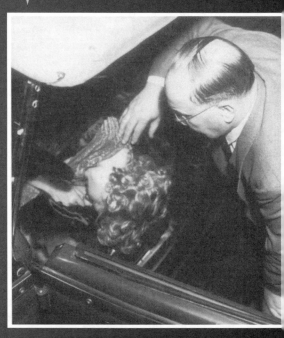

The beautiful and doomed Thelma Todd with her violent, physically abusive husband, Pasquale "Pat" DiCicco, in the mid-1930s.

Punch Drunks again finds the Stooges appearing as separate characters, but this time within a situation related to their specific personalities. The story, written by the Stooges themselves, has Curly as a waiter who goes berserk whenever he hears the song "Pop Goes the Weasel." Moe plays a fight manager who wants to make Curly the new champ, and Larry portrays a wandering musician hired to provide the music that drives Curly crazy. The plot is decidedly absurd, but the Stooges' emerging personalities keep the film moving at a fast pace.

Their third Columbia short, *Men in Black* (1934), was actually nominated for an Academy Award as Best Short Subject. But the film lost to a Technicolor musical short from Metro-Goldwyn-Mayer, and the Stooges never again starred in an Oscar-nominated film.

While traveling cross-country via train in the early 1930s, Shemp compares hairstyles with a couple of Arizona natives.

(However, sixty years later, the Stooges finally turned up in a movie that took home the Oscar — the crime-themed comedy-drama *Pulp Fiction* included footage from the classic post-war Stooge short *Brideless Groom*.)

It is difficult today to imagine why *Men in Black*, in which the Stooges are cast as inept surgeons, was chosen as a contender for the Academy Award. The short is virtually plotless, and many of the wild sight gags are silly, rather than funny. The best-remembered running joke in *Men in Black* involves a disembodied voice heard over the hospital public-address system, that repeatedly and monotonously calls out the Stooges' names as they race up and down the corridors of the building.

Men in Black was directed by Raymond McCarey, who had helmed Shemp's first five solo films at Warner-Vitaphone. The incongruous script for *Men in Black* was written by Felix Adler, who served as a screenwriter for The Three Stooges until the very end of their Columbia short-subject career more than twenty years later.

Adler was a vastly experienced gagmeister, whose main claim to fame prior to working with the Stooges was his long tenure as Mack Sennett's head writer. Adler hailed from an old show-business family, and he started his own career touring in vaudeville as a comedian and singer during the early twentieth century. But when Charlie Chaplin and the "flickers" began to push Adler's type of vaudeville out of existence, Felix decided to enter the film business himself, and he went to work as a Sennett scenarist.

It wasn't long before Adler developed a reputation for devising sight gags that were sure-fire "howlers," many of which later turned up in his Stooge scripts. He subsequently created material for virtually all of the fledgling industry's top funnymen, including Buster Keaton, Harry Langdon, Harold Lloyd, Will Rogers, Charley Chase, Andy Clyde, and many others, as well as for popular teams like Laurel & Hardy, and, much later, Abbott & Costello. Adler had even served as filmmaker Frank Capra's mentor, when Capra began his Hollywood career as a Sennett gagman in the mid-Twenties.

In his published memoirs, Capra described Felix Adler, the man who would become the Stooges' number-one writer, as "a brash extrovert to whom life was just a bowl of gags."

To Jules White, however, Adler was an unqualified genius, as were all the men who came to join his writing staff. "These men were infallible," he said. "You could say, 'I want this and this and this, see what you can do with it, see what you can concoct,' and you could bet your red apples out of a barrel of rotten ones they'd come up with something good."

White often teamed Felix Adler with veteran screenwriter Clyde Bruckman, especially when he wanted a script that was gag-heavy and loaded with sure-fire laughs. With a career that dated back to the Chaplin era, Bruckman had served as Buster Keaton's head scribe during Keaton's "golden age," and later wrote for Harold Lloyd, at that time the most popular comedian in silent films. Bruckman also wrote some of the Stooges' best scripts, with ingenious sight gags and clever gag situations. Like Felix Adler, Bruckman had hundreds of movie credits under his belt, and in the course of his career he worked with virtually every great slapstick comedian in Hollywood.

Despite the highly-qualified writers and directors available to them, the Stooges, during their early years at Columbia, faced a major problem defining their screen characters. In vaudeville, it was not necessary for the Stooges to portray reasonably believable personalities; in films, however, it was absolutely essential. When they started work at Columbia, they had not yet established definite characters for themselves, and many misfire gags resulted from this. For instance, in *Men in Black*, Larry slaps Moe, but Moe doesn't do anything to Larry in return. This deliberate lack of retaliation on Moe's part never surfaced in the later Stooge comedies, yet this kind of gag occasionally popped up in their early shorts.

This situation was quickly remedied when Del Lord began work with them. He helped

Raymond McCarey's *Men in Black* (1934), the only Stooge short to be nominated for an Academy Award, features Mack Sennett Studios veteran Del Henderson as the boys' befuddled supervisor.

them develop their screen characters into somewhat believable personalities, raising their status from absurd ruffians without much characterization (as in *Men in Black*) to believable, yet farcical, comic figures with clearly identifiable traits and attitudes. As director and script contributor, Lord helped The Three Stooges make the transition from vaudeville performers to big-screen "personalities" with a minimum of difficulty.

Lord's first Stooge comedy, *Pop Goes the Easel* (1935), is highlighted by a hilarious clay-throwing melee in an art school. *Easel* deftly blends the vaudeville-style antics of the Stooges with the broad visual humor and sight gags of silent comedy. In these early efforts with Lord, the Stooges performed with energy and enthusiasm that was often missing from their later films. While the actual scripts of shorts like *Pop Goes the Easel* were often rather flimsy, the masterful direction of Lord and the performances of the Stooges brought the shorts to a respectable level of hilarity.

The April 8th, 1935 edition of *Film Daily* reported, "'The Three Stooges' have been signed to a new year's contract by Columbia. They will appear in shorts and features. They will write the material for the shorts."

The first short in which the Stooges supplied material from their vaudeville act was *Pardon My Scotch* (1935). Directed by Del Lord, the film is highlighted by a sequence in which the Stooges are seen as carpenters trying to saw a board. One of the most breathtaking stunts ever performed in a Stooge comedy — and the biggest bellylaugh in *Pardon My Scotch* — has Moe taking a spectacular, albeit unintentional, pratfall.

As the sequence begins, Moe is standing on a table. Curly, supervised by the equally-

This full-page trade-paper advertisement for the Stooges' Columbia short *Uncivil Warriors* (1935), directed by Del Lord, evidences the team's burgeoning popularity.

The boys attempt to help out a frustrated painter in Del Lord's classic *Pop Goes the Easel* (1935), rated at the time by *Film Daily* as one of the team's all-time funniest endeavors.

dumb Larry, unknowingly saws through the table with a power blade. When Moe turns to address his partners, the table suddenly collapses and Moe crashes to the floor, falling onto his side. The effect is awe-inspiring, but in executing the gag Moe landed incorrectly and broke several ribs.

Moe actually completed the scene before passing out, much to the surprise and gratitude of director Lord. A mere second after his harrowing, rib-crushing accident, the injured Stooge got up from the floor, delivered his dialogue, and gave Curly and Larry the "machine gun"-style double slap! Moe accomplished this without losing any aspect of his razor-sharp sense of timing, and, even more amazingly, without giving the slightest indication of the mind-numbing physical agony he was suffering. After finishing the scene, Moe fainted and was carried off the set on a stretcher. He subsequently was hospitalized and remained so for several days.

When Moe finally returned to work at Columbia, he enjoyed a hero's welcome. Although still in his thirties, Moe had already acquired a reputation amongst his peers as a Hollywood trouper of the first rank.

"The Stooges would try anything to make a scene better," said Edward Bernds. "And Del Lord was the same way. 'The play is the thing,' as far as they were concerned. Of course, Del was no stranger to hazard, having worked as a stunt driver for Mack Sennett. And many of the film stunts the Stooges were involved in turned out to be quite dangerous. But Del really loved the Stooges, and he and Ray Hunt, their propman, really looked out for them, protected them. But sometimes things can go wrong, and that's just a fact of life in terms of doing stunt work. And in *Pardon My Scotch*, Moe was truly doing the work of a stuntman."

The best of Lord's early shorts with the Stooges — and probably the least "dangerous" in terms of do-it-yourself stuntwork — is *Hoi Polloi* (1935). Fifty years after its release, movie critic Gene Siskel would pronounce the film "one of the greatest slapstick comedies ever made." The story, devised by Moe Howard's wife Helen and scripted by Felix Adler,

Shemp visits the set of Del Lord's *Pardon My Scotch* (1935), and finds the Stooges in conference with prop man Ray Hunt (standing).

The three Howard brothers on the set of Del Lord's *Hoi Polloi* (1935), in which Shemp serves as a behind-the-scenes joke writer and gagman.

is a gag-laden approach to George Bernard Shaw's *Pygmalion*, with a couple of clever twists added.

The plotline finds a wealthy professor betting an equally wealthy colleague that he can transform the Stooges into gentlemen within a matter of weeks. During this time, he subjects the boys to lessons in reading, table manners and ballroom dancing, with hilarious results. The highlight of the film arrives when the Professor hosts a black-tie soiree in honor of his newly-refined pupils. After behaving themselves for a few minutes, the Stooges allow their instincts to overpower them and they quickly turn the party into a melee of slapstick mayhem. Soon all of the party guests are slapping, punching and poking each other in an orgy of comic violence. Repulsed by the behavior of the crude upper-crusters, the Stooges leave the party in disgust.

This theme, in which the Stooges find themselves pitted against high society, turned out to be one of their more popular story formulas. In fact, the original script was minimally rewrit-

In the Stooges' "comedy of manners," *Hoi Polloi,* Curly gets his hand stuck in a spittoon while trying to retrieve someone else's half-smoked cigar.

ten and filmed as *Half Wits Holiday* more than a decade later, with new sequences including a massive pie fight. *Half Wits* was itself remade ten years after that, virtually shot-for-shot, as *Pies and Guys*. No one, least of all Del Lord, would ever accuse The Three Stooges of not milking their material for all it was worth.

Columbia comedy writer Elwood Ullman said the Stooges developed quite a rapport with Lord, who was, at that time, their most frequent collaborator. Ullman recalled that story sessions between Lord and the Stooges were, to say the least, rather informal meetings.

"Del would be in his office, going over a script with the Stooges," said Ullman. "He'd describe the plot to them, saying '. . . and then she makes the telephone call to the help-wanted people, and you bastards come in,' meaning the Stooges. And they wouldn't bat an eye!"

In addition to their work with Lord, the Stooges turned out several top-notch shorts under Jack White's direction in the early 1930s. White's initial effort with the Stooges, *Ants in the Pantry* (1936), is one of his best. This one has the Stooges as exterminators who drum up business by bringing their own pests with them. *Ants in the Pantry* was the boys' first short to receive unanimous praise from trade reviewers, and as a result, Columbia devoted even more attention to the production of their Stooge comedies. The film was so well-regarded that it was reworked a couple of years later by director Del Lord, and was remade fifteen years later as *Pest Man Wins*, with Jack White's brother Jules directing.

Jack White directed a number of Stooge films after *Ants in the Pantry*, several of which managed to capture the fast-paced lunacy of his first outing. White's next short with the

In 1936, Ted Healy wants former sidemen Moe, Larry and Babe to join him in the cast of Fox's all-star musical spectacular *Sing, Baby, Sing,* but Columbia boss Harry Cohn refuses to loan them out; the Stooges are subsequently replaced by The Ritz Brothers (above), who become major feature-film stars as a result.

Jack White's *Ants in the Pantry* (1936) turns out to be The Three Stooges' most successful comedy to date.

team, *Half Shot Shooters* (1936), has the boys accidentally enlisting in the Army, a premise that would later be repeated by the Stooges, as well as competing comedy teams, over and over again. But *Shooters'* real significance exists in its providing the initial screen confrontation between The Three Stooges and former Mack Sennett Studios star, Vernon Dent.

The heavyset actor had appeared in literally hundreds of silent comedies, rubbing shoulders with such greats as Charlie Chaplin and others in the process. Dent spent sever-

In Jack White's Army comedy *Half Shot Shooters* (1936), the boys cross paths with silent-screen foil Vernon Dent for the first time.

al years playing Harry Langdon's partner and foil in short subjects, and eventually rose to the level of Langdon's co-star (as in "Harry and Vernon"). Dent later appeared opposite Langdon when he was making talkie shorts at Fox-Educational, then at Paramount, and, finally, at Columbia in the 1930s. In fact, Dent appeared with virtually every comedian in Columbia's Shorts Department during the Thirties, including Buster Keaton, Charley Chase, Andy Clyde and, most frequently, The Three Stooges.

The formidable Dent was an excellent foil for the Stooges, and his talent as a character actor enabled him to play everything from cranky landlords to mad scientists. Jules White quite accurately compared him to "the mounting for the ten-carat diamond." In time, the versatile and affable Dent would even come to replace the legendary Bud Jamison as the Stooges' lead antagonist figure and co-star.

"Vernon was a great guy," remembered Edward Bernds, who cast Dent in his first Stooge comedy as writer-director. "And he was no youngster. He goes way, way back to the Mack Sennett days. Every once in a while I'll see a film clip from a silent comedy, and I'll see a young Vernon Dent! Vernon was a real trouper, a very hardworking guy."

Essentially, Dent played what might be described as a variation of the "Ted Healy role" opposite the Stooges. Jules White had determined that the boys were funniest when playing off a straightman or foil or some sort, and he constantly sought to place them in situations enabling this kind of interaction.

As the Stooges were finding their niche at Columbia, their original foil, Ted Healy, was planning to introduce yet another trio of Stooges. Still working at Metro-Goldwyn-Mayer, Ted had been slated for the comedy lead in *San Francisco* (1936), an all-star epic featuring such luminaries as Clark Gable, Spencer Tracy and Jeanette MacDonald. Healy was eager to re-activate his reputation as "King of Stooges," so he cast old pal Red Pearson along with two newcomers, Jimmy Brewster and Sammy Glasser, as his latest trio of sidemen.

Pearson, Brewster and Glasser had been stooges for come-

In what his wife described as his all-time favorite screen role, solo Stooge Shemp Howard stars as "Knobby," the eccentric fight manager of Warner-Vitaphone's hugely popular "Joe Palooka" short-subject series.

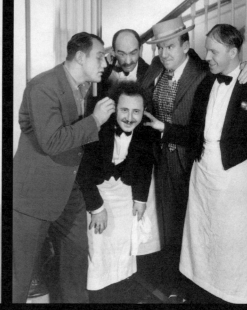

Spencer Tracy (far left) and other co-stars from Metro's *San Francisco* (1936) check out Ted Healy's latest trio of Stooges: Sammy Glasser (later known as "Sammy Wolfe"), Jimmy Brewster and Red Pearson.

Ted's old stage partner Betty Healy, and Shemp's former screen wife Daphne Pollard, appear as the spouses of Oliver Hardy (left) and Stan Laurel in *Our Relations* (1936), written by Felix Adler and reworked twenty years later for The Three Stooges as *A Merry Mixup*.

dian Charlie Foy, yet another of the Seven Little Foys and a close friend of Ted's. Foy suggested his boys might make good Stooges for Healy as well, and Ted wasted no time in announcing that they would co-star with him in *San Francisco*.

But Moe Howard was disgusted that these Stooge "pretenders" were scheduled to appear in a big-budget, feature-length spectacular, while the "real" Three Stooges were more or less confined to stardom in the less-prestigious short-subject field. The big-budget *San Francisco* was to be the sole "Stooge" feature film for the 1935-36 season, and the Howard group was nowhere in sight.

As it turned out, however, Moe and his partners had little to worry about. Sammy, Red and Jimmy, cast as singing waiters in several scenes with Ted, were scissored out of the final print of *San Francisco*. Apparently their performance as a trio was so lame that even Healy agreed it was a disaster. The group was disbanded almost as quickly as it had been formed.

To replace his latest departing trio, Healy attempted to rehire his other set of Stooges from several years earlier, Mousie Garner, Dick Hakins and Jack Wolf. They had returned from their European odyssey and were touring the States in the musical-comedy revue *Spices*, a Broadway-bound show in which they co-starred with fellow Healyite Joe Besser. Ted wired Mousie and his pals, and asked them to return to his act, not as mere Stooges, but as his *Super* Stooges. The painful lesson Healy had learned from *San Francisco* was to hire Stooges who were already working as a trio.

But Jack Wolf was suffering from chronic kidney stones, and had already decided to retire from full-time performing. Jack went into business for himself in his native Washington, D.C., but continued to perform free of charge at major show-business charity benefits in New York, Philadelphia and Baltimore, as well as his hometown. After leaving the Stooges, Jack and wife Rosemarie started a family; in the decades to come, their son Warner Wolf would become one of the most popular and highest-paid sports commentators in American television.

Jack Wolf was subsequently replaced in the act by

Sammy Glasser. Sammy was, of course, a member of Ted's most recent set of Stooges, that unfortunate trio that had been deleted from the release print of Metro's *San Francisco*. Many believed Glasser was simply another Healy hanger-on, who allowed himself to be re-christened "Sammy Wolfe" in an attempt to cash in on the name recognition of the man he was replacing.

It was Charlie Foy who persuaded Ted to bring Sammy back into the fold, arguing that he would make a fine Stooge once he had a chance to work out some routines and business appropriate to Healy's act. Ted agreed to give him another shot.

"I told Healy it was too late to start another Stooges act," said Mousie Garner. "I said The Three Stooges had made it big on their own, and we'd missed the boat. But he insisted we get back together with him."

Ted asked Mousie, Dick and Sammy to go out on the road in vaudeville and get some experience interacting with each other before live audiences. Healy hoped that when they returned to Hollywood in a few months, they would be performing as a well-oiled machine, a true "team."

When Mousie and company returned from their nationwide tour, Ted Healy had already lined up a feature film appearance for them. The boys thus appeared as lead comedians in an all-star musical, *The Hit Parade* (1937), based on the hugely popular radio series of the same name and produced by one of Hollywood's major studios, Republic Pictures. They were later signed for an appearance in a low-budget musical-comedy called *Swing It, Professor* (1937), as well as for a series of starring shorts at Warner-Vitaphone.

Predictably, Moe Howard was less than delighted to learn that yet another competing "Stooge" feature was in production, this one for the 1937-38 season. Worse still was the fact that Ted had begun appearing on a live weekly radio show, *The Metro Maxwell Hour*, a variety program sponsored by the Maxwell House company that promoted Metro-Goldwyn-Mayer's biggest stars. Mousie, Dick and Sammy were also in the cast, and they were now being promoted as Ted Healy's Stooges.

"I thought this was an idea that could work," says Mousie. "The Three Stooges in the movies, and Dick, Sammy and myself on the radio. It wasn't competitive in any way. They would do their thing, and we would do our thing."

In this 1937 publicity photo shot at Warner Bros.' Burbank studios, Dick Hakins, Sammy Wolfe and Mousie Garner appear together for the first time as Ted Healy's Stooges.

★★★ **The THREE STOOGES** ★★★

Ted's newest Stooge ensemble provides the laughs in *Swing It, Professor* (1937), a feature-length musical produced in Hollywood at a small studio across the street from Columbia Pictures.

From left, choreographer Busby Berkely, emcee Ted Healy, and bandleader Benny Goodman pose with Stooges Dick Hakins, Sammy Wolfe and Mousie Garner in 1937.

Three Buffalo Bills (known as "Buffalo Billious," "Wild Bill Hiccup" and "Just Plain Bill") attempt to infiltrate a gang of cattle rustlers in Del Lord's *Goofs and Saddles* (1937).

Meanwhile, across town at Columbia Pictures, Ted's old sidemen Moe, Larry and Babe were enjoying their status as the studio's top comedians. The October 15th, 1937 edition of *Film Daily* included an article written by Jack Cohn, Harry's brother and the vice-president of Columbia, that discussed the studio's overall investment in the Stooges:

"As proof of the emphasis being placed by Columbia on production values, we may point out that the Three Stooges comedies, for example, are being produced with the care and attention that one would devote to a feature film. Further, these shorts are being supported by a comprehensive advertising and exploitation tie-up that helps make the Three Stooges popular names to all moviegoers."

The centerpiece of the group, Curly, was doing everything he could to live up to his reputation as a bona fide movie star. After a full day's work at the studio, Curly's evenings would consist mostly of dancing, romancing, and bar-hopping — anything in the pursuit of a good time. He was a carefree, well-to-do bachelor, living the life of Riley in the glamour capital of the world.

But brother Moe felt it was time for Babe to settle down, perhaps start a family of his own. And when Curly met Elaine Ackerman, the beautiful daughter of a Los Angeles businessman, Moe urged him to pop the question.

Curly and Elaine tied the knot in 1937, embarking on a marriage that would last only a few years, but would momentarily provide the youngest Howard

with a sense of stability and domesticity, as well as his first child, Marilyn. Moe, meanwhile, was relieved his baby brother finally had someone to look after him. Curly was indeed a movie star, but at least now he was a *married* movie star.

As the Stooges' popularity increased and the boys more fully developed their screen characterizations, the style and tempo of their comedies finally began to develop as well. Many of their early efforts suffer from a sluggish, ponderous pace. The Three Stooges based their comedy on fast-paced, cartoon-like action, and, basically, the faster is was, the funnier it was. Once the Stooges and their directors started snapping up the pace of the gags and speeding up the action,

the Stooge shorts found their niche in film comedy as some of the fastest-moving, liveliest shorts ever made.

"When I came upon the Stooges," said Emil Sitka, "they were unique, believe me. They were different. When they started acting, it was like electricity turned on all of a sudden. Fast tempo and farcical, the timing was split-second. With guys like Hugh Herbert it was what they said and how they said it, but with these guys it was what they did."

More than any of their other Columbia colleagues, it was Del Lord who nurtured and developed the screen characters of the Stooges. Edward Bernds, who served as a soundman under Lord, commented that the Stooges probably would

Curly marries a prominent jeweler's daughter, Elaine Ackerman, in the late 1930s, momentarily ending his career as a hard-drinking, free-swinging bachelor.

In Del Lord's *Cash and Carry* (1937), the Stooges are luckless prospectors who travel to Washington, D.C. for a private audience with "President Franklin Roosevelt."

Future Three Stooges foil Emil Sitka arrives in Hollywood from the East Coast in the late 1930s to begin his professional career as a comedian and comic actor.

Ted Healy co-stars with President-to-be Ronald Reagan in the latter's first major movie, Warner Bros.' *Hollywood Hotel,* filmed in 1937.

never have survived as movie personalities if they had not had the benefit of Lord's comic know-how and expertise. Ted Healy had given the Stooges little opportunity to develop characterizations for themselves, since he was practically the whole show. Now, of course, the Stooges were carrying the ball themselves.

One of the Shorts Department's staff writers, Elwood Ullman, would concoct some of the best material the Stooges ever performed. In 1937, Ullman, a former scenarist and gagman for producer Bryan Foy at Universal, began writing what are probably the funniest of the Stooges' film scripts, each one brimming with hilarious visuals and dialogue.

Like silent-era scribes Felix Adler and Clyde Bruckman, Ullman was experienced and well-respected in his field, even though the former journalist did not attempt a career at comedy writing until after the advent of talkies. In addition to innumerable scripts for the Stooges, Ullman's writing credits also included material for such popular teams as Mitchell & Durant, Abbott & Costello, and Martin & Lewis. He also had the opportunity of writing for literally all of Columbia's top solo comedians. Later, after leaving Columbia in search of feature-film gigs, Ullman even contributed screenplays for the then-popular "Bowery Boys" series at Monogram. More than one critic has noticed the similarity between the antics of The Three Stooges and their younger counterparts — particularly in Ullman's "Bowery Boys" films.

Ullman pointed out the secret of writing a Three Stooges comedy — especially during the team's heyday — was devising one sight gag after another. "It was gags, gags, gags," he reflected. "If it didn't get the laugh, you cut it out."

Despite the fact that he contributed some of the funniest visual gags the Stooges ever performed, Ullman himself was not particularly a fan of slapstick. Perhaps this is one reason why his screenplays usually included a good deal of clever dialogue, rather than simply one slap or poke after another.

"Clever dialogue," in fact, had already become old pal Ted Healy's stock-in-trade, now

During a personal appearance tour, Columbia's Three Stooges take time out for a quick bite with an unidentified friend.

A 1937 publicity photo for Ted Healy's upcoming weekly radio series.

that he was a radio personality with his own weekly series in the works. Mousie Garner contends that Healy was well on his way to bigger and better things — now at Warner Bros. instead of Metro — when he rehired his original "replacement" Stooges ensemble.

"Warner Bros. had Healy on loan-out," says Mousie, "and they wanted to make a big star out of him. He had done a picture called *Varsity Show,* and then *Hollywood Hotel,* for them. And he stole both pictures, even without Stooges. As Stooges, we were in on the filming of *Hollywood Hotel,* but we never turned up in the final print. Actually, we had nothing to do with the plot. Absolutely nothing! Healy had signed us to a contract for the film while he was drinking!"

★★★ **The THREE STOOGES** ★★★

While Ted's Stooges can be spotted in a crowd shot, all of their dialogue scenes wound up on the cutting-room floor. For Mousie, Dick and Sammy, it would be their last professional collaboration with Healy, even though they had already signed to co-star with Ted in a new radio show he was to host with musical-comedy legend Alice Faye. The show was to be sponsored by the Gillette company, and Healy was poised to join old vaudeville cronies Jack Benny, Eddie Cantor and George Burns as a major network radio personality.

Ted's life was further enriched when he learned his wife Betty was pregnant with their first child. Moe recalled that Healy had always wanted to be a father, and he delightedly told Moe and his family the good news. So happy was Ted about becoming a dad that he was even willing to bury the hatchet with the Howard clan. No longer employer and employee, now they would just be friends. Just like the old days, when they were kids on the beach in Brooklyn.

Sometime after midnight on December 20th, 1937, while celebrating the birth of his son John Jacob "Ted" Healy with a round of drinks at the Trocadero nightclub on Hollywood's Sunset Strip, Healy got into an argument with two other patrons. Sammy Wolfe said he happened to be at the Trocadero that same evening, and he offered his eye-witness account of what transpired:

"Wallace Beery was sitting at the bar with Pat DiCicco. Beery was making a lot of noise. Ted Healy was at the other end of the bar, and Ted told Beery to be quiet. Beery said, 'I won't be quiet.' It went back and forth. Then Beery gets up and punches Ted right in the side of the head, right there at the bar. So Ted says, 'Let's go outside, and I'll take care of both of you!' I guess Beery and DiCicco went out into the parking lot, but there was already another guy out there. And he jumped Ted, and then the other two guys jumped in and beat him up."

In Metro's big-budget comedy-drama *Good Old Soak* (1937), Ted Healy gleefully steals scene after scene from the studio's top character star, Wallace Beery — and in so doing, unknowingly creates his own Frankenstein Monster.

Curly is forced to participate in a heavily-wagered public brawl in Jack White's *Grips, Grunts and Groans* (1937), released the same year as Ted Healy's death.

According to Shemp's wife Babe, Healy himself told the same story to Shemp in a telephone call the night he was attacked. Ted also phoned other friends, repeating his account of what had happened. Dick Hakins said Healy told him he knew two of his assailants were Wallace Beery and Pat DiCicco, but that he didn't know the identity of the third man.

In the days to come, DiCicco's first cousin and crony, Albert "Cubby" Broccoli — later the producer of the hugely-successful James Bond movie series — would tell newspaper reporters that he was present at the Trocadero the night Healy was attacked, and that he had scuffled with Ted at the bar.

In an interview he gave to the *Los Angeles Herald-Examiner*, Broccoli stated: "I knew that Ted was delighted because a son had been born to his wife, and I heard he was celebrating the blessed event. So when he came up to the bar I asked him, in a friendly fashion, to have a drink as a toast to his wife and son. Ted seemed a bit unsteady. He turned to an attendant at the bar and asked, pointing to me, 'Who is that fellow?' However, I ignored that and congratulated him. But Healy came at me, and punched me on the nose. My nose began to bleed. Then he hit me in the mouth, and added a punch to my chin which nearly knocked me out. I shoved him away, because I did not want to hurt him. Attendants then took him into an anteroom."

The *Herald-Examiner* reported, "Healy had fought with Albert Broccoli, 29, wealthy New Yorker. Police, however, said the case was closed and they would not question Broccoli."

Broccoli added, "when Healy left, he did not have a mark on his face that I remember."

By most accounts, however, Healy was savagely beaten that night, with his three assailants wrestling him to the ground, and kicking him in the head, ribs and stomach. The attackers then reportedly left the Trocadero property. Stunned, semi-conscious, and lying in a puddle of his own blood, Ted crawled into a taxicab and instructed the driver to take him to Hollywood's Brown Derby restaurant.

Instead, he should have told the driver to head for the nearest emergency room. For the very next day, Ted Healy would be dead.

From left, Pasquale "Pat" DiCicco, his second wife, heiress Gloria Vanderbilt, and DiCicco's first cousin, future James Bond producer Albert "Cubby" Broccoli, enjoy a visit to Sherman Billingsley's popular nightspot, the Stork Club, during an evening on the town in New York.

By the late 1930s, Ted's offscreen activities have become more interesting to newspaper columnists than his movie, radio or stage appearances.

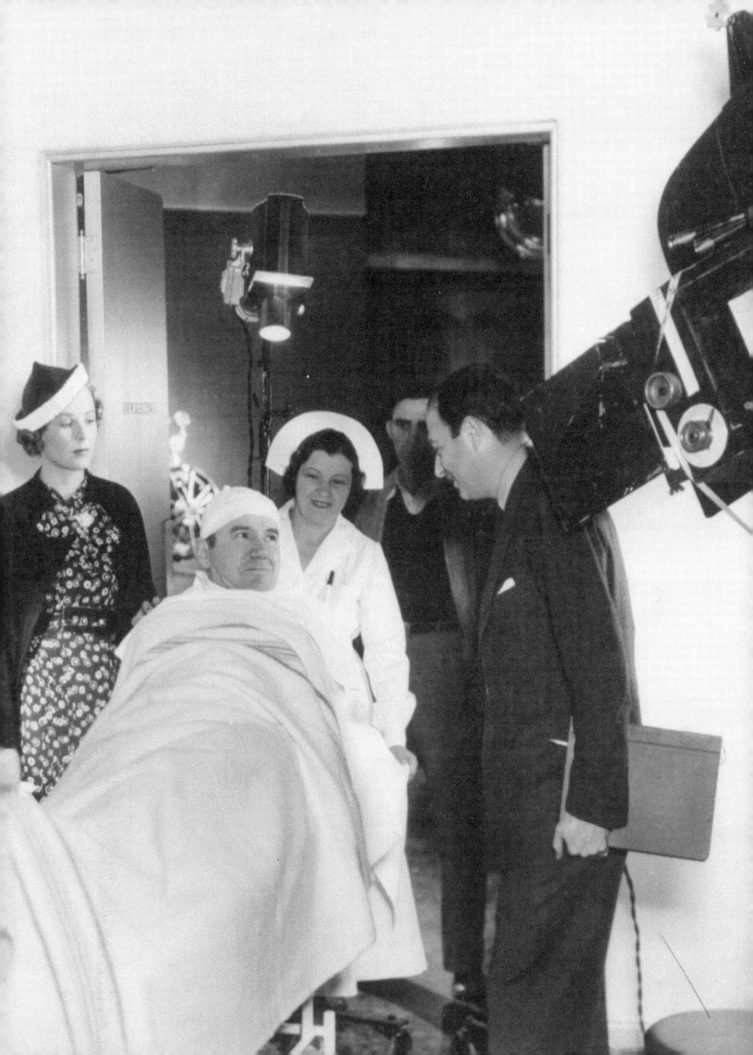

Chapter 3

THE DAY AFTER he returned home from the Trocadero, Ted Healy became violently ill. He began vomiting and suffering convulsions, and talking deliriously for hours on end. These were all deemed symptoms of a fractured skull or brain concussion, according to his family physician, Wyant Lamont. The same man who had just delivered Ted and Betty's baby was now summoned to Healy's Westwood home by Ted's sister Marcia. Ted had fallen into a coma and Marcia, panic-stricken, had no idea what to do.

As it turned out, there was nothing *to* do. It was already too late for Ted Healy, who never regained consciousness and died shortly before noon on December 21, 1937.

The circumstances of Ted's death were so confusing, Wyant Lamont refused to sign the death certificate. The official finding of the Los Angeles County Coroner, Frank Nance, was that Healy had died of "acute and chronic alcoholism." When Dr. Lamont requested an autopsy, Coroner Nance explained that the body had already been embalmed. This, of course, rendered an autopsy useless.

An autopsy was performed nevertheless, and at a press conference Nance made the ludicrous statement that Healy's organs were "soaked in alcohol," apparently in an attempt to bolster his original conclusions.

In the weeks to come, there would be little, if any, investigation into the death of Ted Healy. Speaking for himself as well as his partners, Dick Hakins reported his phone call from Ted to the Los Angeles Police Department. The police took his statement, but no questions were asked of Hakins and he never even received a follow-up call from the L.A.P.D.

Betty Braun Healy, Ted's first wife and a Metro player at the time, complained to the press that Ted's death was not being inves-

Dick Hakins, Sammy Wolfe, and Mousie Garner are signed to appear as Ted Healy's Stooges in Warner Bros. feature films.

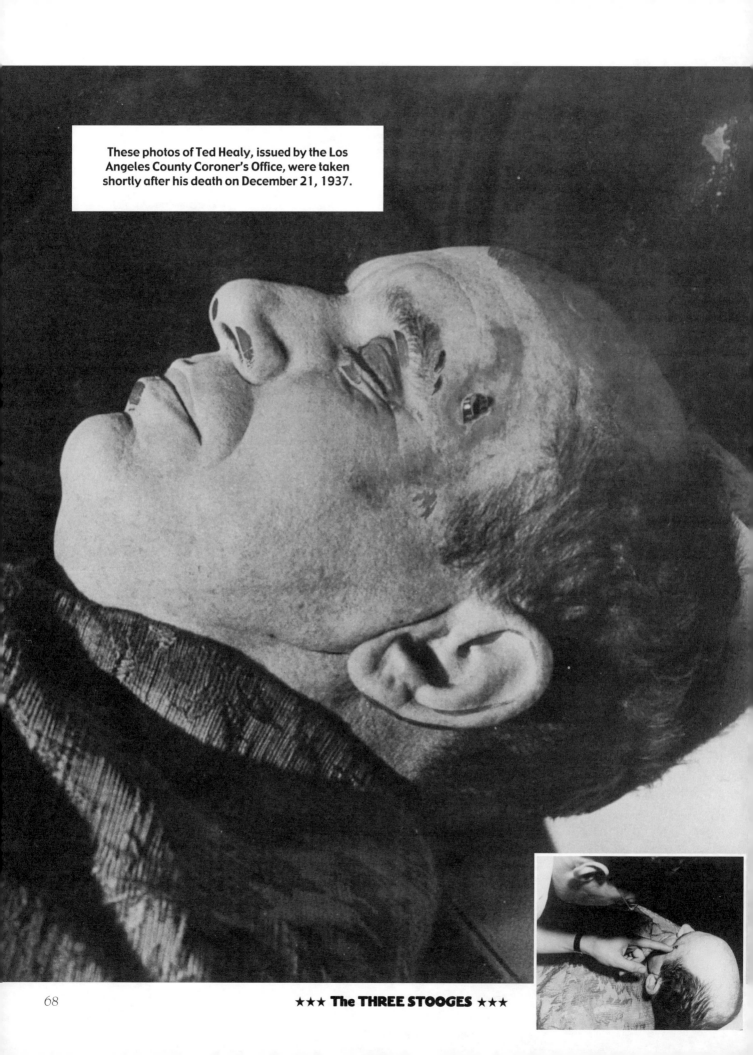

These photos of Ted Healy, issued by the Los Angeles County Coroner's Office, were taken shortly after his death on December 21, 1937.

tigated properly. She promptly found her employment terminated, and she never worked in Hollywood again. The first Mrs. Ted Healy subsequently opened a dude ranch about a hundred miles north of Los Angeles, were she happily avoided show business for the rest of her life.

But it was Curly Howard who summed up the Stooges' feelings about Ted Healy's death when he told a reporter from the *New York Daily Mirror*, "It can't be on the level. He was all right, that guy, and we never heard of him being seriously sick or having anything the matter with him that would cause him to go so quick."

According to Shemp's wife Babe, the Stooges themselves were aware of Beery's involvement in Healy's death, but were too afraid of Pat DiCicco and his vicious gangland connections to make waves. DiCicco would later marry wealthy socialite Gloria Vanderbilt, who would eventually divorce DiCicco as a wife-beater, while DiCicco's cousin, Cubby Broccoli, received his first job in the movies as an assistant director in the months following Healy's death. And Broccoli's then-wife, actress Gloria Blondell, even began showing up in Harry Cohn's short-subject comedies, her first appearance opposite Charley Chase.

Babe also reported the story that Louis B. Mayer had covered up the entire incident in an attempt to protect his biggest character star, Wallace Beery. Samuel Marx, Mayer's own story editor at the time, verified this in an interview conducted shortly before his death.

And according to a report in *Film Daily*, Beery and his family sailed for Europe shortly after Healy's death, ostensibly for a three-month vacation. The overseas trip, of course, made Beery quite unavailable for questioning by L.A. police.

Ted's untimely exit left all of his Stooges in a state of shock. His last trio of sidemen — Mousie Garner, Dick Hakins and Sammy Wolfe — served as pallbearers at his funeral in St. Augustine's Church near Metro-Goldwyn-Mayer Studios. The Stooges were led in the procession by Healy's next-door neighbor and good friend, actor-singer Dick Powell. And even though former co-stars Moe, Larry and Babe were busy playing dates on the opposite end of the continent, all of Ted's remaining Hollywood-based Stooges were at the

Ted Healy's sister Marcia, an actress and comedienne in her own right, plays Curly's wife in Del Lord's *The Sitter Downers* (1937).

A watercolor caricature of Wallace Beery, painted by Ted Healy while the two were co-starring in *Good Old Soak* (1937).

Ted Healy and Wallace Beery in their last known photograph together, a promotional still for *Good Old Soak.* ⟶

At the time of Ted Healy's death, Wallace Beery is not only the biggest character star at Metro–Goldwyn–Mayer, he's the biggest character star in Hollywood, period.

The Three Stooges, out of costume but always ready for a fight, visit Wallace Beery on the set at Metro–Goldwyn–Mayer Studios in the 1930s.

church to bid him farewell.

Healy's official send-off proved to be a traumatic experience for the Stooges, especially Shemp. He was terrified of death, and not only hated funerals, but actually feared them. Recalling the post-funeral gathering at Ted's Westwood home, Mousie Garner said, "Shemp was so nervous he brought along a tiny flask of whiskey to calm his

Ted's last trio of Stooges — Sammy Wolfe, Mousie Garner and Dick Hakins — continue working as a team even after Healy's death.

An overflow crowd attends Ted Healy's funeral, held at ten o'clock in the morning on the day before Christmas Eve at St. Augustine's Catholic Church in Culver City, California.

nerves. He would take a nip at it every once in a while. And Shemp didn't even drink, to speak of. He was really uncomfortable."

Moe and his partners had learned of Healy's death after stepping off a train in New York City. By Moe's own account, he broke down sobbing when he heard the news.

But Emil Sitka, who began working in Hollywood shortly before the time of Ted Healy's death, recalled only Moe's undying animosity toward his former boyhood friend. For the rest of his life, Moe would have ambivalent feelings about Ted, sometimes hailing him as a comedic genius and bosom pal, other times blaming him for any number of the Stooges' career disappointments.

With the death of Ted Healy, show business lost one of its greatest performers. It's ironic that one of the most inventive funnymen who ever lived is today virtually forgotten, remembered only in references to the world-renowned comedy team that he created.

But with Ted permanently out of the picture, The Three Stooges soared to stardom at

In the years following Ted Healy's death, Curly comes into his own as one of the screen's great comics.

Columbia. They became the most valuable comedy property the studio had under contract, bar none. And it was that clever young comedian, that protégé of the great Ted Healy, Curly Howard, who was at the center of it all.

A 1938 *New York Times* interview with the Stooges, focusing on the boys' appearance at Billy Rose's Casa Mañana nightclub, reveals just how much the team depended upon Curly for its success. It was not only his job to provide most of the laughs, but he was expected to serve as the brunt of most of the slapstick as well.

As Moe explained in the interview, "Even if you go out planning to pull your punches, figuring, well, it's a slow house, and what's the use of killing yourself, you get into the spirit of the thing, somebody laughs, and the first thing you know, there you are, darn near killing Curly, the same as ever.

"Why, only last week, Curly is sweating so much around the head my hands slip when I'm supposed to catch him and his head hits the stage with an awful thud!"

Larry offered no comment whatsoever, while Curly cheerfully added, "It got a big laugh."

Obviously, despite the physical dangers involved, getting big laughs was the whole meaning of the Stooges' existence. Curly would ultimately become a virtual gladiator of comedy, a man willing to sacrifice his health and well-being for the sake of other people's entertainment.

Meanwhile, the Stooges' own Caesar, producer Jules White, had finally become Hollywood's undisputed emperor of slapstick, with Hal Roach having abandoned short subjects altogether, and Mack Sennett and Jack White out of business for good. As Columbia expanded its Shorts Department, Hugh McCollum, former secretary to Harry Cohn, also began producing "Three Stooges" comedies. He made his first Stooge short in 1938, initiating a series that in time would even come to be viewed as superior to Jules White's output.

By 1938, The Three Stooges' supporting cast at Columbia was pretty well established. A roster of regulars was formed, with Bud Jamison and Vernon Dent the two mainstays. Character actor Eddie Laughton often appeared in the Stooge comedies as well, usually cast as a tough guy or confidence man but

A few weeks after Healy's death, radio personality Bob Hope begins appearing in big-budget feature films, essentially replacing Ted as Hollywood's top smart-ass comedian.

Former Ted Healy co-star Joe Besser, pictured with straightman Jimmy Little, makes his first Columbia short a few months after Healy's death in 1938.

In the late 1930s, Shemp arrives in Hollywood and establishes his own nightclub, the Stage One Cafe, in partnership with comedian Wally Vernon.

A well-known, real-life Stooge story from the Depression era, in which flat-broke Healy and his boys try to scuttle Ted's wardrobe out of an upscale New York hotel, is depicted by The Marx Brothers in their feature film *Room Service* (1938).

always playing "straight" to the boys.

In the mid-Thirties, The Three Stooges had even hired Laughton to serve as straight-man in their vaudeville appearances, with Eddie stepping into the Ted Healy role. In real life, Laughton and his wife were old show-business pals of Larry and Mabel Fine's from the Twenties, and Larry tried to point his old buddy toward job opportunities whenever possible. Moe Howard had also come to be a good friend of Laughton's, and he lobbied Jules White incessantly to cast him in their shorts.

One of the most memorable performers in the Stooges' stock company was silent comedy veteran Symona Boniface. Miss Boniface was a truly versatile actress, and she played a wide variety of roles in the Columbia shorts. Despite this, she most often found herself cast in the Stooge comedies as a matronly "society" type.

Described by Emil Sitka as "a wonderful person and a real pro," Symona was the ideal straight woman for the Three Stooges. "She was to The Three Stooges what Margaret Dumont was to The Marx Brothers, yet Symona was also very funny and intelligent in real life," commented Sitka.

In addition to the newly-formed cast of identifiable "regulars," the Stooges themselves began to develop their screen characters into easily identifiable personalities. As the 1930s progressed, their characterizations became more and more consistent with each film appearance. Less emphasis was placed on the individual antics of each Stooge, and more time was spent developing ideas and gags for the team as a whole.

Elwood Ullman described the process of creating gags for the Stooges: "Moe was more or less the straightman to Curly, and between them they got most of the laughs. Sometimes we had Larry getting laughs on his own, too. Sometimes we had a melange of all three."

Under the guidance of men like Jules White and Del Lord, the Stooges created identifiable characters for themselves within the traditional burlesque-sketch framework of straightman/talking-woman/comic. "Underboss" Moe was developed into the team's all-purpose con artist and antagonist figure. Larry became the "lynchpin" of the trio, occasionally functioning as a diplomatic buffer between partners. And Curly evolved into the team's fall guy, the "patsy" forever taken advantage of by his so-called pals.

In 1938, silent-comedy giant Harry Langdon (pictured with Bud Jamison and Ann Doran) begins writing gags for Columbia's Stooge comedies.

There was by now no disputing the fact that Moe's character was the domineering leader of the Stooges. Moe had honed his on-screen grouchiness into a downright mean disposition, and his comic personality became that of a somewhat sadistic bully, almost a comic villain. He could fly into manic fits of anger at the slightest provocation from his partners. This, of course, made it all the funnier when his bullying backfired on him. And it usually did, especially in the Stooges shorts directed by Del Lord.

In the team's early years at Columbia, Moe had believed his impersonation of Ted Healy would at long last be properly showcased. He enjoyed top billing in all of the early "Three Stooges" shorts, at least for the first couple of years, playing the wisecracking leader in a virtual carbon-copy of Ted's vaudeville persona. But producer Jules White had no more interest in developing Moe as a star comedian than Ted Healy did. As far as White was concerned, it was Moe's *brother* who was the true centerpiece of the trio. And it wasn't long before this attitude was reflected in the Stooges' film appearances.

"By the time I started working with them as writer-director, Moe was content with his role in the Stooges," recalled Edward Bernds shortly before his death. "I admired him in about every way possible. Moe was a hard worker, and a good family man. And he really cared about what he was doing, professionally speaking."

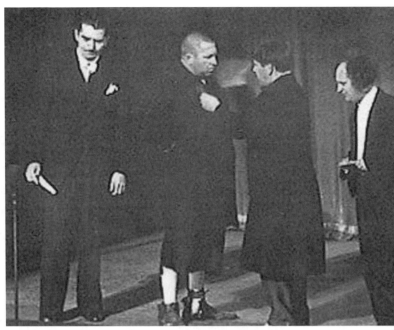

The boys perform Dave Chasen's "circular wave" bit in Del Lord's *Wee Wee Monsieur* (1938), a "French Foreign Legion" comedy reworked the following year by Laurel & Hardy as *The Flying Deuces*.

By 1938, The Three Stooges are full-fledged stars at Columbia Pictures, and their images begin showing up in various forms of themed merchandise.

Hollywood's most prolific comedians in their true medium, vaudeville, with Eddie Laughton as their straightman and master of ceremonies.

Larry's stage persona, on the other hand, came closest to embodying the actual vaudeville definition of "stooge." As the team's perpetual "fence-sitter," he did little more than take orders and physical abuse from Moe, and react with either delight or disgust to verbal nonsense from Curly. Occasionally Larry would make a clever remark, or would actually contribute an intelligent suggestion in order to advance the plot. But for the most part after Ted Healy's death, Larry's contribution to the act was limited to getting pushed around by his partners and looking happy, unhappy, or confused about the situation.

Edward Bernds commented, "The Three Stooges wouldn't have been worth a damn without Larry. He was the glue that held the team together. And as I understood it, he acted in a similar capacity with the Stooges during their Ted Healy days."

In effect, Larry became the synthesis of his partners' personalities, the necessary go-between for "thesis" Curly and "antithesis" Moe. Larry's son-in-law, Don Lamond, says, "If Jules White wanted Curly to be the star, so be it. Larry would smooth it over. Never mind that he was giving up the lead comedian part to a younger, less experienced, partner. Larry had absolutely no problem with being Curly's foil. He was delighted with it! This meant less time in front of the camera, less dialogue to memorize, and a lot less stress in general, but no decrease in salary or celebrity. It also meant more time to relax, gamble, go to the track, go to the ball game, have a good time, and enjoy himself. To Larry, *this* was success. 'If Curly wants to be the funniest man alive, more power to him!' I think Larry was happiest as a performer when the focus was on Curly, because that took the pressure off Larry. Curly was a great talent, and Larry knew they could depend on him to be funny, the way they had depended on Shemp when they were in vaudeville."

Curly, however, had developed a character that was completely distinctive, one that would be imitated by dozens of other comedians in his day and by innumerable others after his passing. The most beloved of all the different members of the trio, Curly's childlike character eventually made The Three Stooges the most popular comedy team in motion picture history. While his partners were allowed their share of funny business, the best gags were created for Curly.

Another interesting aspect of the Stooges' gradual character development was the association between their personalities and their physical appearances. Moe's appearance, short, squat and stocky, crowned by a ridiculous bowl haircut, reflected his character, that of the tough-talking, stubborn simpleton. In character as the boss of the group, Moe's dark-brown bangs looked more like a helmet than a haircut. Moe the Stooge, resultingly, appeared ready to do battle at a moment's notice, and this attitude was mirrored on-screen in his nervous energy, tight-lipped delivery and explosive attacks on his partners. While Moe may have once envisioned himself a breezy romantic comedian in the vein of a Ted Healy, Moe's screen personality was now in fact firmly ensconced in the public's perception as the uptight, ill-tempered supervisor of the Stooges, the manipulative self-appointed leader who created all the tension. And so it would remain for the rest of Moe's career.

Larry's physical features, in turn, were an integral part of his comedy personality. His slight build and short stature gave Larry the appearance of a harmless little character who

Opposite: The boys make occasional appearances on radio beginning in the late 1930s; their first performance is opposite Ted Healy's old vaudeville pal, comedian Georgie Jessel.

In 1938, the Stooges celebrate Christmas by dressing as up Santa Clauses for a series of Columbia publicity photos.

might be bullied about easily. His sparse, frizzy hair always looked as if someone had just grabbed a handful of it. And Larry's tube-shaped nose appeared, in a couple of places, to have already been flattened (perhaps dating back to his teenaged boxing days as "Kid Roth"). All of these attributes complemented his rather diffident, yet newly-evolved, Stooge character. No longer the quick-witted troublemaker of the early films with Ted Healy, Larry now played his Stooge character as a cowering, flinching near-imbecile, a middle-management type whose main responsibility appeared to be keeping an eye on the even more imbecillic Curly.

And Curly's shaven head, cheerful facial expressions and bulging belly were merely physical extensions of his innocent, cherubic character. Since his earliest days on stage with Ted Healy, Curly had worn clothes a couple of sizes too small, with Ted drawing attention to Curly's lack of height and abundance of stomach for comic effect. By the late 1930s, however, Curly had put on so much weight in real life, he no longer needed tight-fitting clothes to make himself look lovably chubby. Once the Stooges' decidedly junior partner, barrel-chested Curly was now unquestionably the lead laughgetter of the team. His "exploited worker" appearance and characterization struck a nerve with Depression-era audiences, who found much to identify with in Curly's on-screen struggles.

Clowning on the set of Violent is the Word for Curly (1938) with writer-director Charley Chase.

The team's first film of 1938 — released within weeks of Ted Healy's death — harked back to a successful concept the Stooges had exploited a couple of years earlier. The pest-exterminator premise first used in *Ants in the Pantry* was reworked for *Termites of 1938,* the title of which parodied the previous season's smash hit *Golddiggers of 1937.* A fast-moving entry in the series, *Termites* was directed by Del Lord, and produced by his longtime friend Charley Chase.

Chase was introduced to the Stooges shortly after his arrival at Columbia, and in 1938 they embarked on an excellent (but, unfortunately, short-lived) series of Three Stooges comedies with the versatile Charley serving as director, screenwriter, lyricist, composer and associate producer.

Although the Stooges made only five shorts with Chase, the quality of these films was more significant than might be expected. As with Del Lord, the Stooges found in fun-loving Chase a comedy creator of the first order.

The Stooges establish no college football records in Violent is the Word for Curly (1938), the title of which parodies Valiant is the Word for Carrie, a feature-length tearjerker released the previous season.

Stooge scenarist Elwood Ullman found Chase to be an easygoing and fun-loving collaborator. "He was a riot. A very funny man; bubbly and good-humored. He had Hugh McCollum on the floor all the time, roaring with laughter. We couldn't do any work!"

But it was in preparing a script for filming that Chase was absolutely top-notch. "I'd exhaust whatever I had to say about the script, and he'd say 'thank you,'" recalled Ullman. "I'd leave, and he'd call his secretary in and dictate it

The boys attempt to divvy up leading lady Lola Jensen on the set of Charley Chase's *Flat Foot Stooges* (1938), remembered primarily as the short that introduced the team's longest-running theme song, *Three Blind Mice*.

➡️

By 1938, all of Ted Healy's former Stooges are co-starring in vaudeville with legendary jazz figures; musical genius and marijuana advocate Louis Armstrong (pictured) even invites nonsmoker Mousie Garner into his dressing room for the purpose of sharing a joint, advising him that the experience will "change his life."

himself — the whole script in one afternoon!"

Probably the most memorable of Chase's Stooge shorts was *Violent is the Word for Curly* (1938). The script, which was written by Chase and Elwood Ullman and directed by Chase, presents the Stooges as service-station attendants mistaken for three European professors. The highlight of the film is the boys' performance of a catchy novelty song, "Swingin' the Alphabet," conceived especially for the Stooges by Chase.

It was during the making of this short that then-soundman Edward Bernds witnessed the shooting of a bizarre gag that almost spelled disaster for Curly. Tied to a revolving spit over an open fire, Curly is "roasted" by his partners in an effort to thaw him out after he has fallen asleep inside of a refrigerated truck.

"Curly was so heavy Moe and Larry couldn't turn the crank," said Bernds. "The straps holding him slipped and he was hanging directly over the fire. Before they could get him off, he was pretty well seared."

Apparently Curly, who weighed more than two hundred pounds, was too heavy even for stagehands to lift off the spit. As they struggled to get the straps loose so Curly could get off, they in turn were getting singed by the flames.

"Curly was hollering his head off, and I don't blame him," said Bernds, adding that "being roasted alive belongs to the Inquisition," not to the making of short subjects.

Despite the occasional mishap, the Stooges developed a rapport with Chase that is evident in the first-rate quality of their films together. Chase emphasized the farcical nature of their comedy, rather than violence and physical abuse; one can only surmise that Chase and the Stooges would have continued working together indefinitely had Chase not died in the early Forties. It's truly unfortunate the Stooges could not have worked longer with him; his vast knowledge and great comic talent were sorely missed in the short-subject field after his death.

After Chase's death, his place as a director was more or less taken over by Jules White. In the late 1930s, White began directing as well as producing the Three Stooges shorts. Altogether, White would direct more than half of their Columbia comedies, with varying degrees of success.

Often regarded as a stern taskmaster, Jules White maintained control over virtually every aspect of the shooting of a Columbia comedy. White later offered his philosophy on the making of short subjects during Hollywood's golden age:

"Economics entered into everything. The artistry of these things was one thing, but they were only as tall or as broad as their financial aspect. My artistic sense often said 'go for broke,' but my economic sense told me I couldn't afford to, actually. So, in other words, 'go as near as you can but don't go for broke.'"

As a director, White often relied on mere violence to get laughs. But White defended his use of slapstick violence as a laugh-provoker. "It wasn't so much violence as it was a *burlesque* of violence," said White. "The violence had a comedic undertone."

White's association with the Stooges would be a long one. Years after his retirement, White had nothing but praise for them, both personally and professionally.

Shemp, seen with popular 1930s Western star Buck Jones, begins making short subjects at Columbia in 1938.

"I liked all of the Stooges, and I had a lot of respect for their ability and cooperation," said White. "And they with me. If I said, 'Boys, this is how we're gonna do it. We don't have any more time to think about it, no more time to rehearse. Let's go out and shoot it,' there were never any arguments. They knew our problem. They also knew that if we spent too much money, we'd be out of business."

White would contribute to the Stooge films as a director, as well as producer, from 1938 until their final year of production nearly twenty years later. White's early Stooges shorts are all quality efforts, ranking alongside the best work of Del Lord and Charley Chase.

As the 1930s drew to a close, the Stooges approached their zenith of popularity. The Columbia Stooge shorts had become increasingly popular with each passing year, and the boys found themselves in demand for live stage appearances throughout the country. In addition, Harry Cohn had finally relented and decided to cast the Stooges in a feature film that would showcase their brand of comedy.

At Columbia, Shemp and moustachioed comedian Andy Clyde pose with supporting player Bruce Bennett.

Start Cheering (1938) was to be the Stooges' feature-length offering for the 1938-39 season. The all-star musical comedy served as a showcase for Jimmy Durante, Walter Connolly, Charles Starrett and a host of variety performers, among them the Stooges. In this "campus" comedy, the boys are all-purpose lackeys forced to serve as human tackling dummies during football practice. The Stooges' appearance was well-received, and Columbia announced its plans to include the team in more feature-length productions. At long last it seemed as if the Stooges' feature-film career was about to blossom.

Shortly after the completion of *Start Cheering*, the Stooge who started it all, Shemp Howard, also signed on with Columbia's Shorts Department as a star comedian and gag writer. Shemp began his performing career in Columbia shorts co-starring with Andy Clyde in *Not Guilty Enough* (1938), a situation comedy which finds Shemp driving Andy

Healy's Stooges On Powers Stage

The Powers' theater stage presentation today offers six well-selected acts, headlined by Garner, Wolf and Hakins, stooges of the late Ted Healy.

The other five acts include the Three Arnolds, athletes, Monahan and Marris, xylophonists; the Banfields in a bouncing ball act; Billie Garland, song and dance girl and Don and Bette Lynne, clever dancers.

The film attraction is a first-run picture, "The Wrong Road," with Richard Cromwell, Helen Mack and Lionel Atwill.

Topping the stage presentation

VAUDEVILLE

POWERS
THEATRE

MATINEE 25c
NIGHTS 35c

HURRY—LAST TIMES SUNDAY—ON STAGE AND SCREEN

IN PERSON
TED HEALY'S
3 STOOGES
The Maniacs of Fun
PLUS—5 OTHER ACTS

ON SCREEN
First Grand Rapids Showing
THE WRONG ROAD

Starting Monday—Complete New Show on

In 1938, Mousie Garner, Dick Hakins and Sammy Wolfe continue to tour the country as The Three Stooges; here they headline a vaudeville bill in Grand Rapids, Michigan.

crazy when the latter suffers a nervous breakdown. It would be the first of a number of films in which silent-screen favorite Clyde served as straightman to Shemp's slapstick antics.

Shemp's co-starring series with the good-natured Clyde was a happy experience for both men, and the two became fast friends. Also, Andy's business manager, Al Winston, at one point handled affairs for both Shemp as an individual, and The Three Stooges as an act. Old-timer Clyde, the Howards and their manager were not only friends and business associates, but neighbors. They all lived within a mile of each other in Toluca Lake, the film-star community nestled north of the Hollywood Hills. The men and their families often socialized together, especially at the home of Shemp and Babe Howard, who were renowned for their comedy-crowd parties.

Meanwhile, Shemp's old Stooge partner, Dick Hakins, was starring with Mousie Garner and Sammy Wolfe in a new series of short subjects for Warner-Vitaphone. The trio had also embarked on a nationwide personal-appearance tour, working under the name "The Three Stooges." They felt that since Ted Healy had created the concept of Stooge comedy, and Mousie and company were in fact Ted's final Stooge ensemble, they had as much right to the name "Three Stooges" as the Howard family.

Healy's second Stooge dynasty headlined the vaudeville circuit, and they frequently crossed paths with the Howard family's "Three Stooges." *Variety* reported that the Howard group had planned to take the other trio to court, in an attempt to stop them from using their name, "The Three Stooges," in their billing. Mousie, however, has denied that the case ever got that far.

"If anything," says Garner, "the publicity would have helped us."

However, a series of legal maneuvers — as well as some pointed gangster-style threats from Harry Cohn — resulted in the "new" trio of Stooges becoming intimidated. They disbanded in relatively short order, and the Howard family's "Three Stooges" finally established themselves as the only Stooge troupe in Hollywood. From that point forward, Garner and company never promoted themselves as "The Three Stooges" without first receiving permission from Moe Howard.

As far as Dick Hakins was concerned, he was just as glad to be through with it. He started noticing that his head had begun to ache every time he came offstage. Years later, when he suffered a series of cerebral hemorrhages, his physician would advise him that these strokes had probably been caused by the head trauma he received while working as a Stooge.

The boys appear in the all-star cast of *Start Cheering* (1938), the first Columbia feature to properly showcase the Stooges' talents; this was in part due to the efforts of the film's producer, Nat Perrin, then best known as co-screenwriter of the classic Marx Brothers comedy *Duck Soup*.

Chapter 4

BY THE LATE THIRTIES, The Three Stooges' popularity was growing overseas as well as at home, so the boys decided to embark on a major personal-appearance tour of Europe. This was half a dozen years after Mousie Garner, Dick Hakins and Jack Wolf had appeared in England with their Stooge act. Moe Howard and company, meanwhile, claimed in a 1938 newspaper interview that they got the idea of "touring their constituencies" from then-President Franklin Roosevelt.

In 1939 the Stooges headlined the London Palladium to an extraordinarily receptive crowd. This was followed by a series of personal appearances at theaters throughout England, Scotland and Ireland. Their tour of the European Continent was canceled, however, when it looked as if World War II might erupt at any moment. The Stooges booked passage on the Queen Mary and sailed for home, all the while watching for German torpedoes in the water below.

Days after they docked in New York, Adolf Hitler's army invaded Poland, and World War II was officially underway.

Later that same year, the Stooges were contracted to star in a Broadway comedy revue, the 1939 edition of *George White's Scandals*. The lavish show was produced by legendary impresario George White (no relation to the White brothers of Hollywood). Many of the routines which pre-

With Ted Healy gone, The Three Stooges climb to new levels of wealth and success; here they discover an oil well in Jules White's *Oily to Bed, Oily to Rise* (1939).

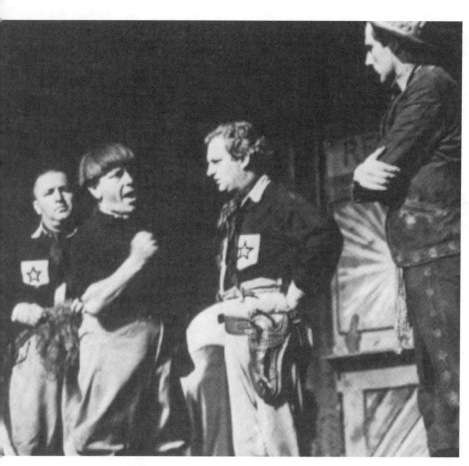

The Stooges appear in vaudeville in 1939, still performing material from their earliest days with Ted Healy.

Curly, Moe and Larry perform their classic sketch, "The Stand-In," in the 1939 edition of *George White's Scandals* on Broadway; it was during the run of this show that the Stooges made their first TV appearance — on closed-circuit television at the New York World's Fair.

In 1939, The Three Stooges sail from New York to Europe for their first overseas person-al-appearance tour.

THE LONDON
PALLADIUM

OXFORD CIRCUS, W.

Telephone - GERRARD 7373

GENERAL THEATRE CORPORATION, Ltd.
Managing Director - MARK OSTRER

Direction - GEORGE BLACK
Resident Manager - C T HUTCHISON

6.25 TWICE NIGHTLY **MATINEES AT 2.30** COMMENCING MONDAY, JUNE 12th, 1939 WEDNESDAY & THURSDAY **9.0**

MAX MILLER

HOLLYWOOD'S
THREE STOOGES

FIRST TIME HERE
JACK DURANT

A New Comedy Impressionist from the States

LESLIE SARONY & LESLIE HOLMES

TWO LESLIES

LAST WEEK

Crazy Stars of Columbia Pictures

WILL CARR
AND ASSISTANT

7 FREDYSONS
SPRINGBOARD GYMNASTS

BATIE & FOSTER
COLOURED COMEDIANS AND DANCERS

DOROTHY GRAY AND BROTHERS
AERIAL THRILLS

ROBINSON & MARTIN
"DESIGN FOR DANCING"

CAPT. TOMMY KAYES AND HIS LIONS

CLOSE HARMONY SINGERS & DANCERS From the COTTON CLUB, NEW YORK

THREE DANDRIDGE SISTERS
FIRST TIME IN ENGLAND

WENGES
"I AM NOT AFRAID"

---

miered in that show popped up in the Stooges' repertoire throughout the remainder of their career.

Indeed, The Three Stooges were so well-received on Broadway that George White reportedly contacted Harry Cohn at Columbia, and asked permission to use the boys in his show for a few more months. Cohn refused, however, and demanded that the Stooges return to Hollywood to begin filming a new series of shorts. The new series included some of the best work the Stooges ever did, including adaptations of many of their vaudeville gags and routines.

For example, the Stooges had performed a sketch on stage in which they ridiculed famous dictators of the era. Curly's specialty was Italy's Benito Mussolini, while Larry contributed his impression of the Soviet Union's Josef Stalin. And Moe's Germanic doubletalk and crackerjack Adolf Hitler impersonation were put to good use in *You Nazty Spy*, filmed in 1939 and released in 1940.

Director Jules White called *You Nazty Spy* his personal favorite of all his Stooge shorts. "I think they were very clever and they were very timely," said White. "And extremely funny."

You Nazty Spy was released more than a year before America's involvement in the war, and, to the immense delight of Jules White, months before the premiere of Charlie Chaplin's much-anticipated Hitler satire *The Great Dictator*. Because it was produced and distributed so quickly, the Stooges' *You Nazty Spy* was able to cash in on the advance bally-hoo for the Chaplin masterwork. And that pleased not only producer White, but studio bossman Harry Cohn as well. Cohn was always happy when his films received free public-

The boys top the bill at the London Palladium in 1939; the show's emcee (and the Stooges' straightman) is singer–comedian Jack Durant, who just months earlier dissolved his comedy partnership with former Ted Healy Stooge, Frank Mitchell.

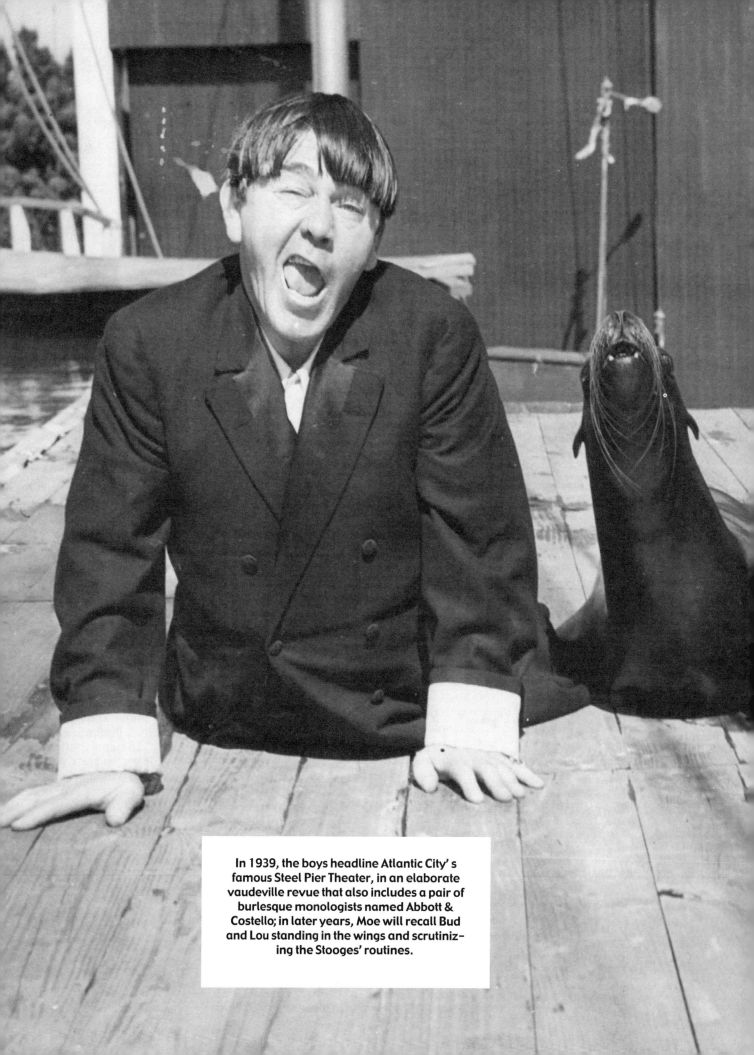

In 1939, the boys headline Atlantic City's famous Steel Pier Theater, in an elaborate vaudeville revue that also includes a pair of burlesque monologists named Abbott & Costello; in later years, Moe will recall Bud and Lou standing in the wings and scrutinizing the Stooges' routines.

In the early 1940s, Curly, Moe and Larry play "Gallstone, Hailstone and Pebble," respectively, in a trio of anti-Nazi Stooge shorts written by Felix Adler and Clyde Bruckman, and produced and directed by Jules White.

The ingenious Buster Keaton (seen here with Dorothy Appleby and Bud Jamison) joins Columbia's Shorts Department as a comedian and gag-man in 1939, providing original material for The Three Stooges and other performers.

ity. He was even happier when said free publicity was provided by an actual competitor, in this case Chaplin.

The Stooge opus pulls no punches in its burlesque of the Nazi regime. "We must find somebody who is stupid enough to do what we tell him," declares Dick Curtis, playing a munitions manufacturer. His associate, played by character actor Richard Fiske, nominates one "Moe Hailstone," a Hitler lookalike who is wallpapering Fiske's home with his two Stooge partners. Curly's obese, womanizing "Gallstone" is modeled on German field marshall Hermann Goering, while Larry's sneaky little "Pebble" is a parody of Josef Goebbels, complete with the Nazi propagandist's nasty limp. Fiske introduces the Stooges to his two partners, and they offer the tyrannical Moe the dictatorship of Moronica. Naturally, Moe accepts, and he predictably becomes a ruthless autocrat.

You Nazty Spy was the first in a series of shorts in which the Stooges parodied the sinister social misfits in charge of the Nazis' "Third Reich." The characters "Hailstone, Gallstone and Pebble" also turned up the following year in a sequel, *I'll Never Heil Again*, as well as in the Stooges' *Back From the Front* a couple of years after that.

Elwood Ullman remembered Del Lord telling him that the Stooges found their way onto Hitler's so-called "death list" because of their anti-Nazi propaganda films. Other prominent Hollywood performers, including Charlie Chaplin and Jack Benny, also made the list of those Der Fuerher wanted killed because of their anti-Nazi movies (Chaplin's *The Great Dictator* and Benny's *To Be or Not To Be*). All told, the Stooges made more films ridiculing the Third Reich than any other performers, so it stands to reason that a megaloma-

The Stooges are census-takers who somehow get on the field during a pro football game in the hilarious *No Census, No Feeling* (1940), written by Elwood Ullman and directed by Del Lord.

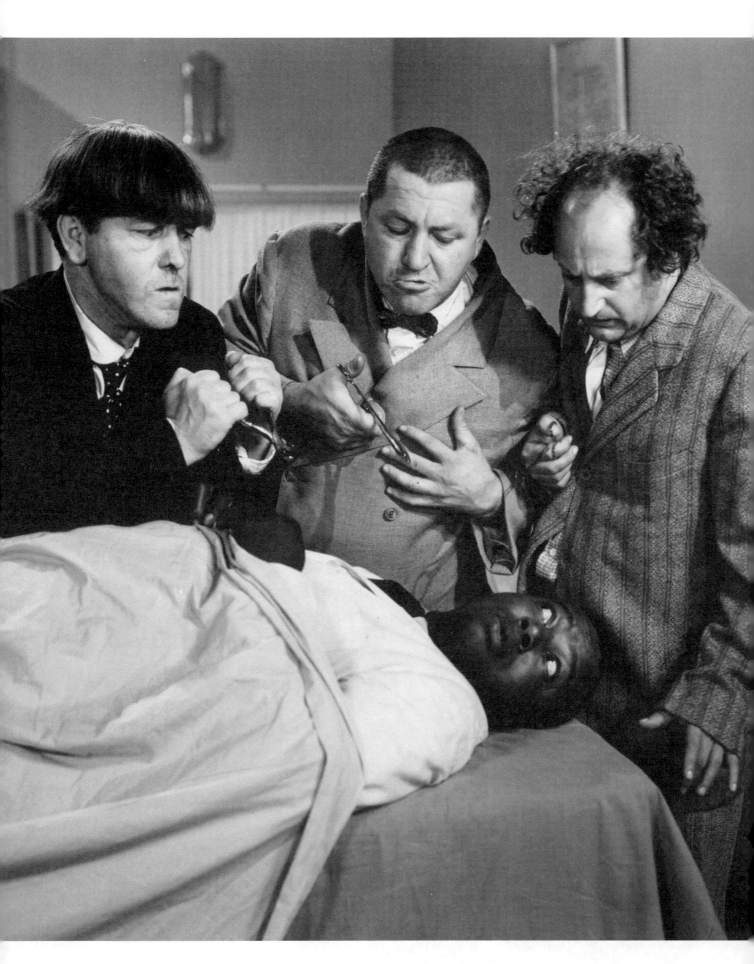

★★★ **The THREE STOOGES** ★★★

The Stooges publicize a "moving picture machine" made especially for kids in this early promotional campaign sponsored in part by Columbia.

niacal egotist like Hitler would have preferred them dead.

Audiences, however, couldn't get enough of the Stooges, and during the Second World War they were more popular than ever. Much of the reason for this was the blossoming of Curly Howard as a performer. By now, Curly had developed into one of the finest broad comics in the business.

Curly has seldom received his due as a comedian, primarily because of the still-existing snobbery by many critics toward the Stooges' brand of humor. Lou Costello, for example, has been referred to as a "comic genius" by more than one American writer, and during his lifetime he was also held in high regard throughout many Spanish-speaking countries. Jerry Lewis, in turn, has received similar accolades; critics in France have even compared him to Chaplin. But while he was alive, Curly Howard never received the credit he deserved.

As brother Moe explained, "He was truly a spontaneous comedian," adding that "in person, he was just as jolly and vivacious as he was in pictures — even more so."

"Curly was generous to a fault, you might say. He'd give you the shirt off his back,"

The boys attempt to terrify comic actor Dudley Dickerson on the set of Jules White's *From Nurse to Worse* (1940), a reworking of a classic Stooge short filmed three years earlier, Del Lord's *Dizzy Doctors*.

"That sonofabitch Bill Fields!," is how Shemp would preface any conversation about the ingenious and insecure W.C., who not only insisted that Shemp be cast as the Greek chorus of his his all-star masterpiece *The Bank Dick* (1940), but also insisted that Shemp's funniest scenes be deleted from the final print.

Draftee Mousie Garner, who served as a soldier in the U.S. Army during World War II and received the Purple Heart for injuries he received during battle, is prevailed upon to resurrect his old Stooge act for a camp show attended by Allied generals Eisenhower, Patton and Montgomery.

said his sister-in-law, Shemp's wife Babe, pointing up the humanity that shone through in all of Curly's performances.

"He really was a genius," reflects Mousie Garner, who often partied with Curly in the Thirties and Forties. "And he was as kind and personable as he was talented. A really good guy."

In *A Plumbing We Will Go* (1940), directed by Del Lord, Curly receives a good deal of screen time as he appears in several solo scenes. Many of the gags in this film, written by screenwriter Elwood Ullman, were repeated in other shorts over the next ten years. Posing as plumbers, the Stooges all but demolish an elaborate mansion with their amateurish "working" methods.

A Plumbing We Will Go turned out to be a huge hit for the Stooges. It was reworked several years later as *Pick a Peck of Plumbers*, produced and directed by Jules White as a Shemp Howard solo vehicle. This short was also remade by the Stooges themselves a decade later, under the title *Vagabond Loafers*, with some of the original supporting cast (as well as some original footage) remaining. Shemp essentially played Curly's role in both of the remakes.

And Curly's style and shtick had started creeping into the performances of other comedians as well. Edward Bernds said that Moe was certain Abbott & Costello were actually stealing material from the Stooges. "I don't know how he knew," said Bernds, "but Moe told me they regularly got prints of the two-reelers, looked at them, and in due course of time, the routines, or the gestures, or the mannerisms showed up in the Abbott & Costello pictures."

Moe was specifically incensed by Abbott & Costello's career-making film, *Buck Privates*,

While former Ted Healy Stooges, Sammy Wolfe, Mousie Garner and Dick Hakins are all serving in the U.S. Military during the early 1940s, they still manage to show up on American theater screens — their feature film *The Hit Parade* is retitled *I'll Reach for a Star* and re-issued domestically during World War II.

The Stooges are about to be exposed to a potent laughing-gas bomb in Jules White's *Boobs in Arms* (1940), based on an original story by Felix Adler titled *All This and Bullets, Too*.

Far right: trade advertisement for *Boobs in Arms*, the most popular of the Stooges' 1940 spate of short subjects.

released by Universal in 1940. He felt the feature-length vehicle was an abject rip-off of the Stooges' own military comedy, *Boobs in Arms*, released earlier in the same year. The basic storyline of the Abbott & Costello film, in which Bud and Lou are street peddlers who hastily join the Army in order to escape an angry pursuer, only to discover he's become their boot-camp sergeant, was virtually identical to the plot of *Boobs in Arms*. And many of the best gags and bits of business from the Stooge opus, such as the famous "drill" routine, turned up in the Abbott & Costello version as well.

It also couldn't have been any comfort to Moe that *Buck Privates'* all-star cast of players included his own brother Shemp, seen playing foil to hapless rookie Lou Costello in a musical number. Shemp would subsequently share the screen with Abbott & Costello in a number of feature films. And while Moe was glad to see his elder brother enjoying a prosperous career, he nevertheless felt that Universal was illegitimately reaping the benefits of top-grade Stooge comedy, simply by casting Ted Healy's favorite funnyman alongside Bud and Lou.

Moe watched helplessly as Abbott & Costello skyrocketed to fame and fortune at Universal, while the Stooges labored like hired hands making curtain-raisers for Columbia. Just when the Stooges were thinking about taking their act to another studio, Harry Cohn gave them exactly what they had been begging for — a feature film in which they had the comedy lead.

Time Out for Rhythm (1941) was the Stooges' feature-length outing for the 1940-41 season. To no one's surprise, the Stooges steal the film from such established stars as Ann

Shemp struggles with Lou Costello and Bud Abbott in this scene from Universal's all-star musical comedy *In the Navy* (1941), much of it filmed on location in Pearl Harbor just months before the enemy sneak attack on December 7th.

Miller, Rudy Vallee, Rosemary Lane and others, mostly by enacting sure-fire routines they had performed on stage for years.

The highlight of the film, the Stooges' presentation of their classic "Maharaja" routine, is a clever melange of slapstick action and double-talk patter. A running gag has Curly wearing a pair of inch-thick spectacles that render him nearly blind, causing him to fall out of chairs and bump into walls. Curly's performance is flawlessly funny, and his timing and vocal inflections are letter-perfect.

This routine was adapted from a vaudeville sketch the Stooges had performed in the previous decade. The stage version featured a knife-throwing sequence, in which Curly was aided by Moe in tossing rubber knives at human-target Larry. Elwood Ullman, who saw the Stooges perform the sketch in vaudeville, recalled that the theater's juvenile patrons

Curly (with director Sidney Salkow) on the set of *Time Out for Rhythm* (1941), the best of the Stooges' Columbia feature films.

"I'll never know how we got that title past the censors," is the first thing Jules White remembered when asked about his classic short *In the Sweet Pie and Pie* (1941), a "Stooges versus Society" opus featuring a memorable performance from Symona Boniface (seen over Moe's right shoulder).

would go wild whenever Curly "accidentally" threw one of the rubber knives into the audience.

Despite their success in *Time Out for Rhythm*, the Stooges continued to do their best work for Columbia's Shorts Department, not the studio's feature-film division. In fact, one of Curly Howard's funniest performances can be seen in the 1942 short *Loco Boy Makes Good*, directed by Jules White.

This film features an excellent sequence in which Curly, wearing a magician's coat full of rabbits, mice, pigeons, and so forth, creates a disturbance on a crowded dance floor. Several years after the short's release, however, Columbia was slapped with a $1 million-plus lawsuit from comedian Harold Lloyd, who complained that the studio had stolen the routine from one of Lloyd's earlier movies.

Apparently Clyde Bruckman, who wrote the screenplay, had a penchant for lifting old material, particularly if it was from one of his own creations. He had simply "borrowed" the sketch from a Paramount feature film he had written a dozen years earlier, a big-budget Lloyd vehicle titled *Movie Crazy*. And even though Lloyd had by this time more or less retired from the screen, he owned the rights to the film, and the onetime superstar was not about to allow his intellectual properties to be plundered by Harry Cohn's Shorts Department and re-enacted by The Three Stooges. Lloyd sued Columbia Pictures as a cor-

Harold Lloyd, who sues Columbia Pictures, producer–director Jules White, and screenwriter Clyde Bruckman for stealing his copyrighted comedy material, apparently never notices that White and Bruckman's very next Stooge film together, *Three Smart Saps* (1942), also appropriates a number of classic Lloyd routines.

★★★ **The THREE STOOGES** ★★★

poration, as well as producer-director White and screenwriter Bruckman as individuals, and won the case.

Despite these occasional production blunders, The Three Stooges continued their winning streak as film comedians during this period. With America and the rest of the free world literally fighting for its existence, the early 1940s served as a time of unprecedented popularity for the Stooges and their particular brand of humor.

For moviegoers craving escape, their emotions jangled by wartime stress, The Three Stooges seemed to be just what the doctor ordered. Elwood Ullman recalled that theater audiences would go wild with excitement the moment a Stooge short was unspooled. "From the time I started working with them, they were very popular. Those three heads would come on the screen, and the crowd would scream, and holler, and cheer. But during the Second World War it was like nothing you'd ever seen. It was pandemonium!"

Nearly every film the Stooges turned out during the early 1940s was a gem. And although their films generally received glowing reviews in movie-industry trade publications, most consumer newspaper critics considered the Stooge comedies to be the very dregs of artistic achievement. However, the "Three Stooges" film series was by now unquestionably the most consistently successful property Columbia had. The Stooge episodes were often voted by theater owners as their most popular short-subject attractions, in competition with cartoons and newsreels as well.

But despite their unprecedented success in films, there was trouble looming on the horizon for The Three Stooges. Namely, Curly was no longer a well man. The daily regimen of slapping, smacking and socking he endured had begun to take its toll on his health. He started suffering a series of minor cerebral hemorrhages, and the long-term result

While performing for soldiers at an Army base in the early 1940s, the boys take time out to harass the officer in charge of entertainment.

The boys entertain a huge audience of servicemen during World War II; note that the Stooges are displaying the two-fingered gesture then known as "the victory sign."

Curly not only tries to make time with a married woman, but he does it in front of her hot-blooded husband, in Jules White's *What's the Matador* (1942).

would be devastating. Curly would lose his sense of timing, his ability to remember dialogue, and his once-awesome physical grace.

By mid-1942, Curly was already becoming too ill to do personal appearances. Shemp — now a Columbia contractee — was brought back into the act as a temporary replacement, taking on Curly's role in the team's live performances.

That same year, Curly's doctors ordered him to take a break from filming as well, as his health had grown progressively worse. But Curly's request for a vacation was turned down by his employers. The Three Stooges were a cash cow for Columbia, and studio bossman Harry Cohn refused to give Curly the time off he needed to recuperate. This heartless edict would result in Curly becoming sicker and sicker, and The Three Stooges would eventually find themselves at the edge of professional disaster.

Also in 1942, at New York's fashionable night spot "21," Harry Cohn and gangster Pat DiCicco got into a vicious argument. Shocked patrons heard DiCicco screaming at Cohn, and they watched in horror as the enraged hoodlum chased the powerful studio head out of the club and into the street. (Later that same evening, DiCicco brutally beat his then-wife Gloria Vanderbilt, who also recalled her husband muttering the name "Thelma" over and over.)

Dick Hakins wondered many years later if Cohn was threatening to expose DiCicco's involvement in the deaths of Thelma Todd and Ted Healy. "From what I knew of Harry Cohn, I wouldn't put it past him," said Hakins.

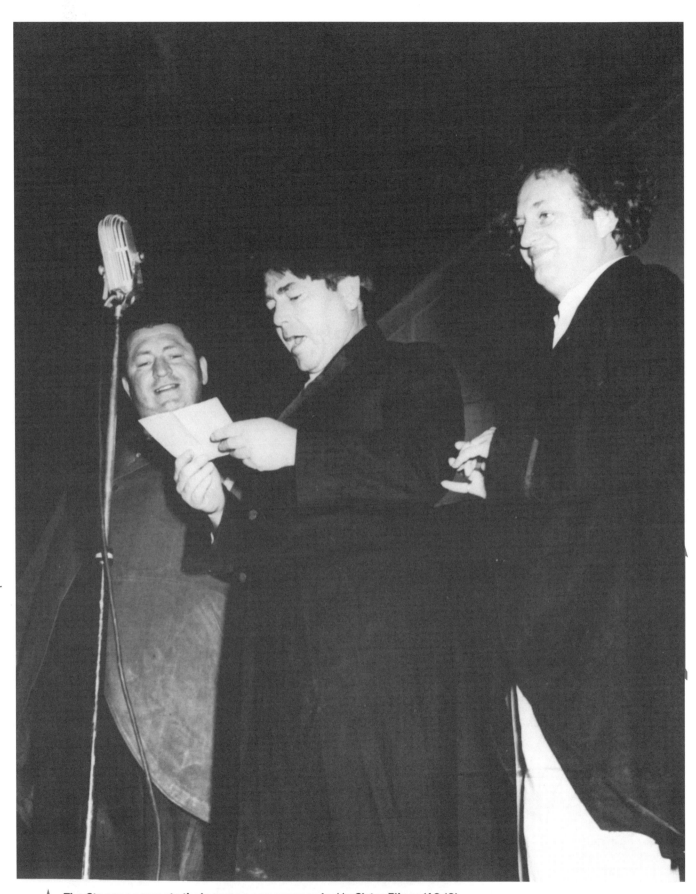

The Stooges promote their cameo appearance in *My Sister Eileen* (1942), a Columbia feature film in which the boys provide the surprise ending.

Harry Cohn, in fact, was already making plans to rein in The Three Stooges like never before. He had insisted they align themselves with a manager, someone to serve as a "liason" in dealings with Columbia. The Stooges, mistakenly hoping this would give them some leverage in salary negotiations, signed with Harry Romm, Mabel Fine's ex-brother-in-law and a longtime family friend, in 1943.

In the years to come, Romm would use his relationship with Columbia's front office to feather his own nest, while seeing to it that the Stooges stayed right where Cohn wanted them. Which was under his thumb. The Stooges could complain all they wanted about never getting a raise or not making enough features. Nothing was going to change now that good old Harry Romm was on board.

By 1943, the bulk of the Shorts Department's directing work was being divided up between Jules White and Del Lord. During the mid-1940s, the separate production entities run by White and Hugh McCollum also developed into significant rivalries.

Consolidating his power, White continued to direct and produce his own shorts, retaining top guns Felix Adler and Clyde Bruckman as screenwriters. Occasionally, Jack White was also brought in to collaborate on a script, although he never again worked at Columbia as a director. The better-paying directing gigs were now snatched up by his brother Jules, who, as head of his own unit, answered only to Harry Cohn.

Jules White was even assigned to work with the Stooges in what was to be their feature-length movie for the 1942-43 season, *Good Luck, Mr. Yates* (1943). The film was an all-star comedy-drama, dealing with America's domestic defense effort during World War II, and the Stooges were slated as lead laughgetters.

Ted Healy veteran Joe Besser becomes a Columbia feature-film star in the early 1940s, appearing in musical-comedy vehicles opposite dancer Ann Miller.

For the film, the Stooges performed their own version of the burlesque classic "Slowly, I Turned," in which Curly plays a poor shnook who repeatedly takes a beating from Moe and Larry. Jules White personally directed the sketch, which is shot against a bandstand as if it is being presented before a live audience.

But when *Good Luck, Mr. Yates* started showing up in theaters across the country, the Stooges were nowhere to be found. Much to their horror, all of their contributions to the film had been deleted. Harry Cohn explained, through reliable Harry Romm, that the Stooges' footage had been scrapped because it had previewed poorly.

According to Shemp's wife Babe, the Stooges later learned that their antics had actually convulsed the wartime preview audience. Cohn, however, had not only ordered the footage be scissored out of the release print, but insisted an entire new Three Stooges

short, *Gents Without Cents* (1944), be built around it! A strange decision indeed, if the footage had in fact been previewed unsuccessfully.

But Cohn knew exactly what he was doing. Better for the Stooges to think that they had bombed, especially since wartime salary "negotiations" were coming up. It wasn't that Cohn didn't think the Stooges were big stars. They *were* big stars, and Cohn knew it. The trick was to make sure the *Stooges* never figured it out.

Toward the end of World War II, as Del Lord began working less frequently at Columbia, Edward Bernds started writing and directing shorts for the Stooges himself. Bernds remained at Columbia for several years, maintaining Lord's tradition of cranking out fast and funny Stooge shorts.

Bernds had wanted to direct films for quite some time before his opportunity came in

A moment of contemplation from Del Lord's *A Gem of a Jam* (1943), which features a wonderfully funny thumb-twiddling routine enacted by Curly and co-star Dudley Dickerson.

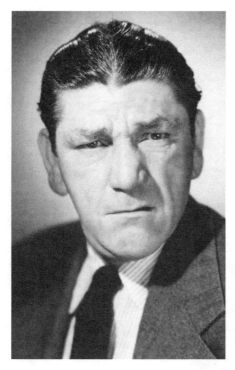

An attempt at re-creating The Three Stooges: Universal Pictures casts Ted Healy veterans Shemp Howard, Freddie Sanborn and Frank Mitchell as "Mumbo, Jumbo and Dumbo" in the all-star feature comedy *Crazy House* (1943).

In a publicity scheme cooked up by Shemp's agent, popular screen actress Virginia Bruce presents Shemp with an award recognizing him as "The Ugliest Man in Hollywood."

the mid-1940s. With a background in radio, Bernds had literally created Columbia's Sound Engineering division in the late Twenties. He was also the studio's top soundman, and throughout the Thirties worked mostly with the studio's top director, Frank Capra. As a Capra crew member, Bernds received a crash course in the art and psychology of film directing by observing the master at work. Recording sound on the Stooge comedies also gave Bernds an education, as he studied the individual directing techniques of slapstick veterans like Del Lord, Jules White, and even Charley Chase. Bernds obviously absorbed quite a bit of knowledge from working with these men. The shorts he turned out with the Stooges are among the best the team ever made.

The longtime soundman recalled how he broke into directing the Stooge comedies: "Elwood Ullman was busy working at Universal, and Hugh McCollum was strapped for writers. He gave me writing assignments with the kind of assurance that when Harry Edwards quit, I would get to direct. . . . I think it was when Roosevelt died in April of '45 that I directed my first picture with the Stooges. Boy, it was a great relief for me when Elwood came back from Universal and began to write scripts. He was very good at it and there was far more than I could handle."

Characteristically modest, Bernds was quick to add that his elevation to the status of studio writer-director was in part due to an attestation from an old boss and friend. Apparently director Frank Capra had put in a good word for him with studio head Harry Cohn. "Capra went to Cohn and told

him I would make a good director. I never even talked it over with Cohn. When I arrived at his office, he just told me to discuss my salary with Hugh McCollum, and shooed me away."

Bernds then learned that another friend and colleague, Del Lord, had already gone to unit producer McCollum with his own testimonial: "Del had assured Mac that I would be successful as a comedy director. He even offered to bail me out if necessary. And Del only made the offer because he knew he wasn't going to have to bail me out."

Of all the comedians in Columbia's Shorts Department, Bernds most enjoyed working with The Three Stooges. So producer McCollum assigned him a Stooge short for his debut as comedy director, one that would require the fledgling filmmaker to write the script as well as supervise the shooting.

Bernds recalled that the Stooges themselves were extremely supportive. "When I came to direct them, they had already known me as a soundman," he said. "I had worked with them on their very first picture at Columbia. This might have worked against me, since they knew me up from the ranks. But they cooperated very fully, right from the start. It was a lot of fun working with them."

Emil Sitka, who appeared in a number of Bernds' Stooges comedies, said Bernds encouraged creativity and fostered a relaxed atmosphere on the set:

"He allowed me to create the character. And I could develop it to such an extent that it would be altogether my own."

Sitka added that Bernds was a "very nice, genial" director. "Many directors are impa-

The Stooges are deliverymen masquerading as newspaper reporters masquerading as servants in Jules White's *Crash Goes the Hash* (1944).

While appearing with the Stooges in Atlantic City in the mid-1940s, Eddie Laughton and a couple of stagehands are pressed into service for this publicity-photo session.

By 1944, The Three Stooges have been major stars at Columbia Pictures for a solid decade, and the studio begins promoting this fact in various trade publications.

BUSY AMERICA IS NEVER TOO BUSY TO LAUGH!

...and movie-goers have been laughing at filmdom's zaniest comedy team for ten years!

THE THREE STOOGES

Laugh-leaders in the two-reel comedy field...these crazy cuckoos are busier than ever...creating more fun than ever!

NOW BOOKING...THE FUNNIEST OF ALL!

PLAY THEM ALL!
THEY ALWAYS PAY OFF!

BUSY BUDDIES

(6th release in their current series of 8)

THE BEST SHORTS OF ALL COME FROM COLUMBIA

The boys pose with their own co-stars, as well as members of the Los Angeles Police Department, on the set of Jules White's *No Dough Boys* (1944).

tient, arrogant and stern. They won't repeat themselves," he said. "But with Ed Bernds you could work it out, reason it out. That's why I liked working with him the best."

This more or less easygoing directing style is reflected in Bernds' Stooge shorts. Good ad libs are always plentiful, and the performances flow smoothly and naturally. Unfortunately, most of the shorts Bernds did with Curly as a member of the team are marred by the ailing Stooge's lack of energy. At about the time Bernds began working with the boys, Curly began losing much of his renowned vitality, and his timing seemed to grow slower with each performance. Although he was not well, Curly continued to make appearances with the Stooges.

Unfortunately, his performance in *Rockin' in the Rockies* (1945), the Stooges' feature film for the 1944-45 season, is one of his most punchdrunk. Moe had begged manager Harry Romm to convince the front office that Curly needed some time off to recuperate, but head man Harry Cohn refused to consider the idea. Now Curly's lack of energy and focus was starting to show up onscreen.

But as far as Harry Cohn was concerned, Curly was going to keep working as long as there was money to be made in Stooge comedies. And there was.

The real question, however, was how long could it *last*?

The boys enjoy top billing in Columbia's feature-length musical *Rockin' in the Rockies* (1945), but Curly is already too sick to carry much of the comedy.

★★★ **The THREE STOOGES** ★★★

Chapter 5

CURLY'S DEDICATION to the Stooges finally caught up with him in 1945, when he suffered what is believed to be his first major stroke. Not surprisingly, Curly resumed work with the Stooges shortly afterward. The Stooges continued filming their Columbia shorts, even though much of the comic load was now focused on Moe and Larry. Although he struggled to continue in the act, Curly simply couldn't recapture the physical vitality and elfin quality that had distinguished him as the star member of the Stooges. Emil Sitka, who appeared in Curly's last comedy as one of the Stooges, recalled that the popular comedian was quite subdued after his initial strokes: "Curly was really quiet, believe it or not, because he would hardly talk at all . . . he wouldn't discuss what he planned to do in the film."

Edward Bernds says working with Curly after his stroke was a struggle. "By the time I started directing them in 1945," said Bernds, "Curly was a sick man. He was a very, very funny guy in his prime, but by 1945 he was not well. He couldn't remember his lines, and he was a little slower in his reactions."

The first comedy Bernds wrote and directed was a short for the Stooges called *A Bird in the Head* (1945), a pretty good offering considering Curly was very ill at the time of filming. This one has a mad scientist (Vernon Dent) after Curly's puny brain—he wants to transplant it into the skull of his pet gorilla. Because of his illness, Curly's actual screen time is comparatively limited. Bernds simply shifted much of the action to Moe and Larry, with better-than-expected results.

Bernds later recalled with horror, however, his first day of shooting, when it became clear from the outset that Curly was a very sick man. Neither department head Jules White, nor Bernds' own producer, Hugh McCollum, had bothered to inform the

Shemp returns to part-time stooging in the mid-1940s, believing he will be finished with the gig and back working as a solo performer within a matter of months.

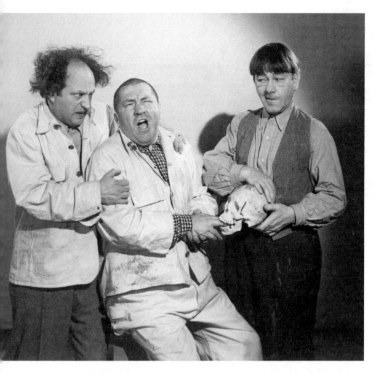

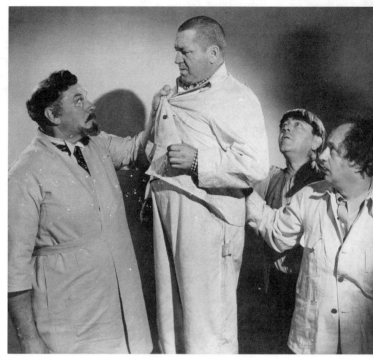

Writer-director Edward Bernds, who films the Stooge comedy *A Bird in the Head* in 1945, describes the experience as "really nerve-wracking, especially since it was the first narrative story I ever directed."

fledgling director that his lead actor was in no shape to appear on camera, let alone take the lead in a high-energy slapstick comedy.

But the Stooges' next short with Bernds turned out to be one of their best, *Micro Phonies* (1945). The film serves as a testimonial to the fact that, next to Del Lord, Edward Bernds more fully understood the comic abilities and limitations of the Stooges than any of their other directors. In fact, many feel that Bernds was probably the best all-around director the Stooges ever worked with in shorts, period. The Stooges themselves held this

The boys are forced to spend the night in a spooky mansion in Jules White's *If a Body Meets a Body* (1945), a remake of an earlier Hal Roach short titled *The Laurel-Hardy Murder Case.*

★★★ **The THREE STOOGES** ★★★

opinion, and as a result, Bernds would continue to work with the team until the very end of their Hollywood career many years later.

Bernds' *Micro Phonies* is a beautiful example of genuine comedic craftsmanship, and is delightfully loaded with memorable gags and routines from start to finish. The supporting cast is also top-drawer, led by Christine McIntyre, a young actress who would quickly become the "first lady" of the Three Stooges series.

According to Edward Bernds, McIntyre was not only producer Hugh McCollum's protégé, but his mistress as well. Her striking physical beauty and graceful manner served as an excellent contrast to the crude antics of the Stooges. "Christine was great to work with," remembered Bernds. "She was a real trouper, and very ladylike, but she learned to slug it out with the Stooges."

The short also exploits McIntyre's fine singing voice and features a number of musical sequences. But perhaps the film's most significant aspect, and another example that says a great deal of Bernds' directorial talent, is Curly's performance. Despite his illness and increasing lack of energy, he manages to turn in a very funny performance, this time maintaining a good share of the comic burden.

Bernds began work on Micro Phonies after his initial short, *A Bird in the Head*, was completed. But *Micro Phonies* was rushed into release first, because producer Hugh McCollum wanted to impress Columbia executives with Bernds' talent as a writer and director on a short that was sure to be a smash hit.

Micro Phonies was the film that won Edward Bernds his position as full-time director. Bernds recalled that he wrote the script for *Micro Phonies* at the request of Hugh McCollum. "I wasn't even aware that Christine McIntyre was a singer," said Bernds, "but after I'd done *A Bird in the Head*, McCollum asked me to write something that would take advantage of her singing voice. She actually auditioned for me."

While the Stooge shorts were now blessed with an excellent new director, a talented leading lady and an abundance of good comedy material, the films themselves were often severely marred by Curly's devastating lack of vitality. It was becoming obvious to his co-workers that Curly was a sick man. Physically, he looked ten years older than his age. Curly no longer had the cherubic facial features and mannerisms that had made him so popular.

Former Ted Healy Stooges, Mousie Garner, Jack Wolf and Dick Hakins, rendezvous in the post-war era for a special appearance at Washington D.C.'s top nightclub, the Cafe of All Nations.

The Stooges are janitors at a radio station mistaken for a classically-trained vocalist and her two accompanists in Edward Bernds' *Micro Phonies* (1945).

On the set of *Monkey Businessmen*, Larry seems to be getting somewhere with co-star Jean Willes, while Curly and Moe happily wait their turn.

According to Edward Bernds, the Curly of 1946 can no longer remember dialogue unless coached on the set by Moe.

During shooting of *Three Loan Wolves* (1946), Curly cannot perform some of the more complicated routines called for in Felix Adler's script, so director Jules White re-assigns most of the funny business to Larry.

Many of these Stooge comedies are almost painful to watch because of Curly's struggling, lifeless performances. In the hands of a sympathetic director, like Edward Bernds, Curly managed to turn in good work. Jules White continued to work with the Stooges as well, although his efforts usually didn't match the quality of the Bernds comedies.

As Curly's energy sapped away, more and more of the burden of being funny was necessarily relieved from his shoulders. The best example of this is *Beer Barrel Polecats* (1946), which has the Stooges as beer barons who wind up going to jail for selling some homemade brew to a cop. Curly is given relatively little to do, and a good deal of his screen time is comprised of old footage from a pair of "prison"-themed comedies, *So Long Mr. Chumps* and *In the Sweet Pie and Pie*, both released some five years earlier.

Occasionally, however, Curly was capable of carrying a good share of the comedy and was able to turn in first-rate work. In *Three Little Pirates* (1946), for example, Curly is the focus of attention, and he turns in one of his best performances.

Curly had performed the classic "Maharaja" routine in the feature-length musical *Time Out for Rhythm*, but its presentation was not an integral part of the story. However, in *Three Little Pirates*, a Caribbean costume comedy directed by Edward Bernds, Clyde Bruckman actually integrated the routine into the plotline, which finds the Stooges passing themselves off as wealthy adventurers in order to escape a ruthless colonial governor (Vernon Dent). Curly's performance is top-notch throughout the double-talk scenes, and, despite the fact that the film was made after his stroke, it's one of the most enjoyable shorts in the entire series.

Directing the Stooge comedies prior to *Three Little Pirates* had been a struggle for Edward Bernds. "But by the time we did

Pirates," he said, "Curly was much better." There was hope that Curly would recover his old comic prowess and stamina, and return to the star position of the Stooges.

But there wasn't much hope for that to be found in the Stooges' feature film for the 1946-47 season, *Swing Parade* (1946), an all-star quickie produced by the team's manager, Harry Romm, at the Monogram studio facility. Curly isn't much better than he was in the previous year's *Rockin' in the Rockies*, and most of the Stooges' routines are fairly stale as the boys attempt to provide the comedy in this all-star musical.

Curly's final appearance as one of The Three Stooges was in *Half Wits Holiday* (1947). The short, produced and directed by Jules White, is a remake of their earlier comedy, *Hoi Polloi*, with most of the original storyline intact.

This version casts the Stooges as plumbers working in the home of a wealthy professor, played by Vernon Dent. Dent hires them to participate in the "heredity vs. environment" experiment, and the results are predictably disastrous. Except this time around, the climactic society party ends in a wild pie-throwing melee.

The boys enact their classic vaudeville sketch, "The Maharajah of Vulgaria," in Edward Bernds' *Three Little Pirates* (1946).

Throughout the pie fight, however, Curly is conspicuously absent. Moe recalled in his memoirs that Curly was relaxing near the set while he and Larry completed a scene by themselves. When it was time for Curly to participate in the shot, the assistant director called out for him. Curly didn't answer.

Moe went for him and found him with his head dropped to his chest. Curly was unable to speak or even raise his head. Between takes, he had suffered a massive stroke.

While Curly was being taken out of the studio for treatment, Moe and Larry were forced to remain on the set to complete insert shots. Within an hour of Curly's collapse, Jules White had envisioned a way of inserting into the action some previously-existing footage of a tuxedoed Curly, repeatedly getting plastered with pies

The Three Stooges provide the comedy in Phil Karlson's *Swing Parade* (1946), a musical feature co-starring virtually all of producer-manager Harry Romm's clients.

Barbara Slater is the leading lady in Jules White's *Half Wits Holiday*, filmed in 1946 and featuring Curly Howard's last appearance as one of the Stooges.

Happy-go-lucky Larry, seen here in costume in the mid-1940s, was occasionally plagued by depression; he suffered most acutely after his adult son, Johnny, was killed in an automobile accident.

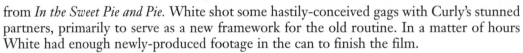

from *In the Sweet Pie and Pie*. White shot some hastily-conceived gags with Curly's stunned partners, primarily to serve as a new framework for the old routine. In a matter of hours White had enough newly-produced footage in the can to finish the film.

Despite White's best efforts, *Half Wits Holiday* is occasionally more sad than funny. Curly's performance is so sluggish one can sense he was an extremely sick man. And White never utilized the vintage Curly footage as he had planned. Apparently the contrast between the vibrant Curly of five years earlier, and the stroke-ravaged Curly of five *hours* earlier, was a little too distinct to get by.

Curly's sense of "professionalism" had, in fact, led to the destruction of his career. To satisfy the unreasonable demands of his employers, he had continued working after his first stroke. Now his health was all but ruined.

Curly also suffered through three unsuccessful marriages, and these failures are said to have contributed greatly to his overall misery. According to a report published by the *Los Angeles Times*, his most recent wife, Marion Buxbaum, sued him for divorce in 1946. The *Times* report read as follows: "She said he had used filthy, vulgar and vile language; kept two

★★★ **The THREE STOOGES** ★★★

vicious dogs which she was afraid would bite her; shouted at waiters in cafes; pushed, struck and pinched her; put cigars in the sink."

Curly had reportedly married Marion just two weeks after meeting her. That marriage lasted less than a year.

After Curly's second, major stroke, his partners were faced with the ominous task of finding a replacement for the popular Stooge. Larry and Moe had considered breaking up the act for good, but Columbia Pictures was insistent that they continue producing shorts under their extremely profitable "Three Stooges" banner. After all, the Stooge comedies were still the most consistently popular commodities Columbia had.

Moe recalled that after Curly's illness, he and Larry were presented with many comedians as potential replacements, but none of them fit their requirements. It seemed that everybody was being touted as "a combination of Curly, Lou Costello and Jerry Lewis." And yet none of these so-called comers—film veterans, nightclub comics, even stage actors—seemed to understand the true essence of Curly's humor. Curly was all vaudeville, and vaudeville was dying as well.

It was finally becoming abundantly clear to Harry Cohn and his army of yes-men, that

The comedy duo of Dean Martin and Jerry Lewis: Moe Howard believes the crewcut-wearing member of the team is lifting character traits, inflections and gestures from Curly.

The boys "make a wish" with Emil Sitka, appearing in his first film with the Stooges, *Half Wits Holiday.*

One of Curly's favorite hobbies is collecting dogs, and he continues to do so long after he is no longer well enough to care for them.

the chemistry between the Stooges themselves was a lot harder to reproduce than appearance suggested. The boys had clowned with such apparent effortlessness, with such spontaneity and gusto, that the front office had actually begun to believe anyone could do what the Stooges did and make it work.

But producer-director Jules White, up to his neck seven days a week in the business of making people laugh, knew exactly what a unique combination the Stooges really were. He said, "I think that in their line they were great. When you talk about Charlie Chaplin, for example, you're talking about the diamond of diamonds. Nevertheless, I've seen some of the Stooges' films get bigger laughs than the same amount of footage of Chaplin's. Although Chaplin's were probably done with more finesse, that didn't necessarily make them any better. Because when you're after laughs, you're after laughs no matter how you get them. When you hear an audience shriek so loud you can't hear dialogue for a hundred and two hundred feet at a time, you can't ask for more than that."

Co-star Emil Sitka added, "For farce, for split-second timing, they were

★★★ The THREE STOOGES ★★★

great. You take three other comedians and let them try to do the same things the Stooges did, and you'd see how hard it would be for them to do it."

Even the crew members who worked on their films were aware of the Stooges' peculiar genius. Henry Freulich, the director of photography on many of the best "Curly" shorts, recalled "I had worked on a lot of pictures, with a lot of different comedians, but I never saw anything like The Three Stooges. They were like lightning in a bottle."

Eventually, Harry Cohn and his executive lackeys would come to understand that securing a replacement for Curly was going to be a much more daunting task than they had imagined.

After conducting auditions for "the next Curly," in which Moe and Larry reviewed more than a hundred different performers and still weren't satisfied, it was determined that the Stooges' chances for survival would be increased considerably if Shemp simply came back to the act, at least until a full-time replacement could be found. Shemp was already under contract to Columbia, and was starring in his own series of shorts at the time. Jules White, a friend of Shemp's and the extended Howard family, had arranged for the series. Some of these shorts were even remakes of classic Three Stooges comedies like *Punch Drunks* and *A Plumbing We Will Go*.

Shemp, however, was less than eager to get back into the act. He didn't relish the idea of being looked upon as Curly's "replacement," even on a temporary basis. Shemp was well aware of the fact that Curly would be an incredibly tough act to follow. In a bizarre turn of events, Shemp was now in the same position that Curly had found himself in during the previous decade. Back then, few believed that Curly had "the right stuff" to replace his brilliantly funny brother. Now the shoe was on the other foot, and no one concerned was particularly happy about it. But Shemp actually had little choice in the matter. Harry Cohn and Columbia Pictures made the decision for him, and the new "Three Stooges" went before the cameras, with Shemp as lead funnyman, in 1946. Curly, meanwhile, took time off for some much-needed rest and recuperation.

It was hoped that Curly would eventually regain his health and stamina, making it possible for him to return to the Stooges. This, of course, would have allowed Shemp to resume his lucrative solo career, and Shemp desperately clung to this scenario. He had spent the last fifteen years developing a name for himself as a single, and Shemp was understandably reluctant to throw it all away. He was well aware there was no prestige in returning to an act he had vacated in the first place.

Also, according to Shemp's wife Babe, Shemp was expected to take a *fifty-percent* pay cut upon rejoining the Stooges. At the time Shemp was earning about $50,000 per year as a solo actor in films, while the Stooges collectively were paid $75,000 annually. In splitting the take three ways, Shemp would now be bringing home only $25,000 each year. And even though the Stooges enjoyed a lucrative personal-appearance career in addition to their movie contract, Shemp could earn an even greater sum of money simply by appearing as a single in local nightclubs. As a solo performer, Shemp had more than enough work opportunities in Hollywood. The Three Stooges, however, did not.

And Shemp was dealing with other internal conflicts that had nothing to do with business. He was now over fifty years old, and he did not look forward to the day-in, day-out regimen of physical abuse heaped upon whomever played the "Third Stooge" role. Nor did Shemp look forward to the idea of touring again, because he wasn't particularly fond of "life on the road," nor of being separated from his family for long periods of time. Shemp took his responsibilities as a father seriously, and felt it was important for his teenage son to have a real flesh-and-blood dad on the premises.

Shemp's wife Babe painfully remembered the agonizing decision-making involved in her husband's return to the act. "Columbia could make Shemp do whatever they wanted

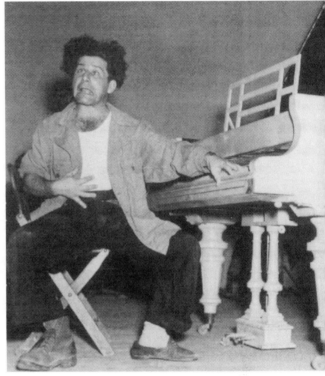

After recovering from injuries sustained in battle at the end of World War II, Mousie Garner returns overseas with the USO to entertain servicemen in Allied-occupied Europe.

Opposite: Shemp is forced to rejoin the Stooges in 1946, essentially bringing to an end his solo feature-film career.

Opposite, lower left: Brothers Shemp and Moe join producer Jules White for a fishing expedition during Curly's illness.

Opposite, lower right: Shemp conducts Harry James' orchestra during an evening at the Hollywood Palladium in the mid-1940s (notice trumpeter James seated at Shemp's left).

him to, because he was under contract. But I do think he could have gotten out of it, if he really objected to rejoining the Stooges. He could have just left Columbia altogether, and settled his contract. I don't think Jules would have held him to it, because he liked Shemp personally and respected his talent. It was really pressure from Moe and Larry, mostly Moe, that made Shemp give in.

"Moe told Shemp the Stooges were through if he didn't come back, and what were Moe and Larry going to do to make a living? Neither one of them could make it as a single. And what would happen to Curly, now that he was sick, if there was no money coming in? Curly was already finished, and without the Stooges, so were Larry and Moe. But that was far from the case with Shemp.

"Anyone who knew him would tell you that Shemp was a real family man. And I can tell you he felt responsible to his brothers and their families, and to Larry and his family. He wanted to do what was right. I begged him not to do it, but he said his conscience wouldn't let him to do anything else. He said the whole family was going to go down the drain if he didn't make the sacrifice. That's why he agreed to go back to the Stooges.

"Shemp was a good man."

In the mid-1940s, Shemp stars in, and writes special material for, several feature-length comedies at Monogram with real-life pals Billy Gilbert (wearing hat) and Maxie Rosenbloom.

As a solo performer, Shemp is at his busiest in the 1940s; here he appears opposite "The Dead End Kids," later known as "The Bowery Boys," in the role of the harassed sweet-shop owner.

Figures of global importance, like Shemp and Albert Einstein, are always popular at Princeton University.

124

Press releases were issued stating how happy brother Moe and former partner Larry were about Shemp's return to the act. Apparently, however, nobody had bothered to ask Shemp's opinion about the whole affair. In truth, Shemp had built a life and a career away from the Stooges. He had fought long and hard to be recognized as a comedian and character actor in his own right, not just as one of Ted Healy's interchangeable buffoons. On his own, Shemp had achieved stardom. Now he was right back where he started. But once he officially rejoined the Stooges, trouper Shemp acted as if he had never been away—both onscreen and off.

"Shemp was a team player if ever there was one," commented Edward Bernds.

And whenever fans would ask him how he could withstand all the slaps, pokes and punches he received as a Stooge, Shemp's reply was always the same: "I'm made of cement."

As one of the Stooges, the good-natured Shemp fit in well, even though his comedic style was remarkably different from Curly's. Even *without* a gag haircut, Shemp was fun to look at. He could get laughs through his facial expressions alone.

"Shemp could be funny even offscreen," recalled Emil Sitka. "He was funny just to look at. He had a big nose like a potato, and slits for eyes. Any place he'd go, people would just stare at his face. They were fascinated by it."

The versatile comedian was also a capable dramatist, holding his own in serious vignettes when called upon. Shemp had the distinction of being a legitimate actor as well as a talented clown.

"Shemp was both, and that's pretty hard to come by," said Edward Bernds. "He was a great character type, and he was great at performing slapstick. He was funny in the way he could take a fall. If you look at his older films, before he was back with the Stooges, he was almost acrobatic in the way he took pratfalls."

Many of Shemp's colleagues believed him to be a top-drawer funnyman as well. Bob Hope, who worked with his own collection of stooges, described Shemp as "one of the greatest laugh-getters ever to come out of vaudeville." Lou Costello's straightman, Bud Abbott, once called Shemp "the funniest guy in the business." And Ted Healy never doubted that Shemp was the most extraordinarily talented of all his protégées.

Often, however, Shemp's natural comic abilities worked against him. His wife Babe recalled that his talent may have actually hindered his career development.

"Lou Costello wanted to put Shemp under personal contract. Just to get him out of the studio! Shemp was doing the Abbott & Costello features at Universal, and he got too many laughs. Costello told Shemp he'd make him a big star if he worked for him. So Shemp asked for $3,500 a week, which was unheard of at that time. Costello didn't hire him, of course, but he still made sure that Shemp didn't get any more laughs. Practically every funny thing Shemp did in the Abbott & Costello pictures ended up on the cutting room floor. And that broke Shemp's heart, because he couldn't help being funny. He was a natural."

All in all, Shemp was decidedly underrated as a comedian, perhaps even more so than his brother Curly. Even some of the staunchest Three Stooges fans dismiss Shemp as a second-rate replacement. But the fact of the matter is that Shemp was not doing Curly's act,

Shemp and wife Babe attend a family gathering in the mid-1940s.

The boys stop to weigh themselves during their tour of military bases with Morton Downey and his orchestra.

nor had he ever made an attempt to do so. He simply integrated his well-known screen personality into the framework of an already-established act. Shemp wisely chose to play the role in a manner that was comfortable to him, rather than try to be a "another" Curly.

Once Shemp was reinstated as a temporary member of the trio, Larry suggested that the Stooges donate a percentage of their weekly paychecks to Curly, to help with his expenses. Moe and Shemp agreed, and all three working Stooges contributed money to the ailing Curly during his period of recuperation.

Curly's retirement from the act was a turning point in the Stooges' career as a team. They would never again capture the lunatic quality of their films with Curly, but nevertheless would continue to produce quality, often hilariously funny, comedies for years to come.

The ailing Curly eventually received treatment at the Motion Picture Country House, a top-quality care facility exclusively for employees of the movie industry.

Although the Stooges would continue performing as a team for some twenty more years, Curly's shadow would never quite be erased from the public image of The Three Stooges. He left behind a marvelous film record of some of the most unique comedy ever produced, and has gone down in movie history as one of Hollywood's genuine masters of the art of low comedy.

Curly's brother Shemp rejoined the Stooges for good in 1946, shortly after Curly's debilitating stroke. Shemp had been nervous about head trauma ever since the death of Ted Healy, and he loathed being on the receiving end of slapstick—especially Stooge-style slapstick. But he was willing to rejoin the team, as long as it was on a temporary basis only.

Little did he know that circumstances would force him to remain one of the Stooges until the day he died.

Moe's son-in-law Norman Maurer creates a series of "Three Stooges" comic books in the late 1940s, all featuring the character of Curly as "Third Stooge."

Curly Howard's last solo publicity photo, taken at Columbia in 1946.

★★★ **The THREE STOOGES** ★★★

SHEMP'S REPLACEMENT of his brother resulted in some minor changes in the Stooges' performing style. Often routines and entire plotlines that would have worked well with Curly failed with Shemp. But when in the hands of a talented director, like Edward Bernds, the new set of Stooges was allowed to develop a style that was in harmony with Shemp's distinctive Stooge characterization.

Jules White, however, persisted in employing the "living cartoon" style of comedy that was frankly better suited to Curly's talents than Shemp's. In the White Stooge shorts starring Shemp, the veteran comedian is often forced to perform the same gags and gestures originated on film by Curly. This, of course, only resulted in the appearance of sloppy imitation.

But in the months following Curly's departure, White had convinced himself that the secret to the popularity of The Three Stooges resided in the "Curly" character. To this end, he began looking for "another" Curly, a search that was doomed to failure from the start.

White's first choice was veteran stage comedian Joe DeRita, then in his thirties and starring in burlesque. In the coming decade DeRita would acquire the nickname "CurlyJoe" and become famous to millions of moviegoers, but in 1946 he was still working under the name that had headlined innumerable burlesque marquees throughout the country. At White's urging, Harry Cohn signed DeRita to a short-subjects contract, and the pudgy comedian began starring in his own vehicles at Columbia at the same time the Stooges were making their initial shorts with Shemp.

"Jules White was a schmuck," opined CurlyJoe. "He wanted me to act like Curly. I told him I do my own thing, my own type of comedy. I don't imitate *nobody*."

While Shemp vacillates about appearing with Moe and Larry on weekly television, Mousie Garner (right) assembles his own "Three Stooges" act with Ted Healy veterans Sammy Wolfe and Bobby Pinkus for NBC–TV's *The Kraft Music Hall*.

DeRita refused to alter his established personality, and Jules White eventually gave up on trying to make him the next Curly Howard. CurlyJoe finished up his contract at Columbia with a handful of shorts, and White focused his attention on trying to make Shemp seem more like his baby brother.

Despite the fact that the Stooges lost much of their charm and inherent appeal to children when Curly left the trio, some of the best Stooges shorts are actually those that feature Shemp. A great improvisational comic, Shemp was often at his best when left alone to do his own thing. Emil Sitka recalled that Shemp's frequent ad libs would have director Edward Bernds on the floor with laughter:

"Ed Bernds would fracture himself watching him. Shemp would go on forever until he heard the word 'cut.' And I mean he'd be funny every second of the time! Sometimes Ed Bernds would just let him go on, and he'd die laughing, even though he knew they couldn't use that much material in the film."

Jules White reflected upon his own relationship with Shemp: "A finer, more entertaining, more comedic man I never met. He'd keep you convulsed with laughter all the time with the stories he'd tell. And I don't mean jokes, but things that happened to him."

DeRita in his funniest solo film, Edward Bernds' *Slappily Married* (1946), produced during Jules White's ongoing search for "the next Curly."

Edward Bernds considered Shemp his favorite of all the Stooges. "Shemp was a honey," said Bernds. "He was a very, very nice guy, a real trouper. He'd try anything; he'd work his head off. He liked working with me, and he really put out."

Virtually all of the shorts the Stooges made during this phase of their career were directed by either Bernds or Jules White. Del Lord made one short with Shemp as a member of the trio, and producer Hugh McCollum even tried his hand at

helming a Stooge comedy, but White and Bernds shared the bulk of directorial duties.

There were also a few minor changes in the Stooges' supporting cast during this period. Bud Jamison had died in the mid-Forties, but Vernon Dent remained with the Stooges until his retirement in the mid-Fifties. Christine McIntyre and Symona Boniface continued to work with the Stooges as well, and with greater frequency.

Emil Sitka began appearing with the Stooges more and more as the years passed, often in the role of an elderly scientist or crusty old codger. Sitka was quite adept at playing eightyish old men, even though he was only in his early thirties at the time. A remarkably talented character actor, Sitka often added the finishing touch to a Stooge comedy with a clever characterization or bit of business.

"Emil was very good," said Jules White. "He could play anything. It's not easy to be able to play a gangster in one shot, and a governor in the next. But he could do it. And he did it very well."

Elwood Ullman pointed out that Sitka was one of the few supporting players for whom the writing staff would specifically devise character parts. "I never saw him refuse to do a thing," said Ullman.

Sitka remembered how he came to play the "old man" character in the Stooge shorts. "This is the story I got from Moe," said Sitka. "The Stooges were doing their vaudeville act in a theater one night, and after they finished, a two-reel comedy was shown [Edward Bernds' *Billie Gets Her Man* (1946)]. I was playing an old man in that particular short. By the time the short came on, the Stooges had already taken off their makeup and costumes. They were headed out of the theater toward a coffee shop to grab a bite after the show. On their way out of the theater, they heard the audience howling

In the late 1940s, Shemp and wife Babe enjoy a second honeymoon in Niagara Falls, shortly after the Stooges return to Broadway for a series of personal appearances and a guest spot on Milton Berle's hugely popular NBC-TV series, *Texaco Star Theater.*

As lead comedian, Shemp receives twice as much pay as his partners, a tradition that started with Ted Healy and continues until the end of Shemp's life.

131

with laughter. They had to go back inside and see what was so funny! So they went inside, and saw that it was my character that was getting all the laughs. They later decided they would like me to play that kind of character in one of their pictures, too."

Sitka was a wonderful co-star for the boys, and he quickly became one of their favorite supporting players, a true "stooge for the Stooges." Moe enjoyed his performances so much that, with Larry's blessing, he even asked Emil to become an actual member of the Stooges years later when Larry became too ill to work. Sitka continued to appear in the Columbia Stooge shorts until their final year of production.

The first "Three Stooges" comedy featuring Shemp Howard as one of the trio, *Fright Night* (1946), was directed by Bernds from a Clyde Bruckman screenplay. Bernds really got the series off to a good start; the film moves along briskly and is full of material well-suited to the "new" Stooges team, with the boys cast as fight trainers in trouble with a gang of thugs.

Fright Night is significant in that it shows how quickly and easily Shemp made himself at home as one of the Stooges. One of the reasons for this is, undoubtedly, the fact that Shemp had spent so much time in vaudeville as one of Ted Healy's Stooges. In addition to this, Bernds allowed Shemp to play his Stooge character as he saw fit. As Bernds saw it,

Comedian Jackie Gleason, who performs at Shemp's L.A. nightclub, the Stage One Cafe, and is well-acquainted with all of the Stooges, shares his closest friendship with Curly, who considers Gleason a genius and one of the greatest entertainers in the business.

The Stooges on tour with Morton Downey and his orchestra, entertaining the U.S. military both domestically and abroad.

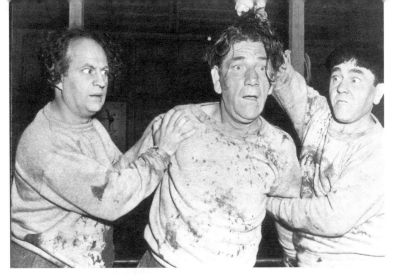

Shemp's character was that of a middle-aged adolescent. If Curly had played a five-year-old kid trapped in the body of an adult, then Shemp was playing an overgrown teenager, complete with greasy hair, bad complexion, and a decidedly rebellious attitude.

"He never used Curly's mannerisms," said Edward Bernds. "He brought his own style to the act, but he did fit in well. Shemp had his own style of comedy. He was a very funny guy, if you let him alone. At lot of times I'd just let the camera run, just to see what he'd do. Sometimes we couldn't use it, but he'd never quit until I yelled 'cut.' It was a lot of fun to just let him go."

Shemp may have had fun exercising his craft, but behind the scenes it was a different story. He complained to his partners about how little the Stooges were earning for their Herculean efforts.

But team leader Moe Howard was too afraid of Harry Cohn to rock the boat. The Stooges' manager, Harry Romm, constantly reminded Moe that "the last thing you wanna do is piss off Harry Cohn." According to Shemp's wife Babe, Cohn's gangland connections made the Stooges fearful of asking for more money.

In addition to their on-camera performances, the Stooges were also expected to contribute to the creation of their films as well. Edward Bernds worked in collaboration with the boys on all of their scripts together, with Bernds often suggesting the basic idea, and the Stooges embellishing it with gags and routines of their own.

After Bernds and the Stooges developed a story, it was then turned over to one of the Columbia writers, who wrote the screenplay. As director, Bernds then completed the final draft, and made all necessary preparations for any gags that required special effects or stunt work.

"The hardest part," remembered Bernds, "was devising the original concept, the starting framework. The rest was hard work, digging for laughs, but getting started was the tough thing."

Edward Bernds credits Moe Howard as being "a reservoir of routines." Moe devised a good many of their story formats, recalling old sketches and routines the Stooges had used over the years.

Out West (1946), Bernds' second film with the "new" Stooges, evolved from a basic gag suggested by Moe, that of a physician's handwritten diagram being mistaken for a hidden-treasure map. Screenwriter Clyde Bruckman wrote the actual script, developing Moe's idea into yet another of the Stooges' Western parodies that hits the bull's eye.

According to Bernds, however, Larry's story suggestions were usually of little value. Although some of Larry's offbeat concepts were occasionally developed into workable ideas, Bernds says that Moe frequently and openly showed his disgust with Larry's lesser ideas. Moe would insult Larry, calling his suggestions "stupid." Shemp, on the other hand, saved most of his ideas for the actual filming. These ideas emerged, basically, as improvisational routines.

There was very little improvisation involved when Curly returned to appear with his old partners in *Hold That Lion!* (1947), the third short released starring the "new" Three

The first Columbia comedy reuniting Shemp with former partners Moe and Larry, Edward Bernds' *Fright Night* (1947), becomes the all-time favorite Stooge short of the boxing-obsessed Shemp.

Edward Bernds finds directing the Stooges a pleasure once Shemp steps in for the ailing Curly.

Danny Kaye, who began his career emulating both Shemp Howard and Harry Ritz of The Ritz Brothers, becomes a huge screen star in the postwar era.

Stooges. With a full head of hair and visibly thinner, Curly could easily have gone unnoticed as just another bit player if not for his trademark snoring routine, performed here with a clothespin over his nose.

Curly's gag appearance was intended as a morale-booster for the comedian, as well as a reminder to audiences that Curly was still around. It turned out to be his final screen appearance, and the first and only time that brothers Curly, Moe and Shemp Howard appeared together in the same theatrical film.

Emil Sitka recalled that during the filming of *Hold That Lion!*, the boys were quite wary of a live lion that appeared with them in several scenes. But while all of the Stooges were uncomfortable around the animal, Shemp was deathly afraid of the beast.

"Shemp wouldn't work if the lion was in the same scene," said Sitka. "And the lion was sickly-looking. It had flies buzzing around its head. But the propmen put a big plate of glass between the Stooges and the lion when they were filming. And when they finished shooting, Shemp wanted to be a mile away from it."

While relaxing between scenes, however, Shemp discovered he wasn't quite as far away from the lion as he had thought. When the animal's trainer came looking for the lion to shoot another scene, he found it curled up asleep on the floor directly behind where Shemp was sitting. So much for Shemp's sense of security!

Around the time *Hold That Lion!* was filmed, the retired Curly met his future wife, Valerie Neumann, at Charlie Foy's nightclub on Ventura Boulevard in Studio City near Los Angeles. She was introduced to Curly by Foy himself, and the two hit if off immediately. Within weeks Curly would ask her to marry him, and Valerie would prove to be a ray of sunlight in his otherwise drab life.

The Stooges were delighted that Curly had found a kind and attractive young woman to look after him and lift his spirits, and they hoped her love and affection would speed

After Shemp rejoins the Stooges, there are changes in the team's style and attitude; the ogling of women, however, continues unabated.

Jules White's first film with the "new" Three Stooges, Hold That Lion! (1947), features a brief cameo by Curly that took virtually an entire afternoon to shoot.

Curly's recovery.

Meanwhile, the Stooges continued to labor at Columbia, and in 1947, with Curly supposedly on the mend, they produced one of their all-time greatest comedies, *Brideless Groom* (1947). Directed by Edward Bernds, *Brideless Groom* is an extremely fast-moving comedy, replete with hilarious sight gags and a riotous premise. Many admirers of The Three Stooges, particularly Shemp fans, actually consider this episode the team's funniest film, period. Performances by series "regulars" Christine McIntyre and Emil Sitka enhance the sparkling quality of this entry, and Shemp turns in what is quite possibly his most memorable performance with the Stooges.

The premise of the film has Shemp as a middle-aged, bachelor music teacher, who must get married within a matter of hours in order to inherit a huge sum of money. The plot consists of attempts by Moe and Larry to find him a prospective bride, resulting in one disaster after another.

Pianist Larry, music teacher Shemp, and business manager Moe study the good professor's little black book in Edward Bernds' *Brideless Groom* (1947), a fast-paced comedy written by Clyde Bruckman that was based on his original story for the classic Buster Keaton silent feature *Seven Chances*.

A lobby card advertisement for *Brideless Groom*, considered by many to be the Stooges' funniest outing; note that Dick Wessel, seen in the insert photo, appears nowhere in the film.

The funniest scene in the film arrives when Shemp attempts to propose marriage to a beautiful stranger, one Miss Hopkins, played by Christine McIntyre.

Miss Hopkins all but physically attacks Shemp the moment he shows up at her apartment door. She assumes Shemp is her Cousin Basil, whom she's never met, but from whom she's expecting a visit. Miss Hopkins hugs and kisses Shemp, not allowing him to get a word in edgewise. Before Shemp can explain he's not the woman's relative, the real Cousin Basil telephones her to say he's going to be late. Miss Hopkins goes berserk and accuses Shemp of impersonating her cousin. She lets loose with a series of brutal slaps across Shemp's face, culminating with a stiff punch to Shemp's jaw that sends him crashing through the door.

Director Edward Bernds called this sequence one of his personal favorites.

"Christine was quite a lady—she really was—and it was not in her nature to slap people around.

"We made several takes in which she just kind of held back, and they were no good. And finally Shemp said, 'Honey, do me a favor. Let's do it once, and do it right—go ahead and let me have it.' On the take that's in the picture, she really nerved herself up and she really belted him! I can look at old film a lot of times and see ways that it could have been done better. But that was one sequence that, in my mind, was perfect. The way we nerved her up to perform! The timing was utterly perfect. Damn! It was timed to perfection!"

Some of Edward Bernds' most enjoyable outings with the Stooges were the "scare pictures" he created in collaboration with writer Elwood Ullman. One of the most familiar themes of the Stooge shorts with Shemp has the boys encountering murderous criminals or madmen in a spooky atmosphere. Frequently the Stooges were cast as relatively inno-

Jules White's first Stooge episode without Curly in the cast, *Sing a Song of Six Pants* (1947), nevertheless includes a number of "Curly"-style gags, enacted under protest by the Stooges and character actor Cy Schindell.

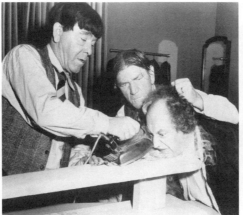

The boys await their execution in Edward Bernds' classic *Squareheads of the Round Table* (1948), remade by Jules White several years later as *Knutzy Knights*.

THE THREE STOOGES
SHEMP · LARRY · MOE
PARDON MY CLUTCH

A COLUMBIA SHORT-SUBJECT PRESENTATION

The famous "marshmallow gumbo" routine from Jules White's *All Gummed Up* (1947), in which the Stooges and Christine McIntyre involuntarily blow bubbles while eating a cake laced with chewing gum, is accomplished by having each of the four players stretch a condom over his or her tongue.

Edward Bernds' *Pardon My Clutch* (1948) becomes the first Stooge comedy starring Shemp to be shot outside the stuffy soundstages of Columbia.

In Jules White's *Fiddlers Three* (1948), a reworking of an early Curly episode titled *Restless Knights*, the Stooges and company go ga-ga over a magician's assistant.

Curly returns for a cameo role in Jules White's *Malice in the Palace* (1948), but his crabby-chef routine winds up on the cutting-room floor.

Moe, surviving partner Larry, and their chiseling attorney Vernon Dent can't see him, but Shemp has just returned from the dead to haunt his old pals in Jules White's offbeat comedy-fantasy *Heavenly Daze* (1948).

cent bystanders, drawn into dangerous situations by the lure of easy money or a beautiful young woman. Without fail, however, the boys found themselves in more trouble than they could handle, and spent the remainder of the film being chased by evildoers.

Both Bernds and Ullman considered the "scare routine" to be sure-fire for getting laughs. Bernds pointed out the appeal of "scare" comedies:

"We'd go to previews and think, 'My God, we've done this before, there's nothing new in it! What can you do new with scare pictures? The audience must be getting tired of it.' But we'd put one of those scare pictures on and, Jesus, the whole theater would come to life! The audience would scream and holler; they never seemed to get tired of scares."

Bernds and Ullman's first "scare" short with the new trio of Stooges, *The Hot Scots* (1948), has the boys as Scotland Yard gardeners who yearn to become investigators for the legendary British law enforcement agency. Desperate for the chance to prove themselves, the boys decide to masquerade as bona fide "Yard men" and soon find themselves assigned to guard a cavernous Scottish castle full of phony spooks. A hilarious chase scene highlights the film, as a trio of crooks chase the boys in and out of the castle corridors.

The Hot Scots is especially memorable because of the beautiful castle set used throughout most of the film. Acquiring such a set for a short-subject comedy often depended upon the ingenuity of a particular producer or director. Edward Bernds was walking across Columbia's complex of sound stages one day when he discovered the massive castle interior, constructed for a feature film. Bernds simply thought it was too good to waste:

"I went in and got Hugh McCollum, brought him out and showed him the sets. I said, 'Let's get a couple of scripts ready; when they're finished with 'em, we'll use 'em.' So we had the scripts ready. A lot of times you'd see a set and say, 'Let's do a story there.' But sometimes by the time you had the script written, the set might have been torn down. You had to be ready to move right in, because at Columbia sound stage space was generally at a premium."

Bernds and Ullman's next "scare" comedy, *Crime On Their Hands* (1948), is one of the Stooges' best, with the boys tangling not only with a panting gorilla, but a trio of crooks (Kenneth MacDonald, Christine McIntyre and Cy Schindell) who plan to cut Shemp open when he accidentally swallows a stolen diamond. This turned out to be character actor Schindell's last film with the Stooges.

Edward Bernds explained that Cy had left Columbia at the outset of World War II to enlist in the Marines, and during his tour of duty in the Pacific, Schindell contracted terminal cancer. "A very pathetic thing about Cy," recalled Bernds, "was that he was doing films even though he was dying of cancer." Make-up was used to disguise the gaunt appearance that resulted from his illness.

"Cy kept working because he wanted to accumulate some money to leave his family after he died," added Bernds. The director and producer Hugh McCollum thus sought out as much on-camera work for Schindell as possible. Cy had been slated for the part of Chief of the Palace Guards in Bernds' *Mummy's Dummies* (1948), a costume comedy in which the Stooges are seen as crooked used-chariot dealers in ancient Egypt. But the ravages of illness made it physically impossible for Schindell to take on the role, and he was replaced by character player Ralph Dunn.

As the 1940s drew to a close, and as the essence of Shemp's personality continued to seep into the consciousness of moviegoers, Columbia released *The Three Stooges Festival of Fun* (1949), a compilation of some of the better "Shemp" episodes. This film, which became the Stooges' feature-length vehicle for the 1948-49 season, was comprised entirely of old footage. In many ways, it marked a turning point in the Stooges' career at

Communistic spies think Larry is a rocket scientist, Moe, his lab assistant, and Shemp, their bodyguard, in Edward Bernds' *Fuelin' Around* (1949), a clever Cold War spoof written by Elwood Ullman and co-starring Emil Sitka and Christine McIntyre.

Columbia. From this point forward, every Columbia feature the Stooges appeared in would include a liberal amount of stock footage.

In addition, remakes of earlier successes with Curly became more and more frequent in the Shorts Department. The best of these was Edward Bernds' reworking of *A Plumbing We Will Go* called *Vagabond Loafers* (1949), with Shemp taking on Curly's role. It turned out to be one of the funniest in the series, and one of the few remakes that was actually an improvement on the original.

The laugh-packed *Vagabond Loafers* was written by Elwood Ullman, who had also scripted the Curly Howard version. Some of the better gags were reprised, such as the "maze of pipes" routine. In addition, a subplot involving art thieves was worked into the storyline. Kenneth MacDonald, a "slippery villain" type, and Chrtistine McIntyre, also adept at playing villainous roles, appeared as the crooks. Emil Sitka and Symona Boniface also turned up in this one, as the well-to-do couple who hire the Stooges to repair a simple leak and live to regret it.

Vagabond Loafers was itself remade a half-dozen years later as *Scheming Schemers.* Produced and directed by Jules White, *Schemers* includes much film from the Bernds original, as well as some pie-throwing footage from White's *Half Wits Holiday.* This stock footage proved to be quite useful, as most of the action takes place between the Stooges (minus Curly) and a few unidentified party guests. As a result, the film could be re-used again and again, with other performers stepping in as "Third Stooge" in newly-produced scenes with Moe and Larry.

In 1950, the production team of Hugh McCollum, director Edward Bernds and screenwriter Elwood Ullman began work on a handful of Stooge comedies that, according to Ullman, constituted "a banner year" for Columbia's Shorts Department.

"We had a string there," added Bernds, "where we just kept topping ourselves."

Bernds directed a series of comedies for McCollum, all written by Ullman, that turned out to be the last really good shorts the Stooges ever made. And this in spite of the fact that The Three Stooges remained Columbia contractees for almost another decade.

Ullman fondly recalled previewing these shorts in theaters surrounding the Hollywood area. "We'd preview at an outlying theater on a Friday night, and pack the place with kids. And it would be both pleasing and disappointing. Sometimes a routine would come on, and it would die. And you just couldn't understand why! But after having previewed it, you could do something about it. You could cut out the dead spots, speed the thing up, and improve it."

Bernds' personal favorite of all the shorts he did with the Stooges

While appearing live back east, the Stooges often clown with local college football players in order to create publicity for their stage shows.

was *Punchy Cowpunchers* (1950), an excellent Western spoof complete with continuous melodramatic background music.

The boys play cavalrymen assigned to disguise themselves as desperadoes and sign up with a dreaded gang of cattle rustlers. Assisting the Stooges in their attempt to clean things up is helpless Elmer, played by former stuntman Jock Mahoney, a future big-screen "Tarzan." Elmer is impressive-looking and quick with his guns, but he always seems to miss out on the fight, either by forgetting to load his pistols or by falling off his horse.

Mahoney performs a variety of breathtaking flips and falls, and steals every scene he's in. The short is full of physical mayhem, from the standard slapstick antics of the Stooges to the constant stumbling of "good guy" Elmer.

Christine McIntyre is featured as Nell, Elmer's girlfriend. One beautifully-timed running gag, in which Nell single-handedly punches out a number of lustful badmen, is the highlight of the short. As she wallops each desperado in the jaw with her fist, they fall to the floor, unconscious. She then proves herself to be a true lady by finding a comfortable place to faint after she administers each beating.

Throughout the early post-war era, the Hugh McCollum unit continued to turn out one top-notch Stooge comedy after another. The Jules White-produced Stooge shorts, however, began to slip noticeably in quality during this period.

Back on Broadway in the early 1950s for an appearance on Milton Berle's TV variety program, the Stooges pose for product endorsements with three young fans.

Part of the reason for this was White's insistence on casting non-actresses in crucial supporting roles. "Jules used bimbos," explained Edward Bernds. "He would get them parts in exchange for (*beat*) favors. And when he fell behind on his shooting schedule because these ladies couldn't remember their lines, Jules would simply tell the front office that it was the Stooges who were blowing take after take."

Sometimes, however, it really was the Stooges who were to blame. According to Emil Sitka, Larry seldom "walked through" a scene to acquaint himself with the peculiarities of the set. His partners, however, had fully examined every prop they would use during shoot-

As Shemp, Larry and Moe are considering headlining a weekly television series of their own, Mousie Garner (with guitar) appears regularly with bandleader Spike Jones on NBC-TV'S *The Colgate Comedy Hour.*

ing, thus decreasing the possibility of error. Shemp was particularly thorough in this respect. Larry, however, would occasionally make mistakes due to his lack of preparation. "He might try to open a door the wrong way," said Sitka, "and that would ruin the scene."

Sitka added that Moe usually responded to Larry's mistakes by assaulting him with some sort of acid-tongued remark. "Larry," commented Sitka, "was probably the least conscientious of the Stooges."

Larry could hardly have been happier, then, when it was announced that the Stooges' feature-length attraction for the 1950-51 season, *Gold Raiders* (1951), was to be filmed in a total of

The boys hit the trail in Edward Bernds' *Merry Mavericks* (1951), an entertaining "scare" Western that takes place in a supposedly haunted homestead.

➤

five days. Edward Bernds directed from a script by Elwood Ullman, which finds the Stooges as traveling peddlers tangling with desperadoes out West. According to Bernds himself, the independently-financed film was so hastily assembled that even Columbia refused to release it, and it ultimately wound up being distributed by United Artists instead.

What's more, the short-subject field had begun to wane after World War II, and was well on its way out by the 1950s. With the future of their movie career relatively uncertain, the Stooges decided to take a stab at a television career with a weekly series. *The Three Stooges* program was to be similar in content and format to their Columbia comedies, and regulars were to include veteran Stooge foils Emil Sitka and Symona Boniface.

A pilot episode, titled *Jerks of All Trades*, was filmed at ABC Studios in Hollywood before a live audience. Phil Berle, brother of comedian Milton Berle, served as producer, and said the pilot was filmed as a candidate for the 1950-1951 season.

Emil Sitka, meanwhile, said the script for the initial episode had himself and Symona Boniface as a wealthy couple who hire the Stooges to work in their home, and that both performers were slated to appear in every episode if a weekly series was "given the green light."

★★★ **The THREE STOOGES** ★★★

However, shortly after completion of the pilot, Shemp decided he did not want to pursue a full-time television career, especially in the "Third Stooge" role. A series commitment would have meant thirty-nine brand new scripts to learn in the course of a year, thirty-nine brand new scripts to be performed in front of an audience on live television week after week, month after month without a break. Plus the team's regular schedule of film comedies, released to movie houses every six weeks or so. *Plus* the live appearances in cities throughout the country, dates that had been booked long ago and would have to be honored, regardless of how busy the Stooges might find themselves.

To Shemp, now in his mid-fifties, this sounded like a sure-fire formula for stress and exhaustion, those twin maladies well-known to anyone who ever spent time touring in vaudeville.

At this point, Mousie Garner was con-

tacted and asked to replace him for television appearances with The Three Stooges. "Moe and Larry were all for the series idea," says Mousie, "but Shemp didn't want any part of it. So they were going to use me instead."

The versatile Garner had already been appearing on television's *The Colgate Comedy Hour*, the hugely popular NBC variety show in the early 1950s, in a revival of Ted Healy's old Stooge act. Mousie actually did double duty on the program during this period, performing as a solo comedian with bandleader Spike Jones, as well as serving in his traditional role of "patsy" in Stooge appearances. Sammy Wolfe was now playing the lynchpin or "middleman" role, while Bobby Pinkus, the onetime Stooge from the Shuberts' *A Night in Spain*, had taken on the part of the team's underboss character.

Despite the fact that arrangements were made to replace Shemp with Mousie, the series idea was turned down by ABC. For one reason or another, the pilot episode never even made it to broadcast. Shemp, as it turned out, had nothing to worry about after all.

However, the Stooges continued to do guest shots on television throughout the 1950s, appearing with early stars like Milton Berle, Eddie Cantor, and even Frank Sinatra. One of the team's funniest performances was on the Berle show, in which the boys resurrected the "Maharajah" routine, with Shemp taking Curly's place as the half-blind knife-thrower. For the most part, though, the Stooges continued to receive their greatest amount of exposure on movie theater screens.

As the Fifties progressed, remakes of earlier comedies became more and more frequent at Columbia. *Ants in the Pantry*, for example, was remade as *Pest Man Wins* (1951). The original plot is followed quite closely, but for the finale, producer-director Jules White added the old reliable pie-throwing footage from Curly's last film as a Stooge, *Half Wits Holiday*.

Breathing life into ancient material was in many respects the Stooges' forte, and dur-

Edward Bernds' *The Tooth Will Out* (1951) evolved from a "dental surgery" routine excised from the final cut of *Merry Mavericks*; the deleted sequence was simply too funny to throw away, so Bernds shot some additional footage and built an entirely new short around it.

The boys are pest exterminators getting the best of butler Emil Sitka in Jules White's *Pest Man Wins* (1951), a remake of *Ants in the Pantry*.

Connie Cezon, a favorite of producer Jules White's, can't decide which of her three suitors she dislikes most in White's *Corny Casanovas* (1952).

The boys kill some time while awaiting the arrival of Shemp's Uncle Phineas in Edward Bernds' *Gents in a Jam* (1952), a remake of the Hugh Herbert comedy *Hot Heir* which starred Emil Sitka as a befuddled millionaire.

ing the "Shemp" years, they would draw upon this ability more than ever. What many assumed to be routines created by The Three Stooges were, in most cases, time-honored sketches from burlesque and vaudeville that had been reworked to accommodate the boys' personalities. This was as prevalent in their live act as it was in their films.

Meanwhile, every few months it was announced that Curly was "almost ready" to return to the act, but this never happened. Curly was not only not improving, but he had no more interest in getting slapped around all day than did Shemp.

Then, in early 1952, Curly's health took a decided turn for the worse, and the Stooges were forced to come to grips with the fact that their beloved star was dying.

Larry, Moe and Shemp are election delegates in Jules White's *Three Dark Horses* (1952), a political spoof based on a story by Felix Adler titled *Small Delegates at Large*.

More than ever, Shemp wanted out of The Three Stooges. After seeing what had happened to his baby brother, Shemp felt that the same fate awaited him if he continued taking hits on the head. In an effort to appease Shemp, comedian Buddy Hackett was asked to take Curly's place.

"They asked me to come in because Curly was dying," confides Hackett.

Hackett, then the latest "cross between Curly, Lou Costello and Jerry Lewis," was amenable to the idea, until he was invited to attend a Stooge rehearsal. There he witnessed the boys hitting each other with various pain-inducing implements.

"I dropped by where they were rehearsing, and they were banging each other around and hitting each other over the head with great big pipes and everything. I took one look at that and said, 'Nope!'"

Moe was then forced to break it to Shemp that he would have to remain a Stooge a little while longer, as no suitable replacement was forthcoming.

Meanwhile, the event the Stooges and their families had been dreading finally came to pass on January 18th, 1952. Curly Howard, the baby of the group, died at the age of forty-nine. He was survived by his widow, Valerie Howard, and their three-year-old daughter, Janie Howard, as well as his daughter from his marriage to Elaine Ackerman, Marilyn. Curly was outlived by his three former wives, as well as elder brothers Shemp and Moe.

The day after Curly's funeral, Shemp, Larry and Moe were back at work at Columbia, filming *Up in Daisy's Penthouse*, a remake of a "Curly" classic from the late Thirties titled *Three Dumb Clucks*. Understandably, Shemp was not feeling up to par during shooting. He was already suffering from depression over his brother's death, as well as his inability to free himself from the Stooges. It was while he was in this frame of mind that Shemp suffered a stroke himself, just weeks after Curly's death in 1952.

Like his brother, Shemp at first suffered only a minor cerebral hemorrhage. And although it didn't force Shemp into retirement, it did seriously affect his ability as a performer.

According to Shemp's wife Babe, "he was sitting at home playing

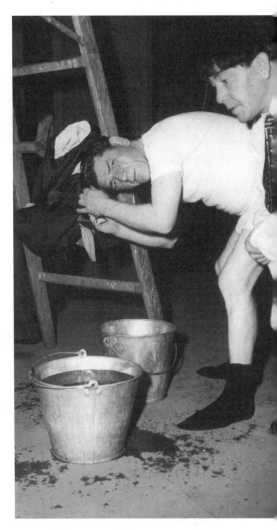

Backstage at the Shorts Department, Head Stooge Moe watches carefully as Shemp rinses out his hair following the shooting of a particularly sloppy routine.

In the early 1950s, Larry, Moe and Shemp show off their most recent Laurel Award, given by the association of movie exhibitors to the most popular short–subject attractions.

cards with a friend, and all of a sudden, he just wasn't acting right. He was in a daze. We later found out he had had a cerebral hemorrhage. Afterward, Shemp never even remembered having the stroke."

Shemp and Babe Howard soon moved out of their home in Toluca Lake, just north of Hollywood, and turned the property over to their son, Morton, and his wife Geri. The elder Howards wanted to remain in their Toluca Lake neighborhood, however, so they bought and moved into an apartment building on Riverside Drive.

"We filled it with show people," said Babe. "Upstairs we had a trio of nightclub comedians called The Three Jokers, and we'd have parties until three, four o'clock in the morning. I was doing it to keep Shemp going, to keep him 'up.' After a while, he was back working with the boys again, going on tour, doing the shorts, and everything. But he was never quite the same afterward. He was never a hundred percent perfect."

Not unlike Curly, Shemp suffered from a decided lack of energy and focus after his stroke, and it became obvious in some of the Stooges' later shorts with him. Fortunately, stock footage was used to take up a good deal of the Stooges' screen time, so it was not necessary to relieve much of the comic burden from Shemp's shoulders.

Around this time, there were some significant changes in Columbia's Shorts Department. Most of these resulted from the culmination of the

While on tour in the early 1950s, the boys and their favorite chef help manager Harry Romm celebrate another birthday.

America's Favorite Funny Men!   10¢

THREE STOOGES

EDITED BY NORMAN MAURER AND JOE KUBERT

In 1953, Norman Maurer revives the Three Stooges comic-book concept with a new series of 3-D "specials," all featuring the character of "Shemp."

The boys pose with supporting player Barbara Bartay on the set of Jules White's *Pardon My Backfire* (1953), the team's final screen venture filmed in the 3-D process.

Jules White-Hugh McCollum rivalry, which had reached its peak in the mid-1950s.

Confidantes say White and McCollum had always shared a "mutual antipathy," and it eventually came to the point where one of the two had to go. Since McCollum had served as Harry Cohn's secretary, he had been rewarded the position of producer. White, however, had been the official head of the Columbia shorts unit since its inception in the early Thirties. When it came to a final showdown, White apparently had more power, and McCollum was fired. White regained complete control of the department in 1952, and from that point on, the production of the Stooge shorts became his sole responsibility.

At that point Edward Bernds and Elwood Ullman left Columbia, and they were subsequently hired by Allied Artists for work on the "Bowery Boys" feature-length comedies. All of these films included Stooge-style humor. Some, in fact, had entire routines and sequences repeated almost verbatim, with Leo Gorcey filling in for Moe, Billy Benedict taking on Larry's part, and Huntz Hall playing the Shemp role.

But with Bernds and Ullman gone from Columbia, the quality of "The Three Stooges'" shorts took a definite nose dive.

The popularity of their films, however, remained relatively consistent. The Three Stooges were given numerous awards from movie exhibitors for the continued success of their short comedies. For several years in the 1950s, the Columbia Stooge shorts were among the nation's most popular box office attractions. In the category of short comedies, they were named the industry's top moneymakers for five years in the early Fifties.

Shortly after Jules White was put fully in charge of the Shorts Department, he made an attempt to capitalize on both the Stooges' continued popularity and the 3-D craze of the early Fifties. White had planned to produce a spate of "Three Stooges" shorts filmed in the 3-D process. He envisioned a whole new series of 3-D Stooge comedies, all of which would capitalize on the nonstop violence and visual action inherent in the Stooge shorts.

By the time the Stooges began making 3-D shorts in 1953, however, the craze was already on its way out. Only a couple of Stooge comedies were filmed in that process, both of which coincidentally showcased old pals from the Ted Healy era. The first of these, *Spooks* (aka *Tails of Horror*), featured the onetime Stooge, Frank Mitchell, as co-star. The follow-up short, *Pardon My Backfire*, presented dialect comedian (and former vaudeville star) Benny Rubin in his first major appearance with the Stooges. According to Jules White, a third 3-D episode had also been planned for the team, but was instead reworked to suit the talents of then-popular TV comedian Harry Mimmo, and released under the title *Down the Hatch* (1953).

According to Jules White, the 3-D Stooge shorts were later packaged, along with *Down the Hatch*, as *The 3 Stooges 3-D Fun Feature* (1953). This compilation of unedited episodes would serve as the Stooges' feature-length release for the 1952-53 season.

Despite the apparent lack of enthusiasm over 3-D film comedies, a series of 3-D "Three Stooges" comic books also emerged in the 1950s, featuring the "Shemp" character as "Third Stooge." The series started in 1953 and lasted several years. The comic books could be viewed by wearing a special pair of glasses, enclosed free with each book. The comics were actually conceived and drawn by Norman Maurer, Moe Howard's son-in-law. Maurer would later become an important influence on the Stooges' career, writing, directing and producing their films himself in the years to come.

Aside from the 3-D experiment, remakes of earlier Stooge shorts, comprised mostly of old footage, became quite abundant at Columbia. This may have been a blessing in disguise, considering Shemp's compromised health and reduced level of stamina.

The first of these shorts, *Booty and the Beast* (1953), was a remake of *Hold That Lion!*, with new footage featuring the Stooges as unwitting accomplices in a home burglary. Curiously enough, Curly Howard's original gag appearance was repeated in this version as well, even though it was not integral to the plot and Curly himself had been dead a year before the film went into release. According to Jules White, the footage was re-introduced as a "tribute" to the Stooges' fallen comrade.

Footage from *Hold That Lion!* also popped up in two more Stooge shorts that year: *Loose Loot* (1953), which has the trio cutting up backstage at a burlesque theater, and *Tricky Dicks* (also 1953), which casts the boys as cops failing miserably in their attempt to solve a murder.

Perhaps the most interesting aspect of this recycling practice was that the Stooges were forced to appear in the same costumes

According to Shemp's wife Babe, Shemp suffers his first stroke shortly before filming begins on *Loose Loot* (1953), one of Jules White's reworkings of *Hold That Lion!*

Character actor Murray Alper helps the Stooges put their heads together on a murder case in Jules White's *Tricky Dicks* (1953).

The boys search for a wanted criminal they believe is hiding out in their tailor shop in Jules White's *Rip, Sew and Stitch* (1953), a remake of his earlier *Sing a Song of Six Pants*.

As Shemp is no longer physically or mentally capable of performing in complicated sketches, the Stooges' popular "live seafood" routine is enacted instead by Larry in Jules White's *Income Tax Sappy* (1954).

The boys use a meat-grinder as a makeshift machine gun in Jules White's *Pals and Gals* (1954), a remake of Edward Bernds' vastly superior *Out West*.

Christine McIntyre is back with the Stooges in Jules White's *Scotched in Scotland* (1954), a remake of Edward Bernds' classic "scare" short, *The Hot Scots*.

Emil Sitka presides over a triple wedding in *Shot in the Frontier* (1954), Jules White's Stooge parody of the previous season's blockbuster Western, *High Noon*.

they had worn in the original movie, in order to "match" the old film. The Stooges actually wear identical garb in all three of the above comedies, which were released to theaters consecutively!

By the 1950s, it had become practice for Columbia to take an old short, delete some original footage, splice in several new sequences, and release the film to theaters under an alternate title as a brand new two-reeler. Jules White explained that this practice was simply an economy measure, resulting from Columbia's continuing budget cuts.

"They weren't entirely old film," argued White. "There was at least fifty percent new footage, if not more, with a different approach to it."

The most obvious reason for this rather confusing practice was that it enabled the studio to sell the old shorts as new ones. In that way, Columbia could charge a theater owner its standard fee for a new release, rather than the much smaller amount obtainable for a reissued film. Such chicanery would never have been permitted in the realm of feature-film production, but few exhibitors paid much attention to short-subject "throwaways," even those starring The Three Stooges. Columbia was thus able to continue this process for several years, churning out retrofitted "Three Stooges" comedies that were actually little more than old shorts with a minimal amount of new footage.

Nearly every film the Stooges made with Shemp during the Forties would eventually turn up as a "brand new" short, with a different title and some newly-produced sequences. By 1954, many Stooge comedies were being shot in a single day, with stock footage accounting for the better part of the completed film's content.

Elwood Ullman remembered that producer White had already obtained his permission to re-use any of his original script material, for the Stooges or otherwise, in future productions. The deal coalesced in the early Fifties when Ullman requested time off to write a Martin & Lewis feature comedy, *Sailor Beware*, for Paramount-based producer Hal Wallis. Jules White proposed a deal: Ullman would receive the requested leave of absence, under the condition that Columbia Pictures would own all rights to his previously-filmed screenplays. Thus, Columbia would be free to do whatever it pleased with Ullman's material, and Ullman would be free to go to work for the hugely-successful Wallis at Paramount. Ullman was so desperate to make the leap into the higher-paid craft of feature-film writing, that he immediately took White up on the offer.

Edward Bernds was less than happy, though, when several of his original writing-and-directing efforts began turning up as "new" films, with Jules White credited as director, and Jules' brother Jack taking honors for the screenplay.

"Columbia used my old film, without my knowledge or consent, and I complained to the Directors Guild," said Bernds. "Columbia was entitled to release them forever, with no residuals, but in using my film without giving me credit, they were violating the Directors Guild contract."

Bernds eventually reached a settlement with Columbia for the token fee of $2,500. In addition to this, Columbia was forced to give Bernds writing credit on films which were remakes of his original scripts. As a result, Bernds was credited with writing the "story," while the writer who concocted the remake version was credited with writing the "screen-play."

"I really didn't care about the credits," explained Bernds. "I just hated to see Columbia getting away with a bare-faced theft. It wasn't right for Columbia to get away with reusing the film the way they did. They butchered a lot of the stories."

Despite Bernds' complaints, Columbia continued to release the patchwork shorts as brand new entries. This later created much confusion amongst television viewers trying to discern one episode from another.

Jules White later commented, "We made those films for theaters over many years, and

Vernon Dent (seated) makes his final appearance with the Stooges in Jules White's *Knutzy Knights* (1954); it's the last film the actor makes before losing his eyesight to diabetes.

we never expected them to be seen again. On television, you're seeing a whole year's worth of work in one week!"

But by late 1955, the use of recycled footage in their films was the least of the Stooges' concerns. On November 22nd of that year, Shemp Howard suffered a cerebral hemorrhage, followed by a heart attack. He died almost immediately, with business manager Al Winston and several other good friends at his side.

"Shemp had gone out to the fights with some friends," said his wife Babe. "He was on his way home . . . and was telling a joke. He was in the middle of lighting a cigar when he had a heart attack and died." Shemp's friends drove straight to St. Joseph's Hospital in Burbank, where he was pronounced dead on arrival.

The final curtain had descended on the original Stooge, just as he was laughing and having a good time with his buddies. Shemp was only 60 when it happened. As Curly's retirement from the act had initiated a turning point in the Stooges' career, so too did Shemp's demise. Without the old master's behind-the-scenes guidance, The Three Stooges as a comedy team would flounder for some time. And even though they would slowly regain their footing and eventually become more popular than ever, the next few years would prove to be the Stooges' most difficult.

With Shemp gone, Larry would be forced to carry more of the comedy. He would also be forced to take more of the hits, as subsequent Stooges would balk at being on the receiving end of Moe's physical punishment.

Larry had long ago stopped complaining about the headaches he would get after a particularly rowdy slapping routine. Like Curly and Shemp, Larry was proud of being a trouper. And whether he knew it or not, he was already following in their footsteps.

Edward Bernds is enraged when the climactic chase scene from his own *Fright Night* turns up in its entirety in Jules White's hastily-filmed remake, *Fling in the Ring* (1955), with no credit or payment of any kind awarded to Bernds.

The Stooges masquerade as fearless explorers in search of modern-day prehistoric man in *Stone Age Romeos* (1955), Jules White's remake of his own earlier Stooge comedy, *I'm a Monkey's Uncle*.

Jules White's *For Crimin' Out Loud*, filmed in 1955 and consisting mostly of old footage from Edward Bernds' *Who Done It?* (including this "scare" routine with character actor Duke York), is the last Stooge episode to be released featuring new scenes with Shemp Howard.

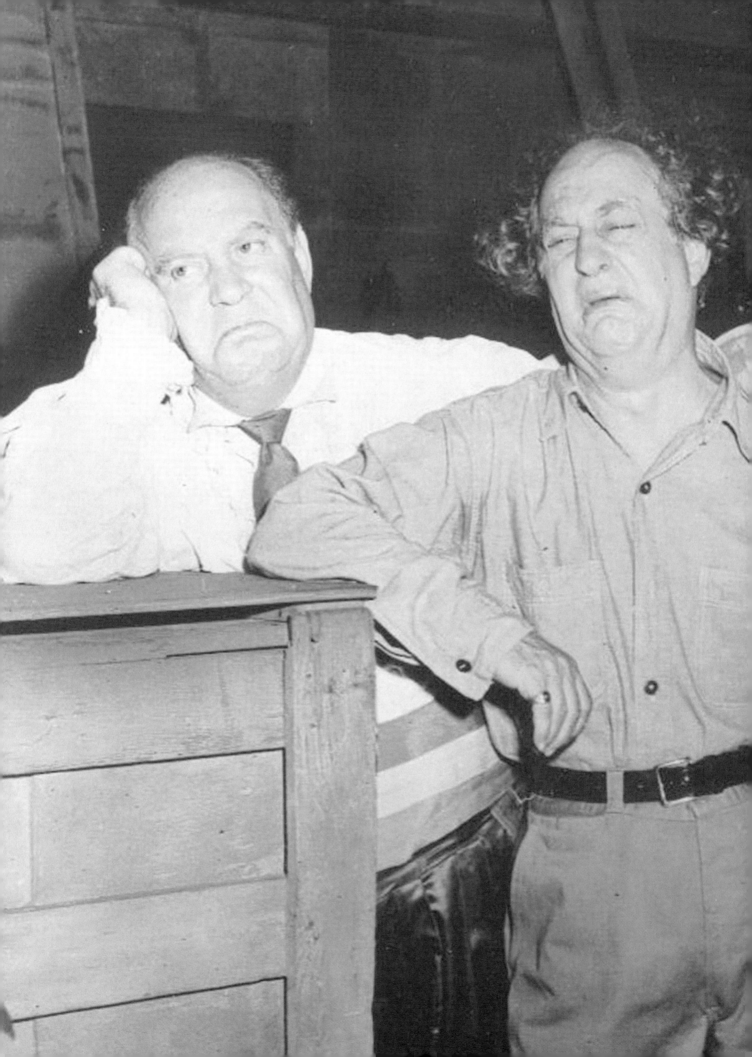

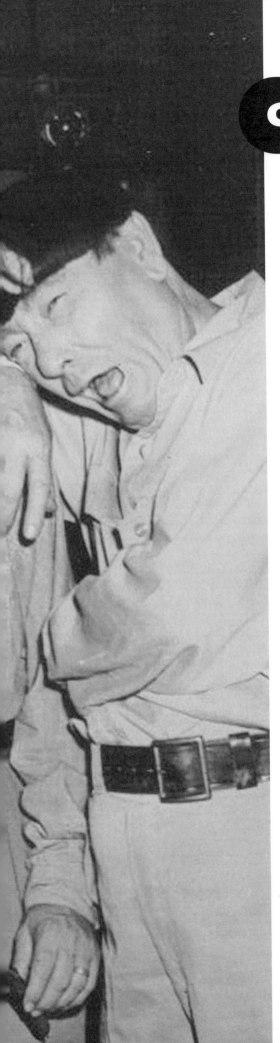

Chapter 7

SHEMP'S DEATH had a devistating effect on the Stooges, particularly his brother Moe. In addition to his personal grief, he could no longer envision a future for The Three Stooges as an act. Losing Curly had been a major crisis, but losing Shemp was a catastrophe. Encouragement from his wife and from Larry, however, led him once again into conference with Columbia executives to find yet another replacement.

Meanwhile Moe and Larry continued to churn out "Three Stooges" shorts—with the late Shemp Howard as a member of the trio!

For several shorts a double was used for Shemp, seen briefly and mostly from behind. Although Shemp Howard was dead, Columbia continued to use the "Shemp" character as one of The Three Stooges through use of the double and a good deal of stock footage. Columbia contract player Joe Palma, who had appeared as a foil in many of the Stooges' previous shorts, was brought in as Shemp's stand-in. When it was necessary for the surrogate Shemp to contribute a line or two, sound editor Joe Henrie would lift the comedian's voice from existing film masters and dub it over the action. Occasionally, however, contract player Palma would be required to grunt a response himself in a deep, gravelly voice, apparently in an attempt to pass himself off as the real thing.

Fortunately, this demeaning practice—aptly described by Edward Bernds as "gruesome"—was discontinued after only a few shorts. The first of these "Fake Shemp" entries, as they came to be known, was *Rumpus in the Harem*, a tedious remake of *Malice in the Palace* with the boys as Middle Eastern cafe owners attempting to save their girlfriends from enslavement by a powerful sultan.

Apparently no one of any consequence who viewed the film noticed that the real Shemp appeared only in recycled footage. This prompted producer Jules White to immediately commission three more

Joe Besser (far left) joins The Three Stooges after Shemp's death, and insists on getting a thousand dollars a week more than partners Larry and Moe.

"cheaters," all with reliable Joe Palma doubling for Shemp: *Hot Stuff* revisited a classic premise from Ed Bernds' *Fuelin' Around*, this time casting the Stooges as undercover agents serving a mythical country. *Scheming Schemers* was a reworking of Bernds' *Vagabond Loafers*, with the three pals as plumbers in search of a missing diamond ring. And *Commotion on the Ocean* was a retooling of White's own *Dunked in the Deep*, featuring the boys as fledgling newspaper reporters who wind up stowaways on a freighter. All of the "Fake Shemp" episodes were filmed in the January following Shemp's death, and all were released to theaters that same year.

In addition to these hybrid shorts, the Stooges appeared in a slapstick compilation film called *Laff Hour* (1955), their "all-star" feature-length entry for the 1954-55 season. This film, in which the boys received top billing amongst Columbia's most popular comedy stars, included a vintage Stooge episode with Shemp, followed by shorts showcasing Andy Clyde, Vera Vague, Hugh Herbert and others. As far as Harry Cohn and Jules White were concerned, they could keep making (or re-making, or at the very least re-*titling*) "Shemp" comedies indefinitely, as long as the public's appetite for The Three Stooges remained unsated.

Shemp's surviving partners, however, had conflicting feelings about appearing in films without a flesh-and-blood "Third Stooge" at their side. Moe in particular found this to be an emotionally devastating experience, and he went about his work more or less in a daze during the long months following his elder brother's death. As always, Larry was supportive of Moe, and remained sensitive to his feelings, but it became clear even to him that The Three Stooges' viability as a big-screen attraction was not going to continue unless a new third man could be found. And soon.

While Moe and Larry were dealing with the reality of yet another partner's death, the studio had finally lined up what it considered a suitable replacement for the lovable Shemp. Bossman Harry Cohn, eager to continue the Stooges' hugely profitable series, had decided that contract comedian Joe Besser would be inducted as the newest "Third Stooge." Like Shemp, Joe had been starring in his own series of shorts at Columbia when he was drafted into the team. Joe Besser officially became a member of The Three Stooges in mid-1956, almost ten years to the day after Shemp had stepped in permanently for brother Curly.

One of Shemp's cronies, Columbia contract star Eddie Quillan, recalled, "Around the time Shemp died, there were very few of us left in the Shorts Department. Andy Clyde had already given his notice that he was leaving when his contract expired, because he was going into television. So there were only three comedians left beside the Stooges—myself, Wally Vernon, and Joe Besser. I would have liked to join the Stooges. I know Wally would have liked it, because he had known them for years. But it turns out Jules White wanted the one guy who absolutely did not want to join the Stooges, and that was Joe Besser. Besser did not like their type of comedy. But Jules thought he looked like Curly, and that was why he was put in. He wanted someone who could imitate Curly, because Curly was Jules' favorite of all the Stooges. Like most producers, I guess, he wanted to repeat his earlier successes."

Physically, though, Joe Besser was similar to Curly Howard in a number of ways: he was short, fat and bald, with a cherubic expression and persnickety mannerisms. And like Curly, his comic character was, in many respects, childlike and patsyish.

"Joe Besser was a very cute man in his own way," said Jules White. "He had a lot of good gestures and expressions. And he was a cute little fat man to look at."

In their first comedy with Joe Besser as "Third Stooge," Jules White's *Hoofs and Goofs* (1957), the boys are in trouble with their no-nonsense landlord (Benny Rubin) when they bring a high-kicking horse home to their second-floor apartment.

⟵

The Stooges get inoculated in *Space Ship Sappy* (1957), the first of three sci-ence-fiction spoofs produced and directed by Jules White, and written by his brother Jack.

⟶

In 1957, the boys light up on the set of *Oil's Well That Ends Well* as a promotion for the Chesterfield cigarette company.

⟶

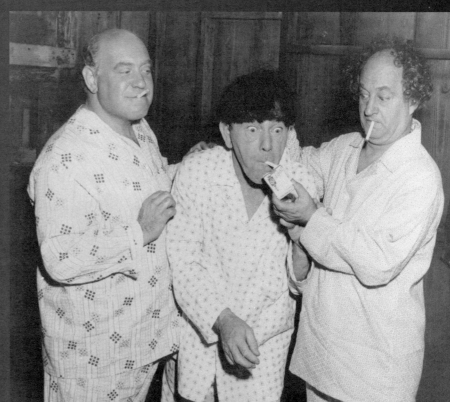

Comedienne Murial Landers plays Joe's sister Tiny, in Jules' White's musical comedy *Sweet and Hot*, filmed in 1957 with each of the Stooges playing multiple roles.

←

Christmastime, 1957: Moe and Larry are left out in the cold in this posed shot from Jules White's *Triple Crossed*, a remake of his earlier Stooge comedy *He Cooked His Goose* and the last film to be shot on the sound stages of Columbia's shorts department.

At first Moe and Larry were equally enthusiastic about the prospect of working with Joe, whom they had known since the early Depression era when they worked together with Ted Healy in Jake Shubert's *The Passing Show*. But the Joe Besser who joined the Stooges in the mid-1950s was not the good-natured, fun-loving imp of decades past. Joe now flatly refused to indulge in the Stooges' brand of comic mayhem, and insisted that a clause be added to his Columbia contract stating that he was not to be slapped, poked or tweaked while playing the Third Stooge role. Despite his desire to keep working, Joe did not wish to sacrifice his health for the sake of slapstick.

Joe also insisted Columbia sign him as a single performer, not as a member of "The Three Stooges." At no point when he was working with the team did Joe ever consider himself anything but a temporary replacement for his old pal Shemp. In time, Moe and Larry would come to view him in the same fashion. And they would eventually yearn to disassociate themselves with Besser when it became painfully clear that their comedic styles simply did not mesh.

Ted Healy's last set of Stooges — Mousie Garner, Sammy Wolfe and Dick Hakins — regularly performs free of charge at the Los Angeles Police Department's annual family picnic.

"Joe Besser was not homosexual, but his character was a rather cruel parody of one," reflected Edward Bernds many years later. "His character was simply too dainty and effeminate for the roughneck Stooges."

Joe's first screen endeavor with Moe and Larry, *Hoofs and Goofs* (1957), is substandard comedy, even though dialect specialist Benny Rubin turns in a funny performance as the Stooges' crabby Germanic landlord. The storyline focuses on Joe's obsession with his long-dead sister, and his belief that she has somehow been reincarnated as a wisecracking horse. Despite the film's derivative premise, a sequel of sorts, *Horsing Around*, was released shortly afterward, and the Stooges repeated the "talking horse" routine in their feature film *Have Rocket, Will Travel* a couple of years after that.

In addition to wholly-original productions, Columbia stitched together a compilation film, *The Three Stooges Fun Festival* (1957), featuring some of the better "Joe" episodes. The film served as the Stooges' feature-length release for the 1956-57 season. At Columbia's request, Joe, Larry and Moe appeared live on stage at the Paramount Theater in Los Angeles in conjunction with the movie. Even Joe had a good time, performing with the Stooges in front of a live audience for the first time since the old Ted Healy days.

"It was a lot of fun," said Joe later, "because we were making people laugh."

When Joe Besser (right) joins Moe and Larry, Harry Cohn promises the skittish newcomer that he will never be hit or injured during the making of a Stooge comedy—but it's a promise that Cohn quickly reneges on, ordering Jules White to "treat Joe Besser no different than you would any other comic."

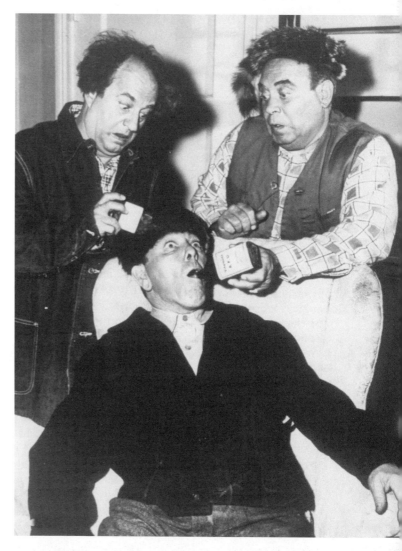

Scripts from earlier shorts that had starred Shemp or Curly were also retooled for the new ensemble. Stock footage of Curly proved to be quite useful, since Joe resembled him somewhat from a distance. For example, Curly's last short as one of the Stooges, *Half Wits Holiday*, was remade in 1957 as *Pies and Guys*. This one turned out to be one of Joe's last Stooge shorts as well.

Since stock footage was being used so frequently at Columbia, producer-director Jules White could often turn out a "new" film in a matter of hours. Emil Sitka, who repeated his *Half Wits Holiday* role in *Pies and Guys*, remembered how he was approached to do the part in the remake:

"I got a call from Jules White. He told me he was remaking *Half Wits Holiday* with Joe Besser, and he wanted me to repeat my role. They even had my old costume ready. All they wanted me to do was take off some weight and read through the old script again."

But the freewheeling, circus-like atmosphere of the Shorts Department's glory days was all but gone by the late 1950s.

"We were shooting the pie fight," said Sitka, "when Moe accidentally sat down on top of a stack of pies that were to be thrown on-camera. The crew broke up with laughter, but Jules White just about had a tantrum. He screamed at the crew, and asked them what was so funny considering Moe was now going to have to change his costume, and production was going to be held up. You would never know we were shooting a comedy from the way Jules was carrying on."

In December of 1957, the Stooges were fired by Columbia Pictures. They had been the only remaining act in the entire Shorts Department, which was disbanded upon their departure. Jules White, their producer and frequent director for nearly a quarter of a century, retired shortly thereafter. The firing of the Stooges marked the literal end of the short-subject comedy era, as lengthier feature films and double features had finally crowded "curtain-raisers" out of the marketplace altogether.

In 1957, Joe steps into Curly Howard's old role in Jules White's *Sappy Bull Fighters*, a remake of *What's the Matador* that becomes Besser's swan song with The Three Stooges.

In the late Fifties, Columbia releases a feature-length compilation of Stooge comedies starring Joe Besser, and the film becomes a huge success via kiddie-matinee showings.

Shortly after they left Columbia, the Stooges began making plans for a coast-to-coast personal appearance tour. Their first-run comedies were still playing in theaters throughout the country, and Moe had hoped to obtain another film contract for the team before The Three Stooges disappeared altogether from the public eye. A successful nationwide tour would prove to industry bigwigs that the Stooges were still a viable attraction.

By this time, however, finicky star Joe Besser had already decided to abandon the team. Now that The Three Stooges were without a movie contract, Joe saw little point in continuing with the act. But the story he gave his ex-partners was that he was unable to accompany them on tour because of a previous feature-film obligation in Hollywood. Joe said his upcoming appearance in Fox's all-star musical *Say One For Me*, with Bing Crosby, Debbie Reynolds and Robert Wagner, would preclude him from carrying on in the role of Third Stooge, particularly if that now meant going out on the road for many consecutive weeks.

Meanwhile, in January of 1958, the man who had promised Joe that he would never be hit had finally stopped making promises he had no intention of keeping. Harry Cohn suffered a fatal heart attack while on vacation in Phoenix, Arizona with his wife, Joan, and Mr. and Mrs. Harry Romm.

At Cohn's funeral in Los Angeles, which was attended by an overflow crowd, comedian Red Skelton was heard to quip, "It's just like Harry always said—If you give the people what they want, they'll come out for it."

As for Joe Besser, he was glad to be done with the Stooges. Years later, when he would suffer a stroke himself, he would wonder aloud if the hits he had received in his years as a comedian had anything to do with it.

SPECIAL **FEATURE LENGTH** LAUGH TREAT!

THREE STOOGES FUN-O-RAMA

You'll laugh! You'll howl! You'll rock! You'll yowl!

THE TALK OF SHOW BUSINESS!

A Columbia Pictures Presentation

★★★ **The THREE STOOGES** ★★★

BY EARLY 1958, Moe and Larry had already begun looking for another replacement. Privately, they were both delighted that Joe Besser had bid them farewell, as they held out little hope that he could ever be integrated into the team like Shemp or Curly. But finding a new third man would not be an easy task, especially since the Stooges no longer had a film contract.

By mid-1958, the future of The Three Stooges as a marketable act looked fairly bleak, at least to the boys themselves. With no impending engagements on the horizon, and no credible Third Stooge forthcoming, Moe Howard began thinking about a career in Hollywood behind the camera in addition to his ongoing pursuit of acting roles as a character player. One Columbia feature from the late 1950s, Harry Romm's all-star musical production *Senior Prom*, even included some Stoogesque comedy material conceived by Moe. However, the veteran comedian was credited on screen not as a writer, but as "associate producer," owing mostly to his having run errands for former manager Romm during production.

Larry Fine, in turn, was considering making a trip back east to scout performing opportunities in his favorite vacation spot, Atlantic City. There he and wife Mabel could enjoy the sand and surf, as well as family and friends from nearby Philadelphia and New York. Larry was entertaining the possibility of appearing in Atlantic City nightclubs as a solo musician and master of ceremonies, an idea he had not pursued since the days of speakeasies and bootleg liquor. He also began making plans to write his memoirs, with an emphasis on his career as the longest-running member of The Three Stooges.

And Joe Besser had already begun accepting movie and television offers as a single, ecstatic to be working once again without

CurlyJoe DeRita (far right) steps in for Joe Besser when the latter decides he's had enough of The Three Stooges.

After Joe Besser's departure, Moe and Larry are joined by CurlyJoe DeRita, who initially wears his hair long and parted down the middle.

the burden of salary-sharing partners. Within a year of his leaving The Three Stooges, Joe would also supplement his performing income by working as an uncredited writer, supplying on-the-set gags for Paramount feature films starring Jerry Lewis and others.

By the summer of 1958, there was definite talk of disbanding The Three Stooges. Moe was torn between his desire to keep working, and his fear that perhaps the Stooges no longer had an audience.

It was while Moe was in this state of anxiety and confusion that Larry and his wife Mabel left L.A. for a brief vacation in Las Vegas. Larry decided to catch CurlyJoe DeRita in the 1958 edition of Harold Minsky's *Follies*. Larry was elated over what he saw, and telephoned Moe to tell him about his great comedy "find."

Moe, already suspicious of any overtly enthusiastic talent appraisal, stopped his partner cold: "Don't tell me—he's a cross between Curly, Lou Costello and Jerry Lewis."

"No," replied Larry, "he's a cross between Curly, Lou Costello and the fat lady at the opera!"

The popular DeRita was not only a well-known roughhouse comedian but, by now, the top burlesque star in America. And like his Stooge predecessor Joe Besser, he was physically similar to the youngest Howard brother.

Although he had toiled alongside them on the soundstages of Columbia's Shorts Department, and had even been asked by Jules White to audition for the Stooges, CurlyJoe had not really known Moe Howard nor Larry Fine prior to meeting with them in the late 1950s. "I had met them years before," said DeRita, "but we were only acquaintances."

In the previous decade, CurlyJoe had been the manager and star of a live theater back east, a "neighborhood house" that was making the transition from Minsky's-style burlesque to family-oriented vaudeville. DeRita had booked The Three Stooges as headliners, and in greeting them in the lobby between shows, the humble comic for the first time stood face to face with the men who would not only make him an international film star, but the moniker "CurlyJoe" a household name.

In a matter of months the Stooges were to become television stars as well as movie personalities. They would amass a huge audience of young children, many of whom had never before seen them in theaters, but would soon be captivated by their classic comedy on the small screen. And, most importantly, the Stooges would form their own production company and finally get the opportunity to star in feature films of their own design.

CurlyJoe's condition for joining The Three Stooges: Moe and Larry must allow him to develop his own character and play it as he sees fit.

All of this came about because Columbia's TV subsidiary, Screen Gems Productions, had released a package of Stooge shorts to local television stations in January 1958 — literally the same month the boys were fired!

According to Jules White, Columbia hadn't expected to profit very much from the old shorts, but he persuaded Screen Gems to release a batch of them on a trial basis. A total of 78 episodes, most of them the bigger-budget entries with Curly Howard, were hand-picked by White himself. At Jules' urging, the package was distributed to a handful of small-market stations on the East Coast, on an experimental basis

★★★ The THREE STOOGES ★★★

only. Supposedly to everyone's surprise, the shorts were an immediate hit, and local stations throughout the country were soon clamoring for the hugely profitable "Stooge" library.

A few months after its premiere in syndication, the film series, packaged simply as *The Three Stooges*, became one of the most popular daytime TV programs available. Within a year, the film package was the top-rated daily-afternoon program on American television, clobbering the competition in virtually every market from coast to coast.

The old shorts were such a hit on TV

that Columbia decided to assemble another compilation film, *The Three Stooges Fun-O-Rama* (1959), released to theaters for the 1958-59 season. The compilation was comprised of some Stooge shorts that had starred Joe Besser, and this incensed Larry, Moe and CurlyJoe. Here Besser was no longer a member of the team, and yet Columbia was promoting him as if he was.

While the Stooges themselves received no residuals from the TV showings of their Columbia shorts, the constant broadcast of the old films kept The Three Stooges in the public eye. Children across the nation became quite familiar with the antics of the threesome, and before long the Stooges were in terrific demand for personal appearances, television guest-shots and, once again, theatrical feature films.

In the late Fifties, the Stooges are on the brink of becoming television superstars, even though Columbia executives never bother to tell them their old films are being released to the small screen.

A program for one of the Stooges' innumerable live stage shows—by the time CurlyJoe joins up, the team is commanding ten to twenty times its usual fee for personal appearances.

One-man band Joe Besser regrets leaving the Stooges for an independent career in the late 1950s.

"When we were on top, nobody liked me," said Moe, in reference to the Stooges' early days at Columbia. "After all, I'm the mean one who does all the hitting. Now the kids come up to me on the street and say they love me. I can't figure it out. A couple of new generations popped up while we had our back turned and they're different, I guess."

By the late Fifties, these "new generations" of fans were responsible for the Stooges enjoying their most profitable years to date. In 1959 alone, Larry, Moe and CurlyJoe reportedly took in more than a million dollars in income, before taxes. When news of the Stooges' extraordinary comeback hit the trade papers, many old-timers who had worked with the boys at Columbia were stunned. Former "Third Stooge" Joe Besser, in fact, was beginning to think that maybe he was a little hasty in divorcing himself from the team.

"I would never have quit, if I'd have known how much *money* they were going to make,"

The boys play before their largest-ever audience—nearly a hundred thousand spectators—at the Canadian National Exhibition.

By the end of the 1950s, the boys are raking in millions; many years later, CurlyJoe would remark, "I road the gravy train with the Stooges, but I pulled my weight."

→

BILL RACH
IN ASSOCIATION WITH
CHARLES A. COMISKEY AND JOSEPH R. VAUGHN
PRESENTS

SPECIAL CHILDREN'S MATINEES

under the Big Top at . . .

MELODY TOP

CONGRESS EXPRESSWAY AT WOLF ROAD EXIT, HILLSIDE, ILLINOIS
ACROSS FROM HILLSIDE SHOPPING CENTER

JULY 14-23
IN PERSON

THE THREE STOOGES

in their own Musical Revue
STAR ACTS
and the
MELODY TOP ORCHESTRA

HUNDREDS OF SEATS AT $1.95!
FOR CHOICE SEATS USE MAIL ORDER COUPON ON REVERSE SIDE.

By winter of 1959, the Stooges are commanding top dollar at theaters and nightclubs throughout the country, where they play almost exclusively to standing-room-only houses comprised of school-age kids and their parents.

remarked Besser.

But with CurlyJoe DeRita now ensconced as "Third Stooge," the Stooges were more than eager to exploit their public image as comedy's reigning "kings of slapstick." By the late 1950s, they were the sole purveyors of Mack Sennett-style humor still active, and the Stooges cashed in on this fact at every opportunity.

As a member of The Three Stooges, CurlyJoe offered a pleasant complement, rather than contrast, to the characters of his partners. As the Stooges began to tone down their comedic violence in the late Fifties, DeRita's passive, less boisterous character blended in easily. Moe and Larry, both of whom were getting on in years, began to relax as well, both personally and professionally.

"Moe especially began to mellow out in his later years," commented his sister-in-law, Shemp's wife Babe.

This "mellowing out" was reflected in the Stooges' movie and television appearances. In the late 1950s, and well into the Sixties, the Stooges relied more on their established comic personalities than violence and roughhousing to get laughs. DeRita, in turn, played the Third Stooge role in his own laid-back style. He simply adapted his burlesque personality for appearances with the Stooges and, like Shemp and Joe before him, frequently performed material originally written for Curly Howard in his own style.

Emil Sitka, who appeared quite frequently in films and on television with DeRita as one of the Stooges, remembered that CurlyJoe had his own notions as to how he wanted to perform. "If you were a director," said Sitka, "the best thing to do was to leave Joe alone. Because he wouldn't take suggestions. He ignored them."

Shortly after acquiring CurlyJoe as a member, the Stooges began popping up everywhere. One newspaper columnist observed that there was seldom a moment when the Stooges *weren't* in the limelight, what with the constant showings of their old movies in theaters and on television, as well as their frequent appearances in nightclubs and other live venues.

As the Columbia "Three Stooges" shorts grew in popularity on television, the Stooges themselves began making appearances on the local TV stations that aired their vintage comedies. The Columbia shorts were excellent publicity for their present act, and they capitalized on their renewed popularity with a series of brand-new, feature-length "Three Stooges" movies.

Moe Howard, of course, had wanted the Stooges to appear in tailor-made feature films for years, but Harry Cohn just as persistently had refused them the opportunity. The fact that teams like Laurel & Hardy, Abbott & Costello and Martin & Lewis had headlined in true "star" vehicles no doubt had an influence on the Stooges' desire to raise their own status, both financially and "artistically."

Columbia thus commissioned *Have Rocket, Will Travel* (1959), which became the Stooges' feature-length entry for the 1959-60 season. In this science-fiction parody, the boys play space-center janitors who accidentally launch themselves into outer space via rocketship. The film, produced by their manager Harry Romm, was sufficiently successful at the box office to prompt Columbia to finance more Stooge features. And while mob-friendly Harry Cohn was no longer around to intimidate them, the Stooges were nevertheless betrayed by Cohn's old buddy, their "loyal" manager Romm.

Unable to get the Stooges to make another feature on Columbia's terms, producer Romm simply slapped together another compilation film, *Stop! Look! and Laugh!* (1960). This feature consisted of clips from earlier Columbia shorts, integrated with newly-produced footage starring kiddie-show host Paul Winchell. Enraged by what they felt was a personal as well as business betrayal, the Stooges fired Romm and hired Moe's son-in-law, Norman Maurer, as their new manager-producer.

The boys then accepted an offer from 20th Century-Fox to star in a lavish, multimillion-dollar epic to be helmed by Walter Lang, who had directed the Stooges in *Meet the Baron* nearly thirty years earlier. *Snow White and the Three Stooges* (1961) was filmed at Fox on a budget of more than three million dollars, making it the most expensive "Three Stooges" movie ever made.

New York Times critic Howard Thompson described the film as "beautiful and tasteful from start to finish . . . Ye Stooges Three, never more subdued, are lively to be sure. If their pleasant, friendly bumbling (the pies fly only once) doesn't exactly enhance Grimm, the boys do quite nicely as sideline sponsors of the hero and heroine."

Snow White and the Three Stooges actually involves very little slapstick, but is an outstanding children's feature nevertheless. Elwood Ullman and Noel Langley collaborated on the screenplay, which deftly utilizes the talents of the Stooges in an unusual manner. (Langley purportedly was brought in because of his prior experience with family-oriented films—he had co-written Metro-Goldwyn-Mayer's *The Wizard of Oz* some twenty years earlier.) The film allows the Stooges to play themselves, more or less, and shows them to good advantage as sympathetic characters. The boys display an ability, however modest, for pathos that previously had been untapped.

Now, far removed from the

Director Del Lord, who helped the Stooges define their screen characterizations back in the Depression era, retires in the 1950s, as does producer Hugh McCollum (at Lord's side).

The boys listen intently to instructions from director David Lowell Rich during shooting of *Have Rocket, Will Travel.*

CurlyJoe makes his big-screen debut with Moe and Larry in Columbia's *Have Rocket, Will Travel* (1959), which, thanks to producer Harry Romm, includes samplings of Curly Howard's voice during a number of DeRita's scenes!

In a deleted sequence from *Have Rocket, Will Travel,* the Stooges are accompanied on their runaway spaceship by a *trained* astronaut.

The size of the "human birdcage" set from *Have Rocket, Will Travel* illustrates the fact that Columbia Pictures was suddenly willing to invest a lot more money in its Stooge comedies.

clutches of Cohn, and his lickspittle Harry Romm, The Three Stooges were finally poised to become feature-film stars who called the shots themselves.

For this reason the Stooges formed their own company, Comedy III Productions, as well as an independent film-producing outfit called Normandy Productions. In the early 1960s, the main thrust of Normandy was the production of feature-length, star-vehicle comedies for theatrical release, with creative control finally resting in the hands of The Three Stooges themselves. Norman Maurer would be the driving force of the "Three Stooges" films throughout the 1960s, producing, directing and even contributing to the writing of the films.

As usual, CurlyJoe, Moe and Larry are fighting over a woman, this time at the black-tie ball held in the Stooges' honor in *Have Rocket, Will Travel.*

Normandy churned out several feature-length Stooge comedies in the 1960s, all of which were characterized by a minimal level of violence in comparison with their earlier Columbia films. Even so, Normandy hired a number of the Stooges' former collaborators to work on the features.

Elwood Ullman wrote all of the screenplays, and Edward Bernds, now a feature-film director with substantial credits, even helmed a couple of productions. The Stooges' favorite supporting player from the old Columbia Shorts Department, Emil Sitka, was also recruited for appearances in the films.

The "spring on the trousers" gag, enacted by Curly Howard in *Hoi Polloi* and other classic shorts, is redone by CurlyJoe in *Have Rocket, Will Travel.*

Columbia financed and distributed the new Stooge comedies, all of which provided considerable profit for the Stooges themselves. For the first time, the Stooges—including newcomer CurlyJoe DeRita—owned a significant percentage of their own movies.

"Moe and Larry were very fair," recalled CurlyJoe. "Everything was a three-way split, as far as money was concerned." Initially, Moe and Larry had decided to make CurlyJoe a junior partner. But they reportedly were so impressed with his willingness to put out for the team, they made him an equally-paid member almost immediately.

The boys owned a full fifty percent of the profits of their first Normandy production, *The Three Stooges Meet Hercules* (1962), their feature-length release for the 1961-1962 season.

Edward Bernds, who directed *Hercules,* recalled that the Stooges had changed relatively little from when he had last worked with them a decade earlier: "Moe and Larry were about the same. Moe was a little touchier, and Larry was a little flightier. In their own ways, they were troupers.

Snow White and the Three Stooges (1961) inspires a record album featuring the boys clowning and singing.

The Stooges are citizens of modern-day Ithaca, New York, who journey back in time to ancient Ithaca, in Edward Bernds' *The Three Stooges Meet Hercules* (1962).

They wanted to do good. I guess Joe DeRita did, too."

Bernds notes that he was aware of the fact that the Stooges were no longer in prime physical condition. "Joe was very fat, and any fat person, if he runs or climbs up stairs too fast, could have a heart attack. And I was aware of that. I was also aware of the fact that Moe and Larry were a lot older than they had been before, so I tried not to strain them too much, either. For instance, if we had to shoot a scene of them running up a flight of stairs, I wouldn't ask them to actually run all the way up the stairs. We would do a shot of them running up a couple of stairs, and then cut to a shot of them reaching the top."

While age and size limited their flexibility, it brought the Stooges a kind of elfin charm. Seeing three aged men slapping each other and indulging in physical mayhem was grotesquely funny in and of itself. Audiences apparently agreed, as *The Three Stooges Meet Hercules* became the team's highest-grossing star vehicle. *Hercules* was followed by another hugely successful feature, *The Three Stooges in Orbit* (1962), with the Stooges cast as TV personalities who get mixed up with Martian spies.

In addition to their feature film appearances, the Stooges continued to be seen on TV five to six days a week, and by the mid-1960s, more stations were carrying the Stooge shorts than ever before. But the small-screen success of The Three Stooges was tainted by one factor, still very much an issue in the television industry: violence. While the Stooges themselves had toned down their often brutal physicality, the Stooges shorts nevertheless were loaded with graphic, visual violence, and parents across the country became outraged when their children began slapping each other and poking their siblings in the eyes. Many believed this was the result of daily exposure to the slapstick Stooge comedies.

Responding to parental complaints, some television stations pulled the Stooges' comedies from their program lineups. The general response to this action, however, was negative, and station managers were sometimes forced to resume broadcast of the shorts. Many stations attempted to alleviate the parental panic by scissoring out the more violent gags, but the roughhouse slapstick remained intact.

On talk shows and in press interviews, Stooge spokesman Moe Howard constantly defended the Stooges' style of comedy, explaining that it was all in fun.

"We're not as violent as we used to be," said Moe. "Our comedy is based on upsetting dignity—something that's very easy for us to do."

But the Stooges did more than upset dignity. They became the scourge of parental groups across the nation, who persisted in their attempt to force the much-loved "Three Stooges" comedies off the air.

Larry's son-in-law and the L.A. host of *The Three Stooges* film series, Don Lamond, catches the boys loafing in *The Three Stooges in Orbit* (1962).

As a result of the outcry against TV violence in the early 1960s, the Stooges toned down their stock-in-trade slapstick considerably. They all but completely abandoned the "poke in the eyes," and at each personal appearance, and in special theater and nightclub shows for kids, Moe would mention, for the benefit of the juvenile audience, that their mayhem was phony, that nobody really got hurt, and that it was all just for laughs. But he also warned children not to try the slapstick on each other, noting that the results could be disastrous.

Edward Bernds was well aware of the possibly harmful effects of a child practicing the "poke in the eyes" stunt on a playmate. Bernds was relatively tolerant of the often excessive violence inherent in the Stooges' routines, but he had his limits as to what he would allow to be filmed under his watch as director:

"Even as a fledgling director, I wouldn't let the boys do the 'poke in the eyes.' That was gratuitously cruel. I told Moe, 'If one kid, anywhere, pokes another kid's eye out, it's no good. It isn't that funny.' So in any picture I directed, there's never

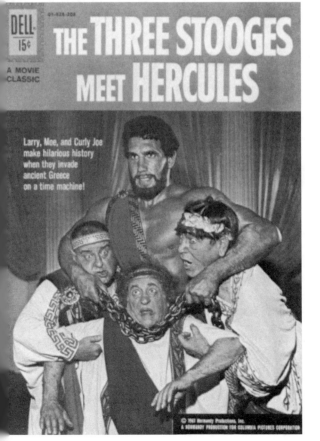

The box-office success of *The Three Stooges Meet Hercules* prompts numerous merchandising tie-ins, including this comic-book novelization of Elwood Ullman's screenplay.

the 'poke in the eyes.' Jules White continued to use it, but I think eventually Moe himself decided they wouldn't do it. It's too real to be tolerated."

Although violence became an important issue of concern for the Stooges in the 1960s, it was not a significant problem during the time in which they were actually making their ever-popular shorts. Elwood Ullman described the situation:

"We used our judgment and we had no particular trouble with censorship. As a matter of fact, when Moe

Emil Sitka, in the role of the oddball scientist Prof. Danforth, shows up at the Stooges' television studio with some startling news in *The Three Stooges in Orbit*.

Moe, CurlyJoe and Larry are marginally impressed with Emil Sitka's plans for a new military vehicle, a combination helicopter-tank-submarine, in *The Three Stooges in Orbit*.

Working as a single, Mousie Garner is cast as "Mousie," the lead funnyman of ABC-TV's *SurfSide Six* series in the early 1960s.

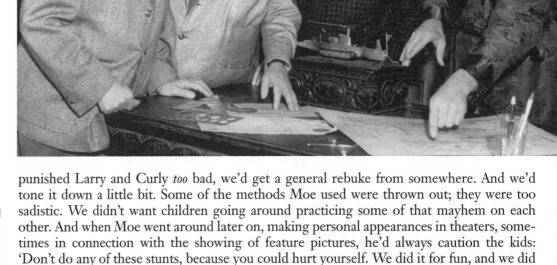

punished Larry and Curly *too* bad, we'd get a general rebuke from somewhere. And we'd tone it down a little bit. Some of the methods Moe used were thrown out; they were too sadistic. We didn't want children going around practicing some of that mayhem on each other. And when Moe went around later on, making personal appearances in theaters, sometimes in connection with the showing of feature pictures, he'd always caution the kids: 'Don't do any of these stunts, because you could hurt yourself. We did it for fun, and we did it "cheating," really, but don't try it.' He always said that during the intermission with the announcements and speeches."

Edward Bernds added, "Violence was our stock-in-trade, but we tried not to be senselessly violent."

But Jules White wholeheartedly believed that the violent aspect of "The Three Stooges'" shorts had been blown out of proportion during the age of television:

"My God, they've been doing violence in motion pictures since the inception of motion pictures. And it's been going on because it's a way of life. They want realism; they've got to take that with it. The trouble is that producers should tell these sob sisters to go to hell! Because they're the ones that create the trouble. Nobody was ever injured because the Stooges had broad-action comedy. Their form of violence was amongst themselves, and it wasn't so much violence as it was a burlesque of violence. If Moe slaps Curly and Curly says, 'Listen, you, remember the good book says turn the other cheek," and he turns over and puts his fanny up in the air on a bench—that has a connotation of 'dirty.' But it's cleaned up because Moe kicks him in the pants, and he deserves it. There was always a provocation for the thing. Nobody ever just went into the scene and went 'slap'; never.

There was always a provocation for the slap or for the other things that they did."

In 1963, during a pause in their film-production schedule, the Stooges made their all-time funniest TV appearance, presenting a favorite sketch from *George White's Scandals* on CBS' *The Ed Sullivan Show*. CurlyJoe DeRita played Curly Howard's role, that of a hapless movie stand-in who continually finds himself on the receiving end of unimaginable physical punishment. The sketch was a huge hit with the studio audience, and it was unquestionably DeRita's finest hour as a Stooge.

That same year, the boys' manager, Norman Maurer, convinced them to let him take the reins as director of their feature film for the 1963-64 season. The result, *The Three Stooges Go Around the World in a Daze* (1963) is, unfortunately, one of the team's slower-paced endeavors. The plotline, which parodies Jules Verne's *Around the World in Eighty Days*, even allowed for the Stooges' old reliable "Maharajah" routine, but the laughs are few and far between. By this time Maurer was directing, producing and writing the stories for the Stooges' films, and his influence was all-encompassing.

While *Around the World in a Daze* was "leisurely paced," to say the least, the pacing of the Stooges' next feature crawled along at a snail's speed. Edward Bernds considered *The Outlaws Is Coming* (1965), a Western spoof with the boys as reporters out to stop the slaughter of bison, to be the team's slowest-moving feature. It was the team's big release for the 1965-66 season, and proved to be the least popular of their feature films. Again, Norman Maurer produced and directed, and wrote the original story for Elwood Ullman's screenplay.

"Norman was a very nice guy," recalled Bernds, "but his ideas about comedy were a little peculiar."

In 1965, the Stooges completed a series of cartoon segments for television release, titled *The New Three Stooges*. The violence

The Three Stooges, back on Broadway at the Ed Sullivan Theater for an appearance on Sullivan's hugely popular CBS variety show in 1963.

The boys reprise their "Maharajah" sketch from vaudeville, as well as the "Pop Goes the Weasel" routine from *Punch Drunks*, in their feature film *The Three Stooges Go Around the World in a Daze* (1963), produced and directed by Norman Maurer.

was kept at a minimum, and the episodes featured live-action introductions and sign-offs by the Stooges themselves.

However, according to producer Dick Brown's wife Margaret, Larry was beginning to have trouble with his verbal delivery. Although he was years away from suffering his own massive cerebral hemorrhage, Larry often found himself slurring his speech and garbling his dialogue. This meant that constant retakes were required, and with Larry no longer working at full capacity, CurlyJoe was more or less forced to carry the bulk of the comedy himself.

Released through a company called Heritage Productions, the series was produced by Norman Maurer, who was initially set to write and direct the films as well. But Edward Bernds wound up writing and directing all of the live-action episodes when, in Bernds' own

According to CurlyJoe, the Stooges' brief cameo in the all-star comedy extravaganza *It's a Mad Mad Mad Mad World* (1963) takes all of five minutes to film.

Moe is about to subject CurlyJoe and Larry to a little head–bopping in Norman Maurer's *The
Outlaws Is Coming* (1965), the least successful of
the Stooges' 1960s feature films.

Jerry Lewis' ex–partner, Dean Martin, plays straightman
to the Stooges in *Four for Texas*, an action comedy also
starring Frank Sinatra, Anita Ekberg, Charles Bronson,
and Ursula Andress.

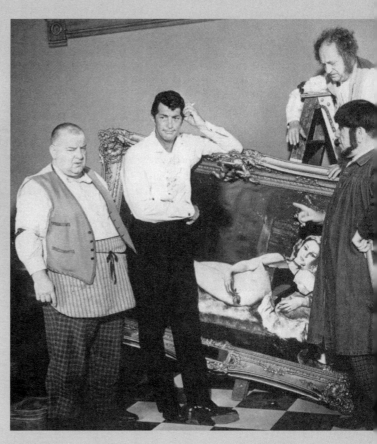

A British program reproduction from the mid–
1960s: Jack Wolf (center), leader of that first trio of
Ted Healy Stooges actually *billed* as Stooges, dies
in 1965 at the age of fifty–six, following his final
appearance with Dick Hakins and Mousie Garner.

Norman Maurer wants the boys to star in a feature film
titled *The Three Stooges Meet the Gang*, to be shot on
location in Canada in 1966, but the deal falls through.

words,"Norman discovered he had better things to do."

Bernds explains that the cartoons were of low quality because qualified animators were difficult to obtain at the time. He adds that directing the episodes was rather nightmarish. Although he received reasonable cooperation from the Stooges, completing the live-action filming was a difficult task, even though the actual screen time of the flesh-and-blood Stooges was minimal.

Also, Bernds personally disliked the series' format, that of the Stooges introducing the cartoons and then concluding them with a quick bit of business at the end of each segment. He felt that switching from scene to scene without explanation was too unnerving for the actors to comprehend. In addition to this, Bernds felt the crew wasn't up to par, leaving him with more on-the-set worries than he really needed.

But when the films were released to television for the 1965-66 season, they were an immediate hit. The novelty of seeing The Three Stooges in color was reason enough for many fans to tune in.

In 1967, the Stooges were asked by the United States Federal Government to appear in a film promoting U.S. Savings Bonds. The feature-length compilation, *The United States Treasury Presents* (1968), is highlighted by a segment filmed at Columbia called *Star Spangled Salesman* in which the Stooges play lighting technicians at a movie studio who sign up for the Payroll Savings Plan. Norman Maurer produced and directed the segment, which features guest appearances by Carl Reiner, Carol Burnett, Milton Berle, and various other comedy personalities.

It was also the last film featuring the Stooges to be released while they were still capable of working.

In 1969, Normandy began pre-production on a *new* series of half-hour television films starring The Three Stooges. A pilot episode, dubbed *Kook's Tour*, was completed in early 1970, with the boys traveling throughout the Western United States and pointing out the natural beauty of America's outdoors. The approach was decidedly relaxed, as the boys, supposedly retired from performing, tour the country and share its marvels with their viewers.

After the completion of principal photography, however, Larry Fine was felled by a stroke. He became paralyzed and, initially, was unable to speak.

The Three Stooges were, at the very least, temporarily out of business for the umpteenth time. Moe was beside himself, wondering if the Stooges would ever perform again. CurlyJoe, on the other hand, was somewhat relieved. Himself a future stroke victim, DeRita was happy to have a break from the constant slapping and head-bopping. Especially since he was beginning to go blind.

The Stooges pose with a group of young admirers during a personal-appearance tour in the mid-1960s.

Larry, CurlyJoe and Moe surround Jean DeRita, CurlyJoe's wife, in this family snapshot.

Moe appears solo in Harmon Jones' *Don't Worry, We'll Think of a Title* (1966), an all-star feature-length comedy released by United Artists.

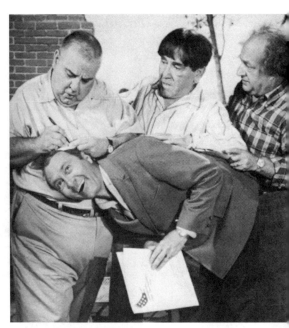

Comedian Howard Morris persuades CurlyJoe, Moe and Larry sign up for the Payroll Savings Plan in *Star Spangled Salesman* (1968).

Emil Sitka takes a pie in the face in this scene from *The New Three Stooges*, the boys' hugely successful syndicated TV series, in 1965.

Norman Maurer (left) directs the boys on location in *Kook's Tour* (1970), the pilot for yet another proposed TV series to star The Three Stooges.

★★★ **The THREE STOOGES** ★★★

★★★ **The THREE STOOGES** ★★★

Chapter 9

SINCE A NEW SERIES of TV episodes starring The Three Stooges had now been ruled out because of Larry's physical problems, plans were made to release their pilot film as a full-length theatrical feature for the 1969-70 season. *Kook's Tour* (1970) played at a handful of small screenings and eventually disappeared altogether. Nearly thirty years later, however, Comedy III Entertainment would release a print of the unedited master to home video, where it would subsequently become a top seller amongst "Three Stooges" titles.

After Larry's initial cerebral hemorrhage, the beloved comedian began physical therapy at the Motion Picture Country House, the same medical facility where Curly Howard had recuperated after his first paralyzing stroke. In the years to come, a number of the Stooges and their co-workers would undergo therapy at the well-known hospital.

By 1971, however, Norman Maurer was already attempting to secure for the Stooges a new contract that would star the team in a series of feature-length comedies. It was hoped that by the time production began on the first film, Larry would be well enough to perform. Emil Sitka was slated for the film as well, and was prepared to take on the bulk of Larry's part if the latter was not in shape for the more strenuous scenes.

Norman Maurer was trying to make a deal to film in the Philippines with the corrupt Ferdinand Marcos regime, and Moe himself complained to friend Emil Sitka that the deal didn't sound *kosher*. In fact, it was the beginning of a series of crooked dealings in which the Stooges became haplessly involved.

Moe was particularly suspicious of making a film in a foreign land, especially a Third World nation like the Philippines. It was widely known that film production in that country was often used

With Moe Howard's permission, CurlyJoe DeRita, Frank Mitchell and Mousie Garner promote their own "Three Stooges" act in the early 1970s.

as a front for laundering money obtained through the sale of illegal drugs. The despot Marcos was eventually run out of the Philippines, due to rumors he had masterminded the assassination of a political opponent. He fled the island nation with billions of dollars, most of it looted from the people he governed.

Fortunately for the Stooges, the entire deal fell through, and Norman Maurer began looking for other sources of feature-film financing.

Despite Maurer's inability to land them a movie deal, The Three Stooges continued to appear on the big screen, if only via recycled footage. *The Horror Hit Triple Threat* (1972), released for the 1971-72 season, was a feature-length compilation of Columbia shorts, including the Stooges' *The Ghost Talks*, *Crime On Their Hands*, and *Who Done It?*.

CurlyJoe, Moe and Larry in their last film together, *Kook's Tour,* **in which producer-director Norman Maurer stands in for the ailing Larry in crucial insert shots.**

Of Columbia's compilation film *The Three Stooges Follies* (1974), *New York Times* **reviewer Nora Sayre writes, "While The Three Stooges weren't our leading national wits, it's a pleasure to see them bashing skulls and tweaking noses while falling about like small children unaccustomed to ice skates."**

Meanwhile, Moe returned to performing that same year as a single, booking personal appearances at major colleges throughout the country. Moe used these lecture-circuit gigs to promote the idea that The Three Stooges were still alive, active, and, most importantly, available. As spokesman of the Stooges, Moe also made several significant guest shots on the popular syndicated TV series, *The Mike Douglas Show*. In each of these Moe showed classic Stooge film clips, and answered queries from the audience about his partners Larry and CurlyJoe. One memorable segment of the Douglas program, and one of Moe's last television appearances, featured a demonstration by the elderly Stooge on the art of pie-throwing. Douglas and several members of the audience wound up covered with pastry as a result.

Although confined to a wheelchair during the early phase of his illness, Larry was eventually able to get on his feet, and he too made live appearances at local schools and colleges. Sometimes he even appeared accompanied by Moe and CurlyJoe. Edward Bernds, who attended one of these shows, said that several Stooge films were shown, and that Larry answered questions from the audience.

"Larry spoke, but his speech was slurred," said Bernds. "It was pretty grim. Having known Larry in his prime, it was a shock to me."

Bernds added, however, that the high school auditorium was packed to capacity with children and their parents. "I didn't realize there were so many Stooges fans," he said.

While in daily physical therapy at the Motion Picture Country House, Larry also

appeared in and helped organize special fundraiser stage shows. In a number of these productions, he was joined on stage by Moe and CurlyJoe, as well as various other celebrities. But although his condition gradually seemed to improve, Larry made no attempt to return to full-time professional performing. He simply didn't want to work himself into another stroke, as Curly and Shemp had years earlier.

Moe performs the "Maharajah" routine on TV's *The Mike Douglas Show,* with Douglas filling in for CurlyJoe and Soupy Sales playing Larry's role.

Larry did keep busy, however, especially for an older man undergoing a great deal of physical therapy. In 1973, he was persuaded to write a book about his experiences in show business. Titled *Stroke of Luck*, with the subtitle *Larry, Moe & Curly,* the book told of Larry's early days before becoming one of the Stooges, his experiences as a member of the trio, and his life as it was at present. Larry even made television commercials promoting the book, which was published by a Hollywood-based company and distributed to consumers via bookstore and mail-order sales.

His old pal Moe, however, was less than pleased with the content of the book, which included numerous inaccuracies. "Moe had a very poor opinion of it," said Edward Bernds. Shortly afterward, Moe began work on his own autobiography, which according to Emil Sitka, was originally titled *We Stooge to Conquer*.

CurlyJoe, meanwhile, made occasional solo appearances of his own, usually at schools or colleges. But while Moe was out selling the concept of the Stooges as a commercially viable entity, and Larry was struggling to fully regain his mobility, CurlyJoe preferred to take a more relaxed approach to life. He enjoyed nothing better than taking it easy at home with family and friends. In particular, he loved having company over to watch the fights on television. Every now and then he was joined by former Ted Healy Stooges, Dick Hakins and Mousie Garner.

As Mousie described it, "You had on the one hand Dick Hakins, who was with Ted Healy back in the Twenties, and you had on the other hand CurlyJoe DeRita, who was in the last group of Stooges with Moe and Larry. It was fun just to sit there and listen to them compare notes!"

Strange as it may seem, The Three Stooges may have reached their peak of popularity years after they left Columbia Pictures. A whole new generation of fans, who had more or less grown up with the Stooges through daily television viewing, came to feel as if the boys were old friends. The demand for Three Stooges comedies never diminished, for theater showings as well as television broadcast.

For the 1973-74 season, Columbia released to theaters a compilation film titled The *Three Stooges Follies* (1974). This feature-length production included,

In 1974, CurlyJoe DeRita, Mousie Garner and Frank Mitchell take to the road as the latest incarnation of The Three Stooges.

amongst other attractions, several classic Stooge episodes from the team's early days at Columbia: Charley Chase's *Violent is the Word for Curly*, Del Lord's *Yes We Have No Bonanza*, and Jules White's *Three Sappy People*. The film was an immediate hit with both audiences and critics, and its success bolstered Moe Howard's theory that there still existed a large and eager audience for the Stooges' antics.

Meanwhile, Moe continued to answer fan mail by hand, as did partners Larry and CurlyJoe. Mail for the Stooges never stopped, even long after they had quit performing on a full-time basis.

Offers to do live appearances also continued to pour in. Eager to keep the concept of The Three Stooges in the public eye, Moe suggested to CurlyJoe that he put together a new Stooge trio and take advantage of the continued public interest in the team. The Stooges had actually been booked for a number of personal appearances long before Larry fell ill, and Moe believed these dates should be honored, lest word get around that the Stooges were no longer in business.

CurlyJoe took Moe's advice and formed a new act in 1974, primarily as a showcase for his "Third Stooge" character. CurlyJoe also brought in Mousie Garner, who simply adapted his own nightclub act for appearances with the new ensemble. Moe, of course, was still alive when the new Stooge group was formed, and he was asked to tour with the boys.

"But Moe wouldn't," said Mousie, "because his wife didn't want him to. She thought he was too old."

Since Moe refused to go on tour, Mousie and CurlyJoe were forced to hire another performer for the role of the team's traditional antagonist figure. Frank Mitchell, who had served as a part-time Stooge under Ted Healy, was hired as Moe's replacement.

Mousie Garner and CurlyJoe DeRita audition burlesque straightman Eddie Ennis for the "underboss" role when Frank Mitchell is unavailable.

CurlyJoe then received permission from Moe to use the "Three Stooges" name in the team's billing and advertising. "When we were putting the act together," says Mousie Garner, "we went over to Moe's house and asked his permission to use the title. He said it was okay, and then we asked him what percentage of the profits he wanted for letting us use it.

"He said, 'I don't want anything. I don't need the money.' I looked around at the beautiful house he had, and I said, 'With this house, you're damn *right* you don't need the money!'"

The team was booked for appearances on the East Coast, in the Midwest, and in the Middle West, before returning home to Hollywood. The boys broke in their newly-configured act at a venue outside Boston in the summer of 1974. "The place we were playing was packed," says Mousie. "We were pretty nervous, because we didn't know how we would go over, not being the real Three Stooges. But it went over great. I'd even say we were a smash. The audience was happy to see anything that resembled the Stooges."

The new "Three Stooges" act featured a good deal of musical comedy, with Mousie doing a variation of his time-honored "Professor Garner" piano routine. "Every time I hit a wrong note, Mitchell would give me a slap," says Mousie. "Mitchell knew how to slap because his old vaudeville act was all physical comedy, like the Stooges."

The act fulfilled all of its scheduled engagements, including local TV and radio appearances, but was forced to disband primarily because of CurlyJoe's failing eyesight. "Joe couldn't get around very well," recalls Mousie, "so we had to break up the act."

Mousie then accepted an offer to appear solo as the "resident comedian" on television's *The Bobby Vinton Show*, a syndicated variety series produced by comedian Alan Thicke. Frank Mitchell, meanwhile, went to work at Hollywood's Universal Studios, performing many of the slapstick stunts he had originated in vaudeville during the Twenties and Thirties.

While Frank and Mousie were busy lining up their solo gigs, Moe Howard received word from Norman Maurer that an independent filmmaker was interested in casting The Three Stooges in his latest feature film production.

Problems arose immediately. Moe was now frail and stiff from decades of taking pratfalls, and his wife did not want him actively performing again. Larry, in turn, was still suffering the lingering effects from his stroke, which included paralysis. And, of course, CurlyJoe's failing eyesight hindered him as well. However, after lengthy consideration, Moe decided to resurrect the act. Somehow, Moe felt, all of their problems would work themselves out.

But Larry's health was not improving, and he finally told Moe it was time for him to start looking for another man. Moe suggested their old friend and colleague, Emil Sitka. Larry approved of Moe's choice, as did CurlyJoe. Sitka was in.

According to Sitka himself, he was chosen to replace Larry primarily because of his comic acting ability and his lengthy association with the Stooge comedies.

"I was kind of taken aback, being asked to be a Stooge," said Sitka, "because then I'd have to forget everything else; I'd be typed as a Stooge."

But Sitka eventually agreed to become an actual member of the team, and he began developing his own frizzy-haired Stooge character. He was determined to play the role his own way, rather than attempt to imitate the legendary Larry Fine. Sitka himself described his proposed Stooge character as "conscientious to the point of being ridiculous."

Sitka's performing resume was retro-fitted to emphasize his appearances with the Stooges, and press releases and publicity photos were issued announcing that the team was again signed to star in a feature-length comedy.

The group was set to appear in *The Jet Set*, an independent production to be supervised by veteran entrepreneur Samuel Sherman, and directed by low-budget maestro Al Adamson. Years later, the affable Adamson would wind up murdered and buried beneath the jacuzzi of his home near Palm Springs, California.

Emil Sitka recalls that trying to get Moe Howard to rehearse the new act was no easy task. "If Moe was here right now," said Sitka, "he'd say we could wing it without rehearsal. Moe felt that we could make a scene right on the spot, that we didn't need to rehearse."

In mid-January of 1975, as the newly-resurrected "Three Stooges" was being promoted, Larry Fine suffered a second major stroke and fell into a coma. A week later, on January 24th, he was dead.

This devastated Moe, who was now the only living member of the trio that had climbed to success as The Three Stooges. On the way to Larry's funeral, the grief-stricken "Head Stooge" collapsed and had to be taken back home. The loss of his best friend and partner of nearly half a century was apparently too much for him to bear.

It was then discovered that Moe, now age seventy-seven, was extremely ill himself.

Moe nevertheless planned to honor the Stooges' new movie deal. But within a matter of weeks, it would become clear to all involved that the veteran performer would never make another public appearance.

The last Three Stooges "totem pole" still, taken in the mid-1970s to promote the team's final personal-appearance tour.

On stage in Long Beach, California, Stooges Mousie Garner and Frank Mitchell perform an impromptu routine while CurlyJoe heckles from the wings.

Larry Fine, surrounded by friends (including actors Strother Martin and Edward Asner), shortly before his death in 1975.

Chapter 10

"I HAD MY BAGS all packed and was set to go film on location," said Emil Sitka, "and then I received a call that Moe was too sick to do the picture."

In early 1975, it was discovered that Moe was suffering from lung cancer, and he was hospitalized immediately. Soon afterward, Moe learned his condition was terminal.

Moe's illness precluded any further plans for the "new" set of "Three Stooges." The team disbanded almost as quickly as it was formed. After a good deal of media fanfare and publicity, the return of The Three Stooges to the big screen faded into the realm of things that might have been.

The Three Stooges were replaced in the film by the once-popular comedy team The Ritz Brothers. The Stooge-less *Jet Set*, an embarrassingly amateurish endeavor peppered with softcore nudity, was released under the title *Blazing Stewardesses* (1975), a cash-in on Mel Brooks' hit comedy of the previous season, *Blazing Saddles*.

Moe's longtime friend Emil Sitka, meanwhile, would have to settle for immortality not as a Stooge, but as the preferred straightman of the most popular comedy team of all time. This was a "disappointment" Sitka could live with, and he deeply cherished his association with the Stooges for the rest of his life.

After a relatively brief battle with cancer, Moe Howard died on May 4th, 1975. At the time of his death, he was still working, still preoccupying himself with thoughts of The Three Stooges, as he hurriedly transcribed his memoirs. These remembrances were later published under the title *Moe Howard and the 3 Stooges*, and the book became one of the most commercially successful autobiographies in recent history.

On the evening of Moe's death, television stations throughout the country announced the news, accompanied by film clips from classic

Emil Sitka (right) is set to replace Larry Fine as one of the Stooges in *The Jet Set* (1975), a comedy to be filmed on location in Palm Springs, California.

Moe Howard, in a publicity photo taken shortly before his death in 1975.

Stooge episodes. The last of the original Three Stooges was finally gone, and with him died one of the most unforgettable acts in the history of screen comedy.

By now, CurlyJoe DeRita had retired to his home in Toluca Lake, located just down the street from Bob Hope's sprawling estate. In his declining years, CurlyJoe often shared his time with Stooge fans, autographing photos and allowing them to visit him at his home. On sunny days he would entertain fans on his front porch, regaling them with anecdotes from his burlesque days, all the while playing with the family dog and contentedly puffing on a huge cigar.

Several years after the death of Moe Howard, the Stooges finally became recognized for their unparalleled contribution to the art of comedy. The unveiling of their commemorative star on Hollywood's Walk of Fame in the early Eighties marked the first "official" salute to the team. Many felt it was a long-overdue tribute, but it was just the beginning of The Three Stooges' ascent toward the pantheon of legendary motion-picture comedians.

In the decade following the Walk of Fame ceremony, the Stooges became revered as true cultural icons. This attitude was bolstered by an endless blur of film documentaries,

After a lengthy stay at the Motion Picture Country House, Alzheimer's disease–sufferer Jules White succumbs in 1985, followed that same year by screen-writer Elwood Ullman, and in 1986 by producer–director Norman Maurer.

→

Dick Hakins, described by Betty Hickman Healy as "Ted's favorite of all the Stooges," expires peacefully in 1991 while taking a nap in the den of his Los Angeles–area home.

←

TV specials and homevideo releases, all saluting the team's legacy of laughter. And Three Stooges merchandise also inundated the market, with hundreds of themed items turning up on retail shelves around the world.

Even that most reluctant of Stooges, Joe Besser, finally came to embrace his connection to the hugely popular comedy team, especially in the years after the Walk of Fame ceremony. Joe died in the late Eighties, and was followed in the early Nineties by Frank Mitchell, Dick Hakins, and CurlyJoe DeRita, all of whom were retired at the time of their deaths. CurlyJoe's story was especially sad, as he had run out of money and was practically broke when he died from Alzheimer's disease. His memorial stone, which reads "CurlyJoe DeRita, The Last Stooge," was donated by three Stooge-history authors. At the time, CurlyJoe's widow, Jean, simply didn't have the money to pay for it.

The years that followed, however, saw a change in Jean DeRita's fortunes. After a lengthy court battle, control of the Stooges' company, Comedy III Productions, was turned over to Jean. Today she serves as the firm's president. Her sons, Bob and Earl Benjamin, are also involved in the company, and they recently executive-produced a well-received "biopic" for ABC Television titled *The Three Stooges* (2000). The two-hour, made-for-TV movie, which credits actor and Stooge fan Mel Gibson as producer, enjoyed spectacular ratings.

In the years following Moe's death, *The Stooge Follies*, a stage revue benefitting the American Cancer Society and based upon scripts from original Stooge comedies, is produced with the cooperation of Columbia Pictures.

Joe Besser, the most prolific solo performer of all the various Stooges, dies in 1988, leaving behind a large contingent of fans and admirers (pictured on Joe's lap is child star Erin Moran).

CurlyJoe DeRita, who enjoyed clowning at home as much as getting laughs on stage, dies in 1993 after a lengthy battle with Alzheimer's disease.

◀—

In 1997, Emil Sitka suffers a massive stroke while entertaining Stooge fans in his living room; he perishes the following year, and is buried under a memorial stone reading "Hold hands, you lovebirds," his signature line from *Brideless Groom*.

—▶

Edward Bernds, posing with a homevideo sleeve for The Three Stooges' cartoon series, dies in 2000 after years of poor health.

—▶

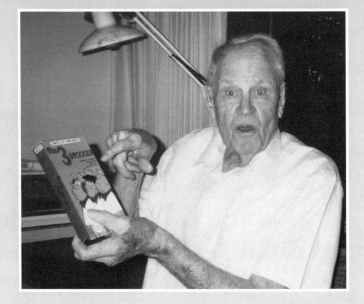

This prompted Warner Bros. Studios to announce plans for a $200 million-plus, theatrical feature film, bringing the antics of The Three Stooges back to the big screen. By 2001, the all-star project was already in pre-production, with shooting slated to begin under the direction of the hugely successful filmmakers, the Farrelly Brothers, in 2002. A 2003 release date was then announced, with the movie promoted as Warner Bros.' big summer blockbuster for that year.

Meanwhile, that last member of the old Ted Healy gang still working, Mousie Garner, recently celebrated his 75th anniversary in show business. With fellow old-timers Bob Hope and Rose Marie retired, Mousie is literally the last true headliner from the glory days of vaudeville still on the job. And the only Stooge to carry their brand of comedy into the new Millennium.

In celebration of his 75th anniversary, Mousie embarked on a nationwide personal appearance tour in 2002. In addition to submitting to countless newspaper interviews, he also made television, radio and live appearances in more than fifty cities, including New York, Philadelphia, Washington, D.C., Chicago, Las Vegas and Los Angeles. But for Mousie, the highlight of the tour was his delivering a lecture on comedy at Princeton University in New Jersey. At the Ivy League school, the hardworking Stooge also received the 2002 Lifetime Achievement Award from the National Comedy Hall of Fame, presented to Mousie at Princeton's James Stewart Memorial Theater and accompanied by a standing ovation from numerous longtime admirers.

Billed as The Grand Old Man of Vaudeville, Mousie does indeed take his work seriously. A week after the terrorist attacks on the World Trade Center and the Federal Government in Washington, Mousie once again volunteered to entertain American military troops wherever they might be. Having performed for servicemen as a child during World War I, as a young soldier during World War II, and now as a ninetysomething veteran in the current global fight against terrorism, Mousie has truly seen it all.

Said Mousie, "They say the story of The Three Stooges is the story of the American Dream. Well, I know it was my dream, that's for sure. My whole life was about being an entertainer. And I know all of the Stooges felt the same way."

But was it all worth it? The years of traveling from city to city, from theater to theater, wondering if you were going to get paid, if you were going to eat, if you were going to survive. The myriad ups and downs . . . the hits and the misses, the smashes and the flops, the triumphs and the tragedies . . . This was the life that Mousie chose, that all of the Stooges chose.

At a recent gathering, Mousie was posed the question, "If you could somehow turn back the clock, if you could go back in time to the day you first met Ted Healy, would you sign up to do it all over again?

"Hand me the pen," he replied, as he leaned forward and extended his finger.

On his 75th Anniversary Tour in early 2002, Mousie Garner clowns with (from left) WCBS' Warner Wolf in New York, WKQX's Mancow Muller in Chicago, and KNBC's Kelly Mack in Los Angeles.

On July 31st, 1999, Mousie Garner celebrates his ninetieth birthday with a gala party in Las Vegas, attended by numerous Stooge fans from around the country.

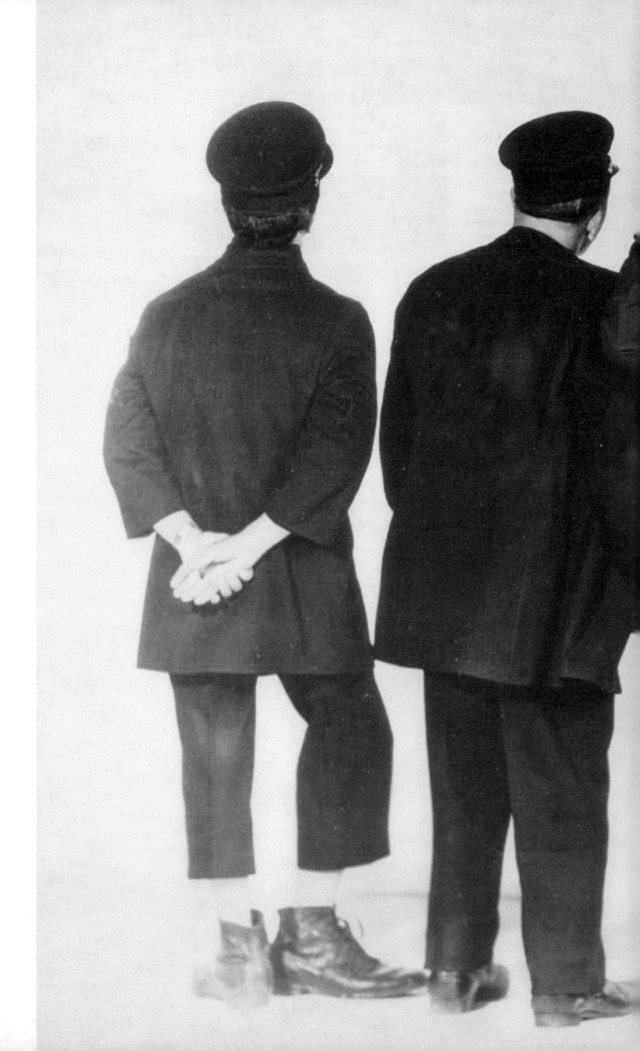

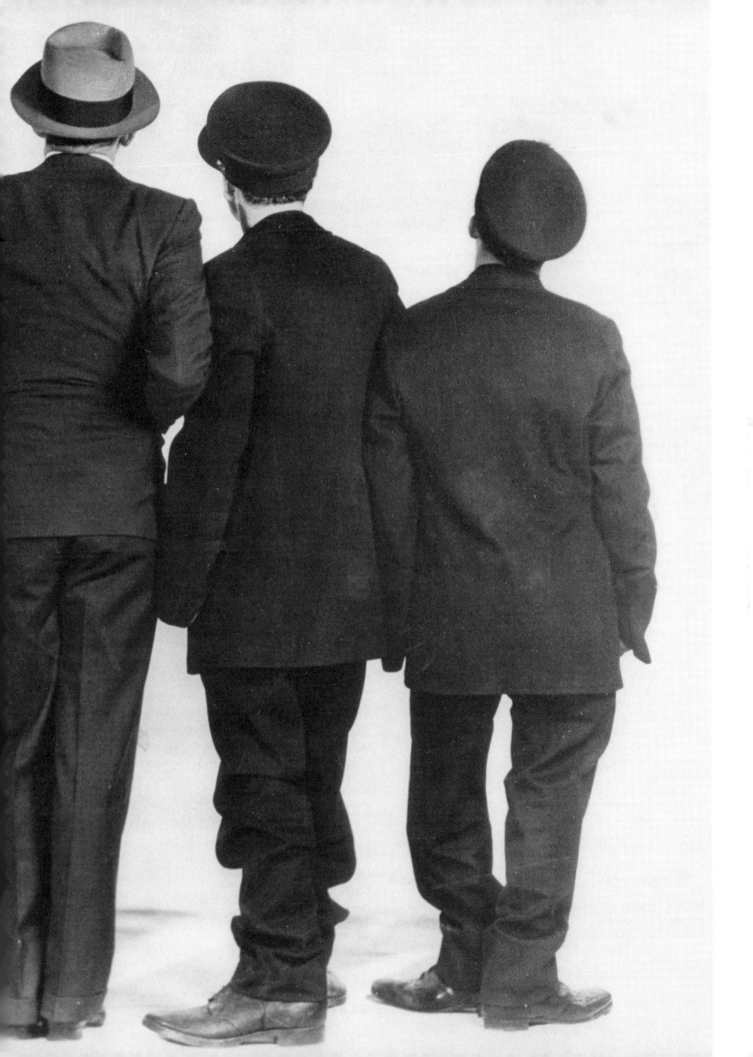

Filmography

* = Feature-length release   ** = Feature-length re-release   *** = Short-subject re-release

Soup to Nuts	(1930)*	We Want Our Mummy	(1939)
Broadway Brevities	(1931)	A Ducking They Did Go	(1939)
Hollywood on Parade	(1933)	Yes We Have No Bonanza	(1939)
Turn Back the Clock	(1933)*	Saved by the Belle	(1939)
Beer and Pretzels	(1933)	Calling All Curs	(1939)
Hello Pop	(1933)	Oily to Bed, Oily to Rise	(1939)
Meet the Baron	(1933)*	Three Sappy People	(1939)
Plane Nuts	(1933)	You Nazty Spy!	(1940)
Dancing Lady	(1933)*	Rockin' Thru the Rockies	(1940)
Screen Snapshots	(1933)	A Plumbing We Will Go	(1940)
Fugitive Lovers	(1933)*	Nutty But Nice	(1940)
Woman Haters	(1934)	The Hit Parade	(1940)**
Hollywood Party	(1934)*	How High is Up?	(1940)
The Big Idea	(1934)	From Nurse to Worse	(1940)
Punch Drunks	(1934)	No Census, No Feeling	(1940)
Men in Black	(1934)	Cookoo Cavaliers	(1940)
The Captain Hates the Sea	(1934)*	Boobs in Arms	(1940)
Three Little Pigskins	(1934)	So Long, Mr. Chumps	(1941)
Horses' Collars	(1935)	Dutiful But Dumb	(1941)
Restless Knights	(1935)	All the World's a Stooge	(1941)
Pop Goes the Easel	(1935)	I'll Never Heil Again	(1941)
Uncivil Warriors	(1935)	Time Out for Rhythm	(1941)*
Pardon My Scotch	(1935)	An Ache in Every Stake	(1941)
Hoi Polloi	(1935)	In the Sweet Pie and Pie	(1941)
Three Little Beers	(1935)	Some More of Samoa	(1941)
Ants in the Pantry	(1936)	Loco Boy Makes Good	(1942)
Movie Maniacs	(1936)	Cactus Makes Perfect	(1942)
Half Shot Shooters	(1936)	What's the Matador	(1942)
San Francisco	(1936)*	Matri Phony	(1942)
Disorder in the Court	(1936)	Three Smart Saps	(1942)
A Pain in the Pullman	(1936)	Even as I.O.U.	(1942)
False Alarms	(1936)	My Sister Eileen	(1942)*
Whoops I'm an Indian	(1936)	Sock a Bye Baby	(1942)
Slippery Silks	(1936)	They Stooge to Conga	(1943)
The Hit Parade	(1937)*	Dizzy Detectives	(1943)
Grips, Grunts and Groans	(1937)	Back from the Front	(1943)
Dizzy Doctors	(1937)	Spook Louder	(1943)
Three Dumb Clucks	(1937)	Three Little Twirps	(1943)
Swing it, Professor	(1937)*	Higher Than a Kite	(1943)
Back to the Woods	(1937)	Good Luck, Mr. Yates	(1943)*
Goofs and Saddles	(1937)	I Can Hardly Wait	(1943)
Cash and Carry	(1937)	Crazy House	(1943)*
Playing the Ponies	(1937)	Dizzy Pilots	(1943)
The Sitter Downers	(1937)	Phony Express	(1943)
Hollywood Hotel	(1938)*	A Gem of a Jam	(1943)
Termites of 1938	(1938)	Crash Goes the Hash	(1944)
Wee Wee Monsieur	(1938)	Busy Buddies	(1944)
Tassels in the Air	(1938)	The Yoke's on Me	(1944)
Start Cheering	(1938)*	Idle Roomers	(1944)
Flat Foot Stooges	(1938)	Gents Without Cents	(1944)
Healthy, Wealthy and Dumb	(1938)	No Dough Boys	(1944)
Vitaphone Varieties	(1938)	Three Pests in a Mess	(1945)
Violent is the Word for Curly	(1938)	Booby Dupes	(1945)
Three Missing Links	(1938)	Idiots Deluxe	(1945)
Mutts to You	(1938)	Rockin' in the Rockies	(1945)*
Three Little Sew and Sews	(1939)	If a Body Meets a Body	(1945)

Micro Phonies	(1945)	Up in Daisy's Penthouse	(1953)
Beer Barrel Polecats	(1946)	Booty and the Beast	(1953)
Swing Parade	(1946)*	Loose Loot	(1953)
A Bird in the Head	(1946)	Tricky Dicks	(1953)
Uncivil War Birds	(1946)	Spooks! *aka* Tails of Horror	(1953)
The Three Troubledoers	(1946)	Pardon My Backfire	(1953)
Monkey Businessmen	(1946)	Rip, Sew and Stitch	(1953)
Three Loan Wolves	(1946)	Bubble Trouble	(1953)
G.I. Wanna Home	(1946)	Goof on the Roof	(1953)
Rhythm and Weep	(1946)	The 3 Stooges 3-D Fun Feature	(1953)*
Three Little Pirates	(1946)	Income Tax Sappy	(1954)
Half Wits Holiday	(1947)	Musty Musketeers	(1954)
Fright Night	(1947)	Pals and Gals	(1954)
Out West	(1947)	Knutzy Knights	(1954)
Hold That Lion	(1947)	Shot in the Frontier	(1954)
Brideless Groom	(1947)	Scotched in Scotland	(1954)
Sing a Song of Six Pants	(1947)	Fling in the Ring	(1955)
All Gummed Up	(1947)	Of Cash and Hash	(1955)
Shivering Sherlocks	(1948)	Gypped in the Penthouse	(1955)
Pardon My Clutch	(1948)	Bedlam in Paradise	(1955)
Squareheads of the Round Table	(1948)	Stone Age Romeos	(1955)
Fiddlers Three	(1948)	Wham Bam Slam!	(1955)
The Hot Scots	(1948)	Hot Ice	(1955)
Heavenly Daze	(1948)	Blunder Boys	(1955)
I'm a Monkey's Uncle	(1948)	Laff Hour	(1955)*
Mummy's Dummies	(1948)	Husbands Beware	(1956)
Crime on Their Hands	(1948)	Creeps *aka* Tails of Terror	(1956)
The Ghost Talks	(1949)	Flagpole Jitters	(1956)
Who Done It?	(1949)	For Crimin' Out Loud	(1956)
Hokus Pokus	(1949)	Rumpus in the Harem	(1956)
Fuelin' Around	(1949)	Hot Stuff	(1956)
The Three Stooges Festival of Fun	(1949)*	Scheming Schemers	(1956)
Malice in the Palace	(1949)	Commotion on the Ocean	(1956)
Vagabond Loafers	(1949)	Hoofs and Goofs	(1957)
Dunked in the Deep	(1949)	Muscle Up a Little Closer	(1957)
Hoi Polloi	(1949)***	A Merry Mixup	(1957)
Uncivil Warriors	(1949)***	Space Ship Sappy	(1957)
Three Missing Links	(1949)***	Guns A Poppin	(1957)
Punchy Cowpunchers	(1950)	The Three Stooges Fun Festival	(1957)*
Hugs and Mugs	(1950)	Horsing Around	(1958)
Dopey Dicks	(1950)	Rusty Romeos	(1958)
Love at First Bite	(1950)	Outer Space Jitters	(1958)
Self Made Maids	(1950)	Quiz Whizz	(1958)
Three Hams on Rye	(1950)	Fifi Blows Her Top	(1958)
Studio Stoops	(1950)	Pies and Guys	(1958)
Slaphappy Sleuths	(1950)	Sweet and Hot	(1958)
A Snitch in Time	(1950)	Flying Saucer Daffy	(1958)
Three Arabian Nuts	(1951)	Oil's Well That Ends Well	(1958)
Baby Sitters' Jitters	(1951)	Triple Crossed	(1959)
Don't Throw That Knife	(1951)	Sappy Bull Fighters	(1959)
Scrambled Brains	(1951)	The Three Stooges Fun-O-Rama	(1959)*
Merry Mavericks	(1951)	Up in Daisy's Penthouse	(1959)***
The Tooth Will Out	(1951)	Booty and the Beast	(1959)***
Gold Raiders	(1951)*	Loose Loot	(1959)***
Hula La La	(1951)	Tricky Dicks	(1959)***
Pest Man Wins	(1951)	Rip, Sew and Stitch	(1959)***
A Missed Fortune	(1952)	Have Rocket, Will Travel	(1959)*
Listen, Judge	(1952)	Sweet and Hot	(1959)***
Corny Casanovas	(1952)	Flying Saucer Daffy	(1959)***
He Cooked His Goose	(1952)	Oil's Well That Ends Well	(1959)***
Gents in a Jam	(1952)	Triple Crossed	(1960)***
Three Dark Horses	(1952)	Sappy Bull Fighters	(1960)***
Cuckoo on a Choo Choo	(1952)	Stop! Look! and Laugh!	(1960)*
Presenting Spike Jones	(1953)	Bubble Trouble	(1960)***

Goof on the Roof	(1960)***	Dunked in the Deep	(1967)***
Spooks! *aka* Tails of Horror	(1960)***	Punchy Cowpunchers	(1967)***
Income Tax Sappy	(1960)***	Hugs and Mugs	(1967)***
Pardon My Backfire	(1960)***	Love at First Bite	(1967)***
Musty Musketeers	(1960)***	Dopey Dicks	(1967)***
Pals and Gals	(1961)***	Self Made Maids	(1967)***
Knutzy Knights	(1961)***	Feulin' Around	(1967)***
Shot in the Frontier	(1961)***	Hokus Pokus	(1967)***
Scotched in Scotland	(1961)***	Who Done It?	(1967)***
Fling in the Ring	(1961)***	Star Spangled Salesman	(1968)
Fox Movietone News	(1961)	The United States Treasury Presents	(1968)*
Quiz Whizz	(1961)***	The Ghost Talks	(1968)***
Fifi Blows Her Top	(1961)***	Crime on Their Hands	(1968)***
Pies and Guys	(1961)***	Mummy's Dummies	(1968)***
Snow White and The Three Stooges	(1961)*	Kook's Tour	(1970)*
Sweet and Hot	(1962)***	The Ghost Talks	(1972)***
Flying Saucer Daffy	(1962)***	Who Done It?	(1972)***
Oil's Well That Ends Well	(1962)***	Crime on Their Hands	(1972)***
Triple Crossed	(1962)***	The Horror Hit Triple Threat	(1972)*
Sappy Bull Fighters	(1962)***	Yes We Have No Bonanza	(1974)***
The Three Stooges Meet Hercules	(1962)*	Three Sappy People	(1974)***
Husbands Beware	(1962)***	Violent is the Word for Curly	(1974)***
Creeps *aka* Tails of Terror	(1962)***	The Three Stooges Follies	(1974)*
Flagpole Jitters	(1962)***	An Ache in Every Stake	(1979)***
The Three Stooges in Orbit	(1962)*	Three Little Sew and Sews	(1979)***
For Crimin' Out Loud	(1963)***	Micro Phonies	(1979)***
Rumpus in the Harem	(1963)***	Men in Black	(1982)***
Hot Stuff	(1963)***	Idiots Deluxe	(1982)***
Scheming Schemers	(1963)***	Pop Goes the Easel	(1982)***
Commotion on the Ocean	(1963)***	Tassels in the Air	(1982)***
It's a Mad Mad Mad Mad World	(1963)*	Three Little Pigskins	(1982)***
Pest Man Wins	(1963)***	Dizzy Doctors	(1982)***
A Missed Fortune	(1963)***	Curly's Movie Mayhem	(1982)*
Listen, Judge	(1963)***	Plane Nuts	(1982)***
The Three Stooges Go Around the World in a Daze	(1963)*	The Big Idea	(1982)***
Four for Texas	(1963)*	Nertsery Rhymes	(1982)***
The Three Stooges Scrapbook	(1963)	Beer and Pretzels	(1982)***
Corny Casanovas	(1964)***	The MGM Three Stooges Festival	(1982)*
He Cooked His Goose	(1964)***	Brideless Groom	(1982)***
Gents in a Jam	(1964)***	You Nazty Spy!	(1982)***
Three Dark Horses	(1964)***	They Stooge to Conga	(1982)***
Cuckoo on a Choo Choo	(1964)***	Dizzy Doctors	(1982)***
Hoofs and Goofs	(1964)***	Gents in a Jam	(1982)***
Muscle Up a Little Closer	(1964)***	Summer Lovers	(1982)*
A Merry Mixup	(1964)***	Fifty Years With the Stooges	(1983)*
The Big Parade of Comedy	(1964)*	Stoogemania: The Movie	(1985)*
Space Ship Sappy	(1965)***	The Stoogephile	(1986)*
Guns A Poppin	(1965)***	Music Box	(1989)*
Horsing Around	(1965)***	Pulp Fiction	(1994)*
Outer Space Jitters	(1965)***	The Long Kiss Goodnight	(1996)*
Quiz Whizz	(1965)***	Gents Without Cents	(1998)***
Hula La La	(1965)***	Micro Phonies	(1998)***
Idiots Deluxe	(1965)***	An Ache in Every Stake	(1998)***
The Outlaws Is Coming	(1965)*	Violent is the Word for Curly	(1998)***
Dizzy Detectives	(1965)***	Squareheads of the Round Table	(1998)***
Slaphappy Sleuths	(1965)***	Brideless Groom	(1998)***
Hokus Pokus	(1965)***	Fright Night	(1998)***
Studio Stoops	(1965)***	Gents in a Jam	(1998)***
Hot Ice	(1966)***	You Nazty Spy!	(2001)***
Dizzy Detectives	(1966)***	Horses' Collars	(2001)***
Malice in the Palace	(1966)***	Slippery Silks	(2001)***
Idiots Deluxe	(1966)***	Oily to Bed, Oily to Rise	(2001)***
Vagabond Loafers	(1966)***	Hold That Lion!	(2001)***

★★★ **The THREE STOOGES** ★★★

Fandom Honor Roll

The Fandom Honor Roll salutes those fans who have loyally supported The Three Stooges and have encouraged others to enjoy their life-affirming antics. (For more information about the Fandom Honor Roll, visit our website at **www.stoogebook.com**.)

A

Abad, Chris
Aballe, Guadalupe
Abdul, Paula
Abel, Dave
Abeyta, Paul
Abraham, Jeffrey
Ackerman, Eddie
Adams, Nick
Agresti, Louis
Aijala, David
Akiva-Plume, Maia
Albarelli, John
Alcorn, Ed
Aldridge, Jason
Alexander, Dave
Alexander, Jason
Alexander, Ric
Allen, Bernie
Allen, Jerry
Allen, Marty
Allen, Tim
Almada, Gabriel
Amaro, Jerry
Amato, Fran
Ambrosio, Jasmine
Amoni, Daniel
Amos, Torri
Anczelowicz, Alan
Anderson, Dave
Anderson, Edgar
Anderson, Jake
Anderson, Jeff
Anderson, Jerry
Anderson, John
Anderson, Leonard
Anderson, Pamela
Anderson, Patrick
Anderson, Robbie
Andreos, George
Andress, Karen
Andrews, Harold
Andrews, Richard
Anisman, Todd
Anker, Rob
Ansel, Sue
Apice, Tom
Appelhans, Brett
Arevalo, Oscar
Arkins, Dan
Arnold, Thomas
Arnold, Tom
Arreola, Alicia
Arsoniadas, Harry
Asheton, Ron
Asheton, Scott
Astbury, Ron
Astronomo, Rashad
Asuncion, Anthony
Asuncion, Tess
Atkins, Jesse
Auriemma, Marie
Austen, Ernie
Austin, Rick
Avoian, Sandi
Axel, Jerry
Aykroyd, Dan
Azaria, Hank

B

Bailey, Bill
Bailey, David
Bailey, Mark
Baird, Don
Baker, Woody
Baldani, Frank
Baldarrago, Jorge
Ball, Charlie
Baltasar, Ben
Bandini, Jimmy
Barbarotta, Mark
Barbier, Joe
Barbour, Steve
Barbutti, Pete
Barger, D.A.
Barnard, Jim
Barnard, Neva-Jane
Barnas, Ray
Baroglio, Phil
Baron, Dr. Robert
Baron, Leonard
Baron, Mel
Barr, Robert
Barrosse, Emilia
Barrosse, Evangeline
Barrosse, Paul
Barrosse, Victoria
Bartko, Daniel
Bartoletti, Lee
Bartoletti, Margaret
Bartruff, Ed
Basten, Bob
Bates, Chris
Bates, Ed
Bates, Lisa
Bates, Lola
Bates, Tyler
Bator, Lisa
Bauerly, Ron
Baulch, Bette
Baulch, George
Baumbach, Robert
Bayer III, Robert
Bayer, Robert
Beachler, Steve
Beattie, Dean
Bechtel, William
Becker, Christopher
Becker, Jim
Beckwith, Kay
Bedner, Donald
Begg, John
Begun, Ben
Belfor, Hal
Belin, Kerry
Bell, Barry
Bell, Colette
Bell, John
Bellamy, Betty
Bellamy, Jimmy
Bellson, Louis
Belushi, Jim
Ben-Victor, Paul
Benavidez, Louis
Benedetto, Eduardo
Benjamin, Eric
Benjamin, Tavi
Bennett, Brad
Bennett, Jessie
Bennett, Reed
Benson, Greg
Berdan, Katie
Berent, Mike
Bergandine, Dave
Bergiadis, Alexis
Bernet, Bob
Berns, Lori
Berru, Steve
Berry, Ken
Besinger, Beth
Best, Pamela
Bettini, Maria
Bettis, Alexis
Bettis, Barbara
Bettis, Robert
Bianchi, Alison
Bianchi, Benet
Bianchi, Brad
Bianchi, Brooke
Bianchi, Bryant
Bianchi, Francesca
Bianchi, Patty
Bianchi, Victor
Bibaz, George
Biener, Tom
Bikun, Dennis
Bilsky, Jeff
Bimmerle, Michael
Bingham, Kyler
Bingham, Lou
Binninger, Jerry
Bionelli, John
Birnbaum, Hyman
Biscaldi, Dario
Bischoff, Bill
Bishop, Joey
Bissell, Trish
Black, Barb
Black, Jack
Blackman, Billy
Blaine, Jerry
Blanco, Alexander
Blanco, Manuel
Blank, Rob
Blatt, Stephanie
Blazevic, Robert
Blazevic, Rosemary
Blazevic, Victor
Bliesener, Eileen
Bloom, Norman
Bobadilla, James
Boe, Kathy
Boe, Kim
Bogar, Barbara
Bohannon, Billy
Bojarski, Tony
Bojarsky, Cezary
Bokoskie, Charles
Boldman, Nathan
Bolger, Ron
Bolin, Rocky
Bon, Michael
Bonacci, Dino
Bonfiglio, Ann
Bonich Jr., George
Bonich Sr., George
Bonich, Chris
Bonich, Kelly
Bonich, Lorraine
Bonich, Nick
Bonich, Tony
Bonilla, David
Bonneau, Steve
Bookbinder, Steve
Bostinto, Robert
Bourne, Kendrick
Bove, Bob
Bowe, Laura
Bowen, Mike
Bower, Tammy
Bowers, John
Bowser, Mark
Bradt, Gary
Brady, Herb
Brahar, Marnie
Brandt, Donovan
Brandt, Eddie
Brantmeier, Pam
Brasich, Tony
Braxton, Cheryl
Briggs, Russell
Briick, Misty
Britt, Pat
Broadwater, J.R.
Broadwater, Jeff
Brooks, Albert
Brooks, David
Brooks, Garth
Brooks, James
Brooks, Mel
Brosius, Chris
Broussard, Jimi
Brown, Brandon
Brown, Jack
Brown, James
Brown, Julie
Brown, Mimi
Brown, Shelly
Bruskin, David
Bryant, Walt
Bryer, Steve
Bryson, Tabitha
Buchan, David
Buchanan, Lovell
Budd, Brian
Buhrman, Elizabeth
Buhrman, Jessica
Buhrman, Mike
Buhrman, Virginia
Buie, Randall
Bulgatz, Howard
Bulmer, Jeremy
Bumb, Rob
Bumbera, Mark
Bunao, Karen
Burch, Yvonne
Burke, Jo
Burmeister, Patricia
Burnell, Chris
Burnett, Carol
Burnley, John
Burns, Bill
Burns, James H.
Burns, Jimmy
Burns, Keith
Burroughs, Calvin
Burry, Dave
Burtch, Jeff
Buscemi, Nick
Busitzky, James
Butler, Joyce
Butler, Lisa
Butterfield, Wayne
Butts, Larry
Byrne, Tom

C

Cabone, Henry
Cadden, Dr. Michael
Cain, Alison
Cali, Frank
Calleja, Dan
Cambria, David
Cambria, Jack
Cambria, Maggie
Campbell, Cheryl
Campbell, David
Campbell, Jon
Campo, Patrick
Candlish, Dave
Caporaletti, Mike
Carey, Drew
Carey, Michael
Carini, Vic
Carlin, Paul
Carpenter, Keith
Carradi, Lou
Carson, Johnny
Casperson, Christopher
Cassata, Mary
Castellaneta, Dan
Castillo, Bill
Cataldo, Tom
Catizone Jr., Nicholas
Catucci, Max
Cauzza, David
Cawhorn, Jeff
Cecchetto, Gino
Cervantez, Peggy
Chaffin, Jeff
Chamberlain, Mary
Chan, Jackie
Chan, Milton
Channell, Steve
Charles, Larry
Chavez, Raul
Cheatham, Anthony
Cherven, Richard
Chesna, John
Chiklis, Michael
Chipchase, Cody
Chipchase, Ryan
Chisano, Tom
Chochole, Jill
Chong, Tommy
Chorba, Chuck
Choren, Angie
Choron, James
Chow, Ricky
Christ, Charlie
Christensen, Henry
Christian, Jean
Christie, Kyle
Christopher, Bob
Chuhinka, Michael
Chun, Joshua
Cicotello, Chris
Clark, Albert
Clark, Michael
Clarke, Bertha
Clarke, Dana
Cleaves, Rodney
Clements, Sam
Cleveland, Dennis
Coates, Brandon
Coen, Ethan
Coen, Joel
Coffey, Neil
Coffield, Eric
Coghlin, Mark
Coker, Stephen
Coladonato, Gary
Coleman, Jason
Coleman, Kimerly
Coleman, Thais
Colen, Kee
Collette, Kip
Collins, Carrie
Collins, Michael

Conley, Gail
Conlon, Mary
Connick Jr., Harry
Conrad, Irene
Conrad, Jeffrey
Cooper, Pat
Copeland, Stewart
Coppel, Clare
Corapi, Albert
Corenbaum, John
Cornell, Ed
Cornell, Gibby
Cosby, Bill
Cossitt, Theodore
Cousins, Ernie
Cousins, Jean
Cox, Donald
Cox, Fanny
Crane, Jason
Crayton, Margaret
Cristoforo, Tom
Crotty, Ada
Crotty, Jim
Crouch, Michael
Crowley, Richard
Crum, Kathy
Crum, Kimball
Cruz, David
Cummings, Chantel
Cunha, Gil
Cutler, Chris

D

D'Alessio, Mario
Dahl, Phil
Dale, Stan
Daly, John
Dammeyer, Tom
Danahey, Mike
Daniel, Alex
Dapsis, Saul
DaSilva, Mark
Daszkowski, Dan
David, Chris
David, Larry
Davidson, Peter
Davidson, Rob
Davidson, Robert
Davies, Horace
Davis, Bob
Davis, Chris
Davis, Grant
Davis, Nathan
Davis, Ronny
Day, Ronald
Day, Stephanie
DeArmen, Stephen
DeBatista, J.R.
DeBoer, Dominic
DeBoer, Kasper
DeBoer, Marten
DeBoer, Thomas
DeCaro, Jeffrey
Dee, Vince
Deeb, Gary
Deezen, Eddie
DeForest, Calvert
Degeneres, Ellen
Del Dotto, Harriet
Del Dotto, Leo
DeLaRosa, Juan
DeLaRosa, Oscar
Delgaudio, John
DeLuise, Dom
DeMarco, Dennis
Demas, Angie
Demas, Jimmy
Demas, Margo
Demas, Sam
Demas, Stacey
Demas, Tony
Demichael, Tom
Dennis, Elaine
Dennis, John
Dennis, Marie
Dermus, Elaine
DeSarno, Michael
Despres, Thom

Deutsch, Ken
DeVito, Danny
Devlin, Paul
Devore, Eddi
Dewis, Carol
Dibari, Jerome
Dickstein, Andrea
Diego, Eugene
Dier, Jeff
Dillon, Mark
DiNiro, Robert
Diorio, Richard
Diorio, Theresa
DiVito, Danny
DiVito, Domenic
Dlubala, Jerry
Dlugosz, Steven
Dobler, Brenda
Dobler, Troy
Dobson, Joe
Dodd, Jesse
Dodson, Douglas
Doerer, Lawrence
Dolan, Thomas
Dolan, Tom
Dolenz, Mickey
Domanico, Cathy
Dorman, Jeff
Dorn, Robert
Dorsey, Kevin
Doss, Gary
Dougherty, Michael
Downey, Rachele
Drake, Laura
Draper, Barry
Drickman, Mitch
Drinnon, Benny
Drost, Teri
Dubie, William
DuBray, Gene
DuBray, Kathy
Dugo, Mike
Dulen, Irma
Dullum, Virginia
Dumas, Dan
Dunham, Doug
Dunn, Kimberly
Dunphy, Randall
Duplush, Jerome
Dvorak, Dr. Gus
Dvorak, Peter
Dyer, Laura

E

Easton, Robert
Echevarria, Tony
Eden, Herb
Eder, Mike
Edmunds, Jim
Edwards, Benjamin
Edwards, Brent
Edwards, Dave
Edwards, Deborah
Edwards, Gary
Edwards, Harrison
Edwards, Joe
Edwards, Marge
Edwards, Nick
Edwards, Steve
Eichler, Susan
Elliot, Andi
Ellis, John
Ellis, June
Ellis, Rick
Emmel, George
Endsley, Kira
Endsley, Roy
Engolia, Janine
Enochs Jr., Joseph
Erickson, Sheryl
Ericson, John
Escabi, Joseph
Escabi, Patricia
Escavido, Sheila
Eskridge, John
Esquivel, Ted
Essers, Charlie
Estridge, Mary-Kate

Evans, Bobby
Evans, David
Evans, Lelah
Evertsz, Darius

F

Fabbro, Jason
Fagen, Donald
Fainberg, Ted
Falcione, Donald
Falk, Marty
Falvo, Ralph E.
Farber, Dave
Farr, Jamie
Farr, S.
Faust, Camille
Faustino, David
Fay, Ryan
Federico, Benny
Feeney, Jim
Ferguson Greene, Scott
Ferns, Eddie
Ferraro, John
Ferris, Bruce
Findley, Jon
Finnegan, Rich
Fisher, Nicole
Fitzgerald, Paul
Fitzgerald, Timothy
Fitzgerald, Ty
Fitzpatrick, Bob
Flaherty, Joe
Flanagan, Bill
Fleming, E.J.
Flemming, Michael
Flores, Bert
Flowers, David
Forbes, Sonia
Forbis, Shane
Ford, Harrison
Ford, Lita
Forester, Tom
Forrester, Ruth
Forsey, John
Forster, David
Forsythe, Anita
Fox, Andrew
Fox, Kenneth
Foxworthy, Jeff
Franks, Jimmy
Franzkowiak, Lynne
Frawley, James
Fredericks, Kay
Fredriksen, Arthur
Freemon, Eugene
French-Sidoti, Catherine
Friedman, Drew
Friedman, Mark
Fries, Carl
Fries, Carrie
Fries, Lauren
Fries, Mary Ellen
Fries, Michelle
Fries, Stefanie
Fryer, Becky
Fryer, Mike
Fuchs, Jerry
Fultz Jr., Larry
Funes, Tony
Furlong, T.C.
Furuta, Amy
Furuta, Bunny
Furuta, Jean
Furuta, Mick
Furuta, Mike
Furuta, Nori

G

Gaeta, Kendra
Gahlon, Thomas
Gakuo, Anthony
Gallagher, Mary
Gallagher, Thomas
Gallo, Marge
Gallo, Rich
Gambino, Sam
Gandelman, Joe
Gandia, Jorge

Gandras, Holly
Ganz, Bill
Garbarini, John
Garcia, Charles
Garcia, George
Garcia, Rosario
Garcia, Ruben
Gardner, Dick
Garner, Donald
Garner, Frank
Garner, Harold
Garner, Jennifer
Garner, Stephen
Gates, Andrew
Gayton, Jason
Gayton, Jay
Gedzhekushyan, Mike
Genotte, Steve
Gentilcore, Jim
George, Wally
Gerard, Sharon
Gerardi, Jerry
Gerson, Matt
Getzinger, Steve
Gezalyan, Bob
Ghayoori, Anthony
Gibson, Mel
Gierucki, Paul
Gilardi, Leonardo
Gilbert, Tom
Gilgrist, Mark
Gillespie, James
Gillis, Ruth
Gillo, Sam
Gilmore, Jerry
Gilmore, Todd
Gipp, Steven
Givens, Rick
Gladem, Al
Glick, Alan
Gluck, Jeff
Glynn, Ron
Gogg, Mike
Goggin, Becky
Goggin, Margaret
Goggin, Michele
Goggin, Mike
Gold, Mickey
Goldberg, Whoopi
Golden, Charles
Golden, Nathan
Goldner, Dan
Goldsberry, Donna
Gomez Jr., Harold
Gomez, Carlos
Gomez, Peter
Gonzales, Carlos
Gonzales, Jennie
Good, Dave
Goodness, Tim
Goodwin, William
Goon, Karl
Goon, Rex
Gorman, Lisa
Gounas, Peter
Graham, Bruce
Graham, John
Graham, Phil
Grande, Jaqueline
Grant, Andrew
Grant, Michael
Grassi, Jamie
Gray, John
Grayson, Eric
Green, J.R.
Green, William
Greene, Debbie
Greenhalgh, George
Gregg, John
Gresh, Andy
Grice, Jennifer
Grice, Judith
Griffin, Eddie
Grimsley, Brandon
Griparis, Ellen
Griparis, George
Griparis, John
Grisham, Bill

Groene, Mark
Groening, Matt
Grohl, David
Grohs, Thomas
Gronert, Philip
Grosch, Dr. Thomas
Grossman, Gerald
Grubb, Robert
Grube, Mark
Gruber, Rick
Guillen, Adrian
Gunterberg, Greg
Gurman, Melissa
Gurney, Linda
Gust, Peter
Gust, Rachel
Guzman, Edward
Guzman, Jordan

H

Haberek, Mary
Haberek, Noel
Hacker, Brad
Hale, Patrick
Hall, Phil
Halle, Lee
Halper, Mark
Halpern, Lisa
Hamer, Tim
Hamilton, Jon
Hamilton, Tom
Handler, Evan
Handman, Elizabeth
Hanrahan, Jack
Hansen, Bob
Hansen, Laurie
Hansen, Tom
Hanuscin, Jerry
Happoldt, Eric
Harako, Richard
Hardee, Al
Hardt, Paul
Haroutunian, Mari
Haroutyunyan, Vahagn
Harpe, Ronald
Harper, Joanne
Harriman Jr., James
Harrington, Tom
Harris, Andrew
Harris, Boyd
Harris, Jonathan
Harris, Ronald
Harris, Trisha
Hart, Mickey
Hartwell, John
Haskell, Jack
Hatfield, Greg
Hathorn, Karean
Haug, Dan
Haverkampf, Dave
Haverkampf, Kim
Haverkampf, Scott
Haverlation, Douglas
Hawking, Steven
Hawkins, Lenora
Hawley, Jane
Hayes, Nick
Hayes, Scot
Hayes, Wendy
Hays, Quay
Hedlund, Erik
Heffentrager, Sally
Heffron, Doyle
Heidbreder, Dale
Heinrich, Kurt
Hellman, Don
Henderson, Marie
Hendrix, Tom
Herbst, Darrell
Herman, Rick
Hernandez, Ruben
Herskowitz, Jeff
Hester, Jennifer
Hickey, Brian
Hicks, Brady
Hill, Brad
Hill, Justin
Hlavacek, Jeff

Hobbs, Richard
Hoffman, Joseph
Holgate, Michael
Holladay, Sylvia
Holland, Thomas W.
Holliday, David
Holmes, Gary
Hoofman, Cynthia
Hook, George
Hopkins, Andy
Hopkins, Ellen
Hoppe, Clara
Hoppe, Erik
Hoppe, Pamela
Hoppe, Steve
Horgan, Mary
Horner, Chris
Hosomura, Koji
Hostetler, Dean
Houlihan, Thomas
Howard, Paul
Howell, Austin
Howell, Mark
Howes, Mike
Hoyle, Scott
Hubbard, Danny
Huck, Chuck
Hughes, John
Huntington, Joyce
Hurlburt, Roger
Huron, David
Hustak, Tim
Hutchings, Gary
Hutchins, Gary
Hylton, Payton
Ilkhan, Jasmine

I

Irvin, Gale
Isaac, Chris
Italia, Bob
Iturbe, Jose
Iverson, Paul
Iverson, Shawn
Izzo, Donna

J

Jaczewski, Ted
Janow, Kevin
Jarvis, Dave
Jefferson, Dave
Jefferson, David
Jefferson, Ernie
Jefferson, Marge
Jefferson, Rich
Jefferson, Rob
Jefferson, Robin
Jensen, Crystal
Jess, Thomas
Jett, Joan
Jewell, Henry
Jinks, Donna
Jischke, Charles
Jobes, Scott
Johannsen, Fred
Johnson, Dave
Johnson, Jennifer
Johnson, Keith
Johnson, Lee
Johnson, Linda
Johnson, Todd
Johnson, Tony
Jones Jr., Spike
Jones, Kevin
Jones, Linda
Jones, Mia
Jones, Orlando
Jordan, Bev
Jordan, Darrell
Jordan, Michael
Jordan, Patrick
Jordan, Paul
Jose, Anthony
Jose, Donald
Joy, Ron
Judge, Mike
Justice, Cannon

K

Kahng, Sejoon
Kaikko, Peter
Kamen, Dan
Kane, Byron
Kane, James
Kanoo, Bassem
Kantor, Jeff
Kantor, Nancy
Karabedian, Jeff
Karamian, Patrick
Karlor, Jeff
Karn, Ron
Karolus, Bryan
Karp, Jessica
Kashnowski, Rich
Kasitz, Eric
Kassir, John
Katzinger, Leon
Kaufman, Eric
Kavet, Matt
Kawaguchi, Gabriel
Keane, Kevin
Keck, Robert
Kellar, Eddie
Kelleher, James
Kelly, Fred
Kelly, Paxson
Kelly, Zane
Kemble, Jan
Kennedy, Jake
Kennelly, Mike
Kenney, David
Keppel, John
Kerpel, David
Kerr, Katrina
Kesow, Mike
Kessler, Angela
Kessler, Kirk
Keys, Barry
Keys, Michael
Khachoian, Ani
Kidd, Fred W.
Kiehl, Alex
Kilgore, Doug
Kilgore, Mark
Killeen, Matt
Killewald, Bob
Kimpel, Bill
King, B.B.
King, Michael
King, Terry
Kinsey, Steve
Kinsley, Bill
Kirchman, Frank
Kirkcaldy, Al
Kirkwood, Katherine
Kirschenbaum, Eugene
Kiser, Helen
Kissane, Sharon
Klasey, Darrell
Kleiser, Danny
Kleiser, Miles
Kleist, Michael
Kliegle, Max
Kloc, Patricia
Knack, Bob
Knight, Dave
Knudsen, Jim
Kobayashi, Tats
Kociemba, Bill
Komorowski, Peggy
Kondrich, Tom
Korman, Harvey
Kornspan, Michael
Koshkaryan, Jack
Kosobucki, Joe
Kotal, Keith
Kovar, Matt
Kozdra, Al
Kozielski, Cap
Kraft, Alison
Kraft, Wilson
Kramer, David
Kramer, Joey
Kraus, Greg
Krieger, Alice

Kroeger, Gary
Kroh, Craig
Krome, Paul
Krueger, Debra
Krupnik, Steve
Kuehn, Jim
Kunkel, August
Kurson, Robert
Kvaloy, Roar
Kyaykedzhyan, Kristina

L

La Bel, Tina
La Flamme, Alan
Ladley, Steve
Laing, Bruce
Lake, Christopher
Laliberte, Bruce
Lam, Sumi
LaMarca, Bruce
LaMarr, Phil
Lamb, Bob
Lamond, Eric
Lamond, Kurt
Lander, Paul
Landry, David
Laner, Alex
Laner, Daniel
Laner, Ken
Laner, Stacy
Langton, Norman
Lanzer, Rob
Lapins, Kim
Larson, Brian
Lassin, Shayna
Lastra Morris, Ernesto
Lawlor, Deborah
Lawrence, Bill
Lawrence, John
Lawson, Ira
Lax, Debbie
Layfer, Scott
Layton, Alex
Layton, Ken
Leahy, John
Leak, Roy
Lear, Robert
Leasure, Daniel
Leasure, Ernest
Lee, Eddie
Lee, Geddy
Lee, Mike
Lee, Ruta
Lee, Wayne
Leener, Craig
Leidelmeijer, Ron
Leidelmeuer, Ron
Leitner, Bonnie
Leitner, Mike
Leitzen, Mark
Lemaster, George
Lemon, Craig
Lenart, Dave
Lenburg, Greg
Lenburg, Jeff
Leno, Jay
Leonard, Brad
Lesh, Phil
Lessig, Tom
Letts, Robert
Levine, Paul
Levitt, Ted
Levy, Eugene
Lew, Homer
Lewin, Robert
Lewis, Al
Lewis, Dawn
Lewis, Scott
Lhota, Frank
Lhota, Kay
Lieberman, Roy
Lien, Gary
Liewald, Dave
Lifeson, Alex
Likar, George
Lilek, Keith
Lilly, Hunter
Lilly, Mark

Lilly, Patrick
Lilly, Peter
Lilly, Sharon
Lilly, Sheena
Lilly, Zachary
Lindsay, Loren
Lingenfelter, Lori
Linsley, Steve
Liotta, Carter
Lippe, Steve
Lister Jr., James
Lithgow, John
Little, Kevin
Little, Scott
Lively, Jonathan
LoCascio, Alex
Long, Shelly
Longhini, John
Longhini, Paul
Longo, Mike
Lopes, Brian
Lopes, Mary Ann
Lopez, Eynar
Lopez, Jennifer
Lopez, Oscar
Lopez, Steve
Lopez, Victor
Lousararian, Edward
Love, Alan
Lozano, Gerardo
Lozano, Rick
Lucas, George
Lucas, Steve
Lucatorto, Eugene
Lucero, Michael
Luckadoo, Clifford
Lueke, Linda
Lupetin, Jeff
Lyker, Rob
Lynam, Jim
Lynch, Dennis
Lyons, Brian
Lyons, Mark

M

Maccagnano, Roger
MacDonald, Fernando
Macek, John
Machak, Deborah
Mack, Dianne
Mack, Kelly
Mack, Skip
Mackail, Craig
Mackey, Joe
Mackin, Steve
Magallanes, Ricardo
Magaro, John
Mahdesian, Greg
Mahler, Bruce
Maines, Chris
Majdi, Pat
Major, Bill
Major, William
Maloney, Jim
Maloney, Myrna
Manganaro, Lynne
Manidis, Andy
Mankey, Bruce
Mapp, Martisa
Margaretic, Steven
Mariano, Raymond
Marien, Pete
Marin, Cheech
Marks, Alan
Marks, Doug
Marquez, Mariann
Mars, Bob
Marsten, Clay
Martin, Bill
Martin, Doron
Martin, Travis
Martinet, Brian
Martinet, Emily
Martinet, Lindy
Martinet, Micae
Martinet, Nicole
Martinet, Olivia
Martinez, Clarissa

Martinez, Erika
Martinez, Felix
Martinez, Gabriana
Martinez, Mickey
Martinez, Pam
Martinez, Patrick
Martinez, Sabrina
Marvel, Scott
Mascus, Charles
Maser, Louanne
Maska, David
Mason, Dalton
Mason, Ruthie
Mason, Sam
Massie, Scott
Mather, Marianne
Matthews, Dave
Matthews, Jerry
Maturin, Joseph
Maurer, Gary
Maurer, Joan
Maurer, Kim
Maurer, Michael
Mauro, Jamin
Maw, Joycelyn
May, Paul
Mayer, Becky
Mayer, John
Mayfield, Les
Mays, Rick
Mazurek, Linda
Mazzoni, Brett
Mazzuca, Mary Ellen
McAnany, John
McBryde, Mark
McCarley, Gary
McCarthy, Kevin
McCarthy, Michael
McCasland, Jeff
McClanahan, Marie
McCool, Kelly
McCool, Roark
McCool, Sean
McCormick, Mike
McCoy, Jeff
McCulley, Flint
McCullough, Ed
McCurdy, Kim
McDonald, Fernando
McGinley, Hugh
McGinnis, Rev. Michael
McKay, Gabrielle
McKay, John
McKay, Laurie
McKay, Lorraine
McKay, Scott
McKay, William
McKenzie, Dan
McKerry, Frank
McLean, William
McLeroy, Ken
McNabney, George
McNulty, Calum
McNulty, John
McPartland, Brian
Mead, James
Meador, Phil
Meadows, Jayne
Mehnert, Robert
Mehrpay, Veronica
Meidinger, Terrance
Meister, Barry
Mellor, Vic
Meltzer, Allan
Mendez, Marvin
Mendonsa, Tim
Menezes, Aubrey
Menti, Vince
Meron, Neil
Mettevelis, James
Michael, Doug
Midura, Mike
Milanek, Blaise
Miller, Amy
Miller, Andy
Miller, Dr. Nora
Miller, Eugene
Miller, Greg

Miller, Keith
Miller, Paul
Miller, Will
Mina, Jeffrey
Minkler, Joi
Minor, Christine
Mintz, Charles
Misup, Steven
Mitchell, Jack
Mitchell, John
Mitchell, Kevin
Mitchell, Steve
Mitrovich, Nick
Moeckel, Rob
Molsoniak, Carmen
Monaco, Vince
Monnier, Gary
Montalbano, Jim
Montgomery, Chris
Montrose, Mitch
Moore, Chris
Moore, Donald
Moore, Eric
Moore, Todd
Morales, Eduardo
Moran, Erin
Morelli, Joshua
Morelli, Ralph
Morelli, Thomas
Morgan, Chuck
Morin, Todd
Morse, Frank
Moses, Sandra
Mosley, Stephanie
Motika, Barbara
Mould, Bob
Moulton, Warren
Mounts, Darlene
Mourao, Tarcisio
Mouzis, Ken
Muchow, Steve
Mudrack, Theresa
Mueller, Brett
Mueller, Jim
Mullen, Pat
Muller, Erich
Muller, Mancow
Mullins, Susan
Munoz, Alice
Munoz, Rick
Munoz, Vera
Muro, Michael
Murphy, Debbie

N

Nadeau, Chris
Nadeau, Raymond
Nagler, Neil
Nahm, Kathy
Nance, Christopher
Nastasit, Robert
Nathan, Billy
Nava, Ricardo
Nawaz, Afroze Anis
Nazloomian, Sacco
Necastro, Maria
Neergaard, Fred
Nelson, Jay
Nelson, Steven
Nelson, Willie
Nestler, Kelly
Newton, Jay
Nichols, Chris
Nickle, Linda
Niedzwiedz, Todd
Nielsen, Leslie
Nievar, Jim
Niles, Chuck
Noe, Gary
Nolan, Brendan
Noreika, Liz
Noreika, Tom
Novak, David
Novak, Rick
Novario, Amy
Novario, Steve
Novicki, Eric
Nowak, Mary Ann

Nugent, Ted
Nusko, Jeff
Nute, Gary
Nutt, Valarie
Nyman, Glen
Nystrom, Debra

O

O'Brien, Conan
O'Connor, Joseph
O'Dea, Richard
O'Donnell, Kathy
O'Malley Jr., Thomas
O'Malley Sr., Thomas
O'Malley, Bill
O'Malley, Charlotte
O'Malley, Don
O'Malley, Erin
O'Malley, Kathleen
O'Malley, Kevin
O'Malley, Meghan
O'Malley, Michael
O'Malley, Patrick
O'Malley, Rita
O'Malley, Ryan
O'Malley, Shannon
O'Malley, Tina
O'Malley, Tom
O'Malley, Tracy
O'Neil, Timothy
O'Neill, Riley
O'Reilley, Mike
Occenia, Caridad
Ochoa, Kenny
Ohman, Kathy
Ohmart, Ben
Okany, Celsus
Olin, Deborah
Oliveri, Sandy
Olsen, Stanton
Ontis, Tom
Ople, Jo
Oravitz, Michael
Orbell, Mike
Ordonez, John
Orkin, Neil
Orr, Colin
Ortega, Gerardo
Ortiz, Cynthia
Ortiz, Hugo
Osbourne, Ozzy
Osterberg, James
Osth, Jennie
Oswald, Cody
Otto, Jason
Ottolino, Frank
Owen, Robert
Owens, Mike

P

Pacyga, Kenneth
Padron, Mark
Pagano, Joe
Pagano, Paul
Panaggio, Brendan
Panaggio, Charlotte
Papadimas, Julie Persing
Paragoutev, Nikola
Parente, Nicholas
Parish, Ann Marie
Park, Michael
Parker, Cheryl
Parker, Gordon
Parker, Kayla
Parker, Mike
Parker, Phoebe
Parnell, Casey
Pascua, Lawrence
Pase, Gary
Paul, Bill
Paul, Jim
Paulson, Bradford
Pautsch, Eric
Pautz, Betty
Pautz, Jarrett
Pautz, Jeff
Pautz, Jennifer
Pautz, Kenny

Pavlich, Jeff
Pavolaitis, Matt
Pawlewicz, Trevor
Paz, Nicole
Peart, Neil
Peeler, Timothy
Pekrol, Brian
Pelrine, Michelle
Penaggio, Brendan
Pentecost, Kevin
Perez, Vince
Perfect, Lissa
Perkins, Stan
Perry, Joe
Perry, Linda
Perry, William
Pesci, Joe
Pesto, Sarah
Peters, Jason
Peters, Rich
Peterson, Bob
Peterson, Etta
Peterson, Oscar
Petlock, Gary
Petryshyn, Andy
Pettinella, Mike
Pfeifer, Will
Pham, Tony
Phang, Jason
Philbin, Danny
Philbin, Regis
Phillips, Clifton
Phillips, Lou Diamond
Piancenti, Stephanie
Pianta, Nestor
Piccoli, Daniel
Pickett, Cynthia
Pier, Ty
Piercy, Kirk
Pigeon, Steven
Pines, Jason
Pirtle, Kathryn
Pitofsky, Peter
Pitt, Jim
Pitula, John
Plake, Wayne
Planamente, James
Plank, Sean
Plummer, Louie
Poche, Audrey
Poderis, Flavio
Poler, Michael
Polhill, Richard
Polk, Jessica
Pollack, Pete
Poplawski, Keli
Porter, Kendrick
Potash, Larry
Powers, Mark
Powers, Wally
Prasad, Sheila
Preciado, Joe
Presto, Alex
Priess, Joel
Procknow, Donald
Pucci, Gregory
Puglisi, Diego
Purser, Chip
Purser, David
Purvis, Michael
Pyzanowski, Gary

Q

Quaglia, Jan
Quimby, Denise
Quinn, Kathleen
Quinn, Peter
Quintana, Cristina
Quintero, Jose
Quinty, Robert
Quirk, Susan
Qvistgaard, Tom

R

Radzik, Ann Marie
Radzik, Jeff
Radzik, Keith
Radzik, Mark

Radzik, Suzanne
Raimi, Sam
Rainford, Maria
Ramaswamy, Ramesh
Ramirez, Ray
Ramos, Joe
Ramsey, Jay
Rapsis, Jeff
Ratliff, Tommy
Ray, Roger
Ray, Roger
Reall, Julieanne
Reames, Jess
Reboul, Scott
Rebsch, Steve
Reddick, Gerri
Reder, Marina
Redfearn, Daniel
Reed, Jason
Reed, Jim
Reed, Lou
Reed, Mike
Reeve, Trent
Reeves, Malana
Regan, Dorothy
Rehberg, Jodi
Rehberg, Keith
Rehberg, Kevin
Rehberg, Kurt
Reichek, Jordan
Reichstein, Manny
Reid, John
Reinisch, Earl
Reiser, Paul
Renzetti, Jeff
Rerrando, Sandy
Reyes-Orlando, Cadan
Reynolds, Bob
Rezula, Chris
Rezula, Jonathan
Rezula, Michael
Rezula, Rebecca
Rheome, Nathan
Rhodes, Kristi
Rial, Luis
Richard, Bill
Richards, Dean
Richards, Jeff
Richards, Jim
Richards, Judith
Richards, Michael
Richards, Paul J.
Richards, Paul T.
Richards, Rob
Richardson, Duane
Richardson, Gwen
Richardson, March
Richert, Bill
Ricotta, John
Ricotta, Mark
Riedle, John
Rieve, Richard
Rihel, Janet
Riley, Greg
Riley, Gwell
Riley, John
Riley, Tim
Rimmel, Nicole
Rinn, Amanda
Rinn, Barbara
Rinn, Bart
Rinn, Katlyn
Rinn, Nick
Rinn, Renee
Rinn, Steve
Ripoli, Midge
Risberg, Joel
Ritchell, Tony
Ritter, John
Roarke, John
Roberts, Karen
Robertson, Allison
Robertson, Annette
Robertson, Anthony
Robertson, Edward T.
Robinson III, David
Robinson, Norman
Robison, David

Rocha, Mirella
Rodriguez, Jennifer
Rodriguez, Ron
Rodriquez, Robert
Roehm, Angela
Roehm, Richard
Rogers, Ian
Rogers, Kirsten
Rogers, Louis
Rogers, Morgan
Rogers, Reigna
Rohr, Sharon
Roker, Al
Rolando, Travis
Roman, Andy
Romanova, Karen
Romanowski, Jim
Romero, Monica
Rooth, Glenn
Rooth, Jaymes
Rose, Roger
Rosenak, Rebecca
Rosenbach, Howie
Rosenfield, Charity
Rosenfield, David
Rosenfield, Tyler
Rosin, Gigi
Rosman, Bill
Ross, Harry
Ross, Jeffrey
Ross, Michael
Ross, Rich
Roth, David Lee
Ruiz, Belle
Ruiz, Rick
Russell, Brian
Russell, Julie
Russo, Frank
Ruth, Don
Rutkowski, David

S

Sabatino, Laura
Sacco, Larry
Sack, Steve
Sagal, Katey
Saksenhaus, Bob
Salak, Mike
Salinas, Jose
Salinas, Victor
Salisbury, Lawton
Salomone, Gino
Salomone, Michael
Sambrano, Dylan
Sampson, Scott
Sanchez, Ramona
Sandwisch, Matthew
Sansing, Jonathan
Santini, Nelson
Saperstein, Steve
Sargent Jr., Bobby
Sargent, Beth
Sargent, Linda
Sargent, Robert
Sarginson, Shane
Satterfield, Robert
Satterwhite, Jerome
Savage, Toi Lin
Savone, Joseph
Sawyer, Jeff
Sawyer, Jerry
Sawyer, Jon
Scacchetti, Frank
Scanlan, George
Scarbrough, Russell
Schaefer, Gary
Schatz, Maria
Schellenberger, Suzie
Schenk, Ted
Schey, Connie
Schiller, Ralph
Schleifer, Fred
Schmelzer, Clay
Schmelzer, Clyde
Schmidt, Charlie
Schneider, Heidi
Schott, Glenn
Schumacher, Matt

Schwartz, Annie
Schwartz, Barney
Schworm, Dave
Schworm, Patti
Sciacca, Joe
Scordato, Ellen
Scordato, Mark
Scorsese, Martin
Scott, Brett
Scott, James
Scott, Jeffrey
Scrafford, Roger
Scribner, Marc
Sebastian, Tim
Segovia, Margo
Seguine, Brent
Seguine, William
Sells, Fletcher
Sendejas, Chris
Seng, John
Servin, Robert
Severson, Cat
Sexton, Mike
Seyller, Sandy
Shanholtzer, Dewey
Shankar, Kumar
Sharma, Paul
Sharps, Evan
Shaw, Burt
Shaw, James
Shelton, Darla
Shelton, Jay
Shelton, Jon
Sheppard, Paul
Shermer, Patrice
Shields, Marie
Shifres, Ed
Shin, Jin
Shmookler, David
Shor, Larry
Shore, Pauly
Short, Kathi
Short, Martin
Shriner, Wil
Sidhom, Roger
Sielert, Diane
Sielert, Rich
Silcox, Grover
Silverman, Dan
Silverman, Joshua
Silverman, Richard
Silverman, Steven
Simmons, Clayton
Simpson, Jessica
Singh, Abhishek
Sink, Jeff
Siriwatanakamol, Roy
Sisson, Rob
Sitka, Saxon
Skorich, Jim
Skratz, G.P.
Skretved, Randy
Skulborstad, Jon
Slawinski, Gretchen
Smiley, David
Smith, Anna Nicole
Smith, Barry
Smith, Brian
Smith, Daniel
Smith, Derek
Smith, Doug
Smith, Janice
Smith, Jason
Smith, Jay
Smith, Julie
Smith, Ken
Smith, Laura
Smith, Lawrence
Smith, Lisa
Smith, Mark
Smith, Michael
Smith, Phillip
Smith, Robert
Smith, Tim
Smith, Wendy
Sneirson, Gregg
Snider, David
Snyder, Greg

Snyder, Jim
Snyder, Larry
Snyder, Shlomo
Sofo, Mike
Sol, Herbert
Sol, Jonathan
Solack, Eddy
Solak, Stephen
Soliz, Victor
Solomon, Dr. Jon
Sommo, Frank
Sorrells, Tommy
Soto, Abel
Soto, Larry
Sousa, Fernanda
Speilberg, Steven
Spence, Jim
Spencer, Lewis
Spencer, Scott
Spencer, Star
Speyer, Michael
Spiegel, Scott
Spillane, John
Sprague, Kent
Springfield, Rick
Stacy, Taylor
Stallman, Gary
Stallman, Jim
Stallman, Shirley
Stanley, Cindy
Stary, Morgen
Stavrou, George
Stavrou, Maria
Steetz, Cara
Steetz, Drew
Steetz, Rob
Steinglass, Sabrina
Steneck, Chuck
Stenmo, Chris
Stephan, Derek
Stephan, Justin
Stephens, Kalaun
Stern, Howard
Stevens, John
Stevenson, Debra
Stewart, Ray
Stiffler, Vern
Stiller, Ben
Stiller, Jerry
Stoever, Eric
Stone, George
Stone, Jack
Stone, Julie
Stone, Larry
Stopfel, Mark
Storrs, Todd
Stoskopf, John
Stout, Amoreena
Stoycoff, Mike
Stratton, Jeff
Strayer, Robert
Strome, Matt
Stuckert, Keith
Suarez, Liz
Sullivan, Charles
Sullivan, Joe
Sullivan, Michael
Summitt, Thomas
Surratt, Joe
Sussman, Sy
Sutherland, Jeffrey
Swaim, Pamela
Swerdlow, Robert
Swiderski, Al
Sykes, Joseph
Syth, Ron
Szymczak, Gordon

T

Taber, Lindsey
Tammenga, David
Tang, Wilson
Tapley, Mike
Tarantino, Quentin
Tarran, Ray
Tartaglia, Paul
Tase, John
Taylor, Clark

Taylor, Joe
Taylor, John
Taylor, Lee
Taylor, Randall
Taylor, Rip
Taylor, Roger
Tedesco, Arthur
Tello, Alex
Terrill, Chip
Terrill, Donna
Terry, Courtney
Theodore, Chris
Theodore, Virginia
Thicke, Alan
Thicke, Todd
Thomas, Hailey
Thomas, John
Thompson, Dana
Thompson, Lynn
Thompson, Oscar
Thompson, William
Thomson, Edward
Todd, Bob
Todd, Jim
Toerber, Michael
Tolentino, Jeff
Tomlin, Lily
Tonge, Bob
Topolski, Jan
Torres, Jamie
Torres, Jorge
Torres, Phil
Torres, Victor
Tovar, Antonio
Townley, Bob
Townsend, Kelly
Trachtman, Don
Traenkenschuh, Roy
Tranchina, Thomas
Traver, Andy
Traver, Becky
Traverso, Mark
Traxler, Kirk
Trefil, Donald
Trepczyk, Don
Trott, Robert
Troxel, Danny
Troxell, Alan
Tucci, Michael
Turner, Barbara
Turner, Ted
Tyler, Austin
Tyler, Gary
Tyler, Steven
Ulm, Chris
Urbanowski, Richard
Urubek, Kenny
Uthe, John

V

Vai, Steve
Valentine, Roger
Valenzuela, Jaime
Valeu, John
Valley, Michael
Vallone, Frank
Vallone, Peter
Vamos, Dave
Vamos, Kimberly
Van Diggelen, Bill
Van Halen, Alex
Van Halen, Edward
Van Hauwe, Barry
Van Hoose, Jim
Van Loon, Christine
Van Meeter, Peggy
Van Milligan, Bob
Vanegas, Christopher
Vangieson, Mary
Vanwagner, Alicia
Vargas, Ana
Vargas, Richard
Vasquez Jr., Gilbert J.
Vasquez Sr., Gilbert J.
Vasquez, Frances
Vasquez, Jerry
Vasquez, John
Vasquez, Pappy

Vasquez, Pete
Vasquez, Terry
Vazquez, Fernando
Vega, Dotty
Velasquez, Timothy
Ventrice, Anthony
Viacava, Tony
Vianzon, Ted
Vicknair, Troy
Viecco, Gabriel
Vignone, Mark
Vinson, Gary
Viriwatanakaskul, Chris
Virtus, Jack
Vlahegiannis, Cathy
Vorenkamp, Mark

W

Wahl, Todd
Wahlund, Garnet
Waldum, Roy
Walker, John C.
Walker, Johnny
Wall, Kim
Wall, Mary
Wall, Mike
Wall, Terese
Wall, Tommy
Wallace, Ronald
Wallenstein, Ray
Wallenstein, Roy
Wallison Jr., Edward, J.
Wallison Sr., Edward J.
Wallison, Gert
Wallison, Mark
Walsh, Donald
Walter, Steve
Walzer, John
Wanamaker, Barry
Warick, Ed
Warnick, Felicia
Warnick, Jared
Warren, Keith
Warwick, Steve
Watkins, Susan
Watters, Sue
Waugh, Steve
Wax, Steven
Weaver, Caroline
Webb, Bucky
Weber, Gerald
Weber, Robert
Webster, John
Weir, Bob
Weisenborn, Shirley
Weisenborn, Wally
Weiss, Dorothy
Welker, Frank
Welker, Sarah
Welles, Torri
Wells, Sue
Wentland, Rob
Wescott, Theresa
West, Billy
West, Frank
West, James
West, Karen
West, Steve
Westfall, David
Westfall, Gail
Weston, Carin
Weston, Kathy
Weston, Mike
Weston, Neil
Whalen, John
Wheeler, Howard
White, Bill
White, Carolyn
White, Jack
White, Kevin
Whitford, Brad
Whitt, Matt
Whittaker, Adam
Whittington, Greg
Wiandt, Steven
Wielgus, Carol
Wielgus, Larry
Wilkinson, Michael

Williams, Brian
Williams, Carl
Williams, David
Williams, Robert
Williams, Shawe
Williams, Steve
Williams, Vince
Williamson, Doug
Williamson, James
Willis, Bruce
Willoughby, Brad
Wilson, Abbey
Wilson, Amy
Wilson, Debra
Wilson, Frank
Wilson, Grant
Wilson, Lucas
Wilson, Nathan
Wilson, Rodney
Wilson, Stanley
Windas-Goodwin, Kathleen
Windt, Vickie
Wingard, Barry
Winit, Mitchell
Winter, Dell
Winters, Margaret
Wise, Martin
Wise, Marty
Wise, Woody
Wissmann, Erik
Witte, Eric
Woelfel, Brian
Woldum, Roy
Wolf, Bruce
Wolf, Chris
Wolf, Susan
Wolf, Warner
Wolfe, Deborah
Wood, Emil
Woodard, James
Worboys, Lawrence
Wozniak, Derek
Wright, Margaret
Wrobel, Andy
Wronski, Bill

X

Xanthos, Jonathan

Y

Yang, Kyungsun
Yaster, Carol
Yiu, Leng Hiang
Yoakam, Dwight
Yonan, Tony
Yonick, Gerri
Young, Dan
Young, Fraiser
Young, Gary
Young, Neil
Young, Todd
Yousse, Jason
Yucht, Stacy
Yukevich, Amy
Yurkiw, Mark

Z

Zabelin, Philip
Zadan, Craig
Zak, Tom
Zangri, Joan
Zangri, Joe
Zarndt, Monique
Zaver, Bill
Zema, Jim
Zenger, Cyndie
Zenger, Larry
Zevallos, Maggie
Zilinsky, Karen
Zippi, Victor
Zirbes, Mark
Zosel, Ken
Zundle, Adam

About the Authors

Jeff Forrester

(b. 1959) is today best known as host narrator of the TV Land Network's flagship series, *Inside TV Land*, a position he has held since the late 1990s. In addition to providing the narration, he also produced, directed and co-wrote the pilot episode for the series, *Inside TV Land: The Honeymooners* (seen by more than 25 million viewers), as well as the series' first feature-length installment, *Inside TV Land: The Dick van Dyke Show*. As a filmmaker, he has helmed productions featuring Academy Award-winning screen talent, and in 1990 Jeff won the American Film Institute's Professional Award (given in conjunction with the American Video Conference) for Best Fiction Production for his original feature-length docu-comedy, *They're Still Breathing*, in which he served as executive producer, co-writer and -director, and played the lead role on camera. Jeff is also a two-time Emmy Award nominee for his work in television as lead performer and producer-writer, and his feature-length video *The Great Gleason*, which he produced, wrote, directed and hosted, was named *People* Magazine's top comedy title the year it premiered. Jeff is the author or co-author of ten books, including several previous volumes on The Three Stooges and, most recently, *Blockbuster's All Time Favorite Movies and Music*, of which more than 10 million copies were published. Jeff also writes a weekly, Sunday-edition newspaper column, *Our Man in Hollywood*, which features entertainment-themed news and humor. He received a Bachelor of Arts Degree in Journalism, with an Emphasis on Broadcast News, from Northern Illinois University in 1981. Jeff, whose professional mentor was the late journalist and screenwriter Elwood Ullman, became a member of the Writers Guild of America himself in 1990. A native of Illinois, Jeff moved to Los Angeles in his twenties.

Tom Forrester

(b. 1963) is a filmmaker who presently works for Technicolor in Los Angeles. Tom has served as producer, director and writer on numerous feature-length film, television and homevideo productions, including the Civil War documentary *A Nation Asunder*, the Black history chronicle *Struggle for Freedom*, and the Hollywood film compilation *The Legend of the Frankenstein Monster*, among many others. For TV's SciFi Channel, Tom produced the restored versions of numerous classic feature films, among them *Metropolis*, *The Thief of Bagdad*, *Nosferatu*, *Dr. Jekyll and Mr. Hyde*, *The Golem*, and *The Lost World*. Additionally, he produced the interview segment accompanying the official digital disc edition of the fully-restored *City Lights*, regarded by many as Charlie Chaplin's greatest film masterpiece. Tom also produced the supplemental section for the digital disc release of George Lucas' *Star Wars*, which includes a never-before-seen, behind-the-scenes look at the Lucasranch production facility. Tom began his career as an author writing cutlines for the books *The Stooge Chronicles*, *The Stoogephile* and *Stoogemania*, and he co-authored *The Stooges' Lost Episodes* as well as six other books, all focusing on classic entertainment. With his brother he wrote the entire Music Catalog for *Blockbuster's All Time Favorite Movies and Music*, reviewing all of the top-selling compact discs in the history of the Blockbuster chain. Tom received a Bachelor of Arts Degree in Journalism, with an Emphasis on Advertising, from Northern Illinois University in 1985. A native of Illinois, Tom moved to Los Angeles in his twenties.

Joe Wallison

(b. 1958), the Forrester Brothers' editor, is a comedy-team historian who has written extensively about all of the major screen comedy teams of the 20th Century. Joe has authored articles for national magazines on such favorites as Laurel & Hardy, Abbott & Costello, Martin & Lewis, Allen & Rossi, and, of course, The Three Stooges, among numerous others. He is also managing editor of *Wildest Westerns* Magazine, which frequently highlights the work of legendary screen comedians and comedy teams. Joe received a Bachelor of Sciences Degree in Business, with an Emphasis on Marketing Research, from Wilkes College in 1981. Joe, who is married, moved to Los Angeles from his native Pennsylvania in his twenties.